Great Power Politics in the Fourth Industrial Revolution

Great Power Politics in the Fourth Industrial Revolution

The Geoeconomics of Technological Sovereignty

Glenn Diesen

BLOOMSBURY ACADEMIC
LONDON • NEW YORK • OXFORD • NEW DELHI • SYDNEY

BLOOMSBURY ACADEMIC
Bloomsbury Publishing Plc
50 Bedford Square, London, WC1B 3DP, UK
1385 Broadway, New York, NY 10018, USA
29 Earlsfort Terrace, Dublin 2, Ireland

BLOOMSBURY, BLOOMSBURY ACADEMIC and the Diana logo
are trademarks of Bloomsbury Publishing Plc

First published in Great Britain 2021
This paperback edition published 2022

The work on this book was funded by the Faculty of World Economy and International
Affairs of National Research University Higher School of Economics, Moscow.

Cover design: Toby Way
Cover image Robotic hand, illustration © Getty Images / Ktsdesign/Science
Photo Library | Concert lighting © Getty Images / Prasert Krainukul

A catalogue record for this book is available from the British Library.

A catalog record for this book is available from the Library of Congress.

ISBN: HB: 978-0-7556-0700-6
       PB: 978-0-7556-4049-2
       ePDF: 978-0-7556-0701-3
       eBook: 978-0-7556-0702-0

Typeset by Integra Software Services Pvt Ltd.

To find out more about our authors and books visit www.bloomsbury.com
and sign up for our newsletters

To my wife, Elena, and our children – Konstantin, Andre and Maria

Contents

Foreword by Dr Vladimir Yakunin,

Chairman of the Supervisory Board,
Dialogue of Civilizations Research Institute
Head of the State Governance Department,
Faculty of Political Sciences, Lomonosov Moscow State University,
Doctor of Political Science

Technological development is one of the key factors determining the social and economic wellbeing of communities, nations, states and civilizations. Scientific progress has led to unprecedented achievements in numerous areas of life in a relatively short period of time in human history. Starting from the eighteenth century, humanity has witnessed an accelerating pace of development, commonly termed industrial revolutions. During this flourishing period of technological development, humankind survived two world wars, at the cost of 13 million and 74 million lives, respectively, around the world. These global disasters occurred because of confrontations among the great world powers, driven by ideas of their exclusivity and the right to determine the shape of the world order of the day based on military might and a system in which the winner takes all.

What awaits the world in the future? Is the so-called 'end of history' real? How will recent technological advances complement the development of human beings and global society? Should new socio-economic models be more human-centred or, better to say, ethics-based? These are key questions that need to be addressed by humanity at a time when advanced technologies have the potential to destroy everything on Earth in a very short period of time.

One of the major advantages of this book is that, unlike other authors writing on the Fourth Industrial Revolution, IT and AI, Dr Diesen researches not only the objective and evident benefits of technological progress in different nations, but provides a complex analysis of possible risks that could emerge in the context of technological breakthroughs.

Great power politics brings forward one of the most challenging questions of our times about technological competition among developed countries. In this regard Dr Diesen brilliantly introduces the concept of technological sovereignty. Moreover, the problem of growing technological inequality between developed and developing countries remains a vast area for deeper elaboration.

Another important advantage of the book is that the author comprehensively systematizes the impact of scientific and technological achievements on all spheres of human life, from transformations in everyday labour and leisure up to the emergence of cyber warfare and the introduction of killer robots.

The conclusions about the prospects and threats of US–China rivalry in terms of developing new technologies, as well as of Russia's long track record as a great global power, are very well founded and thoroughly researched.

'Great Power Politics in the Fourth Industrial Revolution' by Glenn Diesen deserves the attention not only of the academic community, but also of the professional political establishment in both West and East. The book makes us contemplate and understand the sources of upcoming revolutionary changes, focusing on threats to the emerging new world order, which is undeniably determined by the availability of technologies and how they may be used in practice.

Introduction: The geoeconomics of industrial revolutions

The Fourth Industrial Revolution alters the source of power and how states interact in the international system. Technologies that evolve gradually receive less attention because incremental changes are predictable and manageable. In contrast, *disruptive technologies* are revolutionary because they render earlier technologies obsolete, and the changes they cause are often unpredictable and chaotic. Disruptive technologies that make former technologies and industries obsolete also restructure the organization of society, economics, communication, military, ideology, and how great powers cooperate and compete.

The concept of technological sovereignty recognizes that industrial capacity and state sovereignty are closely linked. High-tech industries are strategic due to the limited ability for self-sufficiency and diversification, which therefore creates an asymmetrical interdependence. Excessive dependence of foreign technologies reduces both the autonomy and influence that define great powers. States can augment their technological sovereignty by improving technological self-sufficiency, and diversify partnerships to manage the diffusion of technologies.

Dominant states that fail to extend and cement their technological leadership can descend into irrelevance as the technologies that underpinned their primacy become outdated. In the same way that generals often follow strategies more applicable to past wars, governments generally fail to acknowledge the tectonic shifts and transformations caused by industrial revolutions. However, because technological progress almost always outpaces political thinking and governmental policy, it is imperative that societies assess the opportunities, challenges and limitations inherent in these technologies, as well as their misconceptions about them.

It is puzzling why international relations devote so little attention to technological innovation when technology is arguably the most important variable in great power politics and geoeconomics. Technology is commonly viewed as a 'black box' that brings about major changes in the world, yet rarely are efforts made to pry open that box and understand how it works (McCarthy 2017). Technology shapes economic systems, military weapons, societal structures, political communication, ideologies and all other aspects of human interactions.

Technology has fuelled the economic growth that has become central to both great power cooperation and competition. In the military sphere, new technologies favouring defence have incentivized prolonged periods of peace, while military technologies providing offensive advantages have sparked wars with killings on an industrial scale. Communication technologies – from the printing press to the Internet – have empowered and limited states' ability to impose dominant narratives, construct identities and organize society. Strong societies capable of competing in international affairs have emerged as new technologies have delivered efficiency and prosperity, although the same technologies have also disrupted society by eliminating entire professions and creating a crisis in meaning by distancing mankind from nature and traditional communities.

Learning from the past

The First Industrial Revolution shaped the modern world by restructuring all aspects of human life and skewed the international balance of power. Governments ardently attempted to harness the power of new technologies to develop economic strength, military power and control over political communication. Britain took the lead in the Industrial Revolution and built the world's largest empire by securing access to natural resources and export markets for its manufactured goods. The fear of core–periphery relations due to excessive reliance on British manufacturing industry incentivized other great powers to strive towards technological sovereignty.

France countered Britain's newfound manufacturing and industrial power by constructing the Continental System that subsequently led to Napoleon's disastrous invasion of Russia to enforce compliance. The American System and its German and French equivalents deemed industrialization and a manufacturing base, technological sovereignty at its time, to be a central component of nation-building. Economic nationalism was subsequently embraced as a development strategy using temporary tariffs and subsidies to support infant industries, transportation networks and national banks freed from British economic dominance.

China, formerly an economic giant, fell behind during the Industrial Revolution, and was defeated by Britain in the Opium Wars in the 1850s, which was followed by the 'Century of Humiliation'. Russia's failure to industrialize similarly resulted in humiliating defeat in the Crimean War in 1856, which motivated sweeping and disruptive socio-economic changes to rapidly industrialize. Russia's industrialization in the late nineteenth century mimicked the United States and German development strategy, and made Russia the fastest-growing economy among the great powers. However, the Russian government was unable to mitigate the instability caused by social disruptions.

Competitiveness in international affairs requires states to industrialize and manage the domestic socio-economic and political repercussions from industrialization. Self-reliant farmers whose ancestors had resided in small communities for centuries were displaced from their rural lifestyles and recast as urban factory workers in a centralized society fuelled by coal and steam. Philosophy focused on the struggles of mankind to live in industrial society. The ideology of free market capitalism emerged as the dominant instrument for organizing the relationship between capital, labour and the state. Emancipation movements among workers seeking liberation from outdated feudal structures sparked revolutions. Yet, imbalances between capital and labour spawned bold but flawed ideological rivals in the form of communism and, later, fascism. The relationship between the state and the individual became increasingly mutable because technologies that empowered the individual could also strengthen the authority of the state.

The opening phase of the Fourth Industrial Revolution has only just begun, yet the main pillars of the world order are already trembling. Technological developments and geoeconomic disruptions in recent years have shattered what was seemingly an era of stability after the Cold War. The geoeconomic rise of China will likely shape great power politics in the years to come as it challenges the technological leadership of the United States and five centuries of Western dominance. Moscow aims to shed its technological dependence on the West and pursue wider geoeconomic collaboration with China. It is ending the three centuries-long Occidental era in which Russia both compared itself to and identified with the West. In the United States, the transition to a high-tech economy and the subsequent loss of manufacturing jobs has led to socio-economic upheavals. The United States is gravitating towards economic nationalism as power has concentrated in the tech giants to the extent that the free market cannot sufficiently function. Internationally, the decoupling from American digital platforms unravels a key source of US influence around the world. By successfully harnessing the electorate's growing disgruntlement with the political–media establishment, a reality TV star armed with Twitter entered the White House. Ideological rivalries that were believed to have been settled in the late twentieth century are likely to be revisited.

The unpredictable world of tomorrow

The Fourth Industrial Revolution is producing rapid and simultaneous advances in artificial intelligence (AI), automation, robotics, additive manufacturing (3D-printing), distributed ledgers (blockchain), the Internet of Things (IoT), big data, quantum computing, nanotechnology, neurotechnology, biotechnology, genetic engineering and related technologies with unpredictable applications.

Predicting the potential and limitations of revolutionary technologies and their applications is problematic due to the uncertainty about the speed and scope/function of these technologies. In 1903, Michigan Savings Bank President Horace Rackham had this advice for Henry Ford's lawyer: 'The horse is here to stay but the automobile is only a novelty, a fad'. Albert Einstein concluded in 1932 that 'there is not the slightest indication that nuclear energy will ever be obtainable'. In 1939, Winston Churchill opined that 'atomic energy might be as good as our present-day explosives, but it is unlikely to produce anything very much more dangerous'. Similarly, the potential influence of computers has been and continues to be underestimated because their potential is still far from realized. At the dawn of the computer age in 1943, the president of IBM stated: 'I think there is a world market for maybe five computers'. The developments in computer technology only a decade later demanded a reassessment of previous forecasts. Nevertheless, Digital Equipment Corp President Ken Olson was convinced in 1977 that 'there is no reason anyone would want a computer in their home'.

The increasing speeds and falling costs of computers in the 1970s and 1980s generated growing demand. In the 1990s, the explosion of Microsoft software and the extremely rapid spread of the Internet around the world caused a boom in personal computer use. Digitalization has since reshaped every aspect of society, politics, the economy and the military. We have now become accustomed to the sudden and intrusive presence of computers and have developed a false sense of stability and permanency concerning the relationship between mankind and machine.

Professor Michio Kaku (2018), a leading physicist and futurist (and Star Trek fan), argues that the new industrial revolution will eventually make human beings into Gods by enabling them to simply think about something in order to make it appear. Kaku cites the possibility of developing molecular assemblers in the future capable of restructuring molecules to, for example, remake a piece of wood into glass. Although such futuristic technologies will belong to the realm of science fiction for the foreseeable future, technologies have already been developed that enable us to merely think about something in order for it to appear. Advances in neurotechnology make it possible to detect brain waves that can then be transmitted digitally as an instruction. In an experiment in 2008, a monkey used his mere thoughts to control his prosthetic robot arm. In 2017, a race car was driven using brain waves alone for the first time (Schwab 2018). The next step in this 'God analogy' is to digitalize and transmit brain waves to a 3D printer – also known as additive manufacturing. Successful developments in 3D printing technology have ranged from printing small objects with biological matter such as a functioning uterus for mice to complex equipment with advanced nanomaterials and moving parts and even large objects such as entire houses. A new 3D printer was even nicknamed the 'replicator' by its inventors after a device from Star Trek that can enhance existing objects with new materials, transforming, for example, mushy liquids into complex solid objects.

Popular culture and science fiction have inundated people with stories about new technologies for so long that many now appear distant and unrealistic. The technologies of the Fourth Industrial Revolution, however, are either already here or will arrive in the near- to medium-term future. A Boston restaurant is currently run completely by robot chefs, formerly bustling assembly lines in Shenzhen are now completely automated, self-driving cars are navigating the streets of Moscow, and plans are afoot in Brussels to 3D-print a moon base. The exponential rate of technological change is already making it difficult to follow and adapt to the new realities. How will these changes influence great power politics? In his famous book on machines in society, mathematician and philosopher Norbert Wiener (1950) warned seven decades ago that 'we shall never receive the right answers to our questions unless we ask the right questions … The hour is very late, and the choice of good and evil knocks at our door'.

Identifying which conversation is now most important to humanity remains at the periphery of public discourse. Conflicts between great powers usually arise during tectonic shifts in the international distribution of power because political leaders do not identify the new challenges accurately and become increasingly willing to take greater risks even as their ability to manoeuvre diminishes. The international distribution of power will increasingly be restructured according to technological capabilities. Large and established corporations and states unable to read the shifting landscape will likely go the way of the dodo bird. Meanwhile, start-ups such as Google, Yandex and Alibaba have risen from obscurity to commercial dominance and immense political influence. The winners of tomorrow will be decided by technologies that require capital, skills, time and strategic thinking. Liberal democracies could be disadvantaged as authoritarian states wield a competitive advantage due to their greater ability to extract data and assert control over political communication and economic activity. The broad implications that an industrial revolution has for geoeconomics also warrant an analysis of its socio-political effect. Schwab (2016) argues:

> We stand on the brink of a technological revolution that will fundamentally alter the way we live, work, and relate to one another. In its scale, scope, and complexity, the transformation will be unlike anything humankind has experienced before. We do not yet know just how it will unfold, but one thing is clear: the response to it must be integrated and comprehensive, involving all stakeholders of the global polity, from the public and private sectors to academia and civil society.

Attempting to predict the influence of the Fourth Industrial Revolution on great power politics and geoeconomics compels us to answer a series of questions: Will the great powers need to achieve 'technological sovereignty' in the form of self-sufficient technological ecosystems? Will the international distribution of labour, global value chains and open markets that have defined globalization be dismantled and become nationally or regionally autonomous? When automation and robots in developed states become more competitive, which development strategies will the states with low-wage manufacturing adopt as a comparative advantage? Will digital cash, distributed ledger technology and peer-to-peer lending platforms disrupt the entire international financial sector by creating 'banking without banks' and limiting the scope of monetary policy? Can the free market be trusted with biotechnology, neurotechnology and genetic manipulation? Can capitalism continue to function as technological innovations dismantle meritocracies, concentrate wealth and disrupt the balance between capital and labour? Are we approaching a jobless utopia that provides more time for leisure, art, family and for regaining a sense of our own humanity? Or are we building a dystopia of mass unemployment that deprives people of economic security, human dignity and purpose? Will new technologies empower primarily the individual, corporation or state? Will the current nuclear détente unravel and trigger a return to wars between great powers? Is our international system – that has not changed fundamentally since the Peace of Westphalia in 1648 – prepared to respond to these changes and impending risks?

New technologies are reshaping domestic societies by challenging the economic and political philosophies that underpin the relationship between individuals, corporations and the state. Global governance is similarly fragmenting rather than preparing to manage the technologies that will restructure the world. On the one hand, industrial revolutions are a welcome phenomenon because they provide opportunities and solutions to everything from economic to environmental problems. On the other hand, previous industrial revolutions led to periods of extreme instability, spawning chaos as they tore down the old before societies could plan properly for the new. Is the world heading towards mass unemployment and cyberwars or a more evolved and peaceful coexistence? Increased efficiency by doing more with less can improve the quality of life and security, yet it also enhances the ability of humanity to fight and destroy itself. Nuclear technology can be used to illuminate and incinerate entire cities. Technology can lift millions out of poverty and offset flaws in the capitalist system, but it can also concentrate wealth by decoupling productivity from labour and unleash political instability. Former Russian Foreign Minister, Igor Ivanov (2018), cautioned:

> History has taught us that humanity's transition from one world order to another has always been driven by the accumulation of new production technologies, with wars and revolutions usually acting as a catalyst. Today, a critical mass of new technology for yet another civilizational breakthrough has been accumulated, yet a new cycle of wars and revolutions may prove deadly not only for individual countries, but for humanity. That is why it is extremely important to break this established cycle of world history in order to transition to a new level of civilizational development without another global cataclysm.

Research design

Industrial revolutions are defined by disruptive technologies that render former technologies obsolete, which inevitably impact the conduct and relations between great powers. Technological innovations cannot always be integrated into the existing domestic and international political system. Disruptive technologies often change the very foundations of politics and render the former order obsolete. The international distribution of power undergoes a reorganization and the concept, origin and exercise of power itself must be redefined. Power is defined as 'A has power over B to the extent that he can get B to do something that B would not otherwise do' (Dahl 1957: 202–3). Although this book attempts to shed light on the challenges ahead and make predictions, nobody can anticipate fully how the new industrial revolution will influence great power politics. This book, therefore, explores the variables or factors affected by disruptive technologies based on the historical precedent of previous industrial revolutions. Most research into new technologies explores such influence based on possible future scenarios without assessing the incentives and constraints states face in the acquisition and implementation of technology, and the disruptions that technology causes.

The research question to be answered in this book is: *To what extent will the Fourth Industrial Revolution influence the geoeconomic competition between the great powers?* The hypothesis in this book is that the Fourth Industrial Revolution will increase the significance of technological sovereignty and alter the instruments of power. Instruments of power is a reference to how states can defend their autonomy and project influence in the international system, which includes economic power, military power, soft power, and the control over communication.

Geoeconomics is used here as the point of departure and the main variable to explore great power rivalry. Great power politics after the Cold War has shifted from geopolitics to geoeconomics as power derives increasingly from the control over international markets rather than merely military hardware and territory. New technologies are central to geoeconomics as they lay the foundation for strategic industries, which by definition create economic dependencies that can be converted into political capital. High-tech industries are strategic as they promote asymmetrical interdependence by augmenting both autonomy and influence.

Yet, the shift from militarized geopolitics to geoeconomics is largely a consequence of the digital technologies and nuclear power in the Third Industrial Revolution. These new technologies have elevated the destructiveness of weapons to the extent that it alters the cost–benefit considerations of using military means for power competition between great powers. New technologies have also strengthened the role of market forces due to enhanced economic connectivity between states. The Fourth Industrial Revolution can reverse the trend towards geoeconomics if new technologies contribute to fragment international supply chains and augment the offensive advantage of weapons that unravel nuclear détente.

Domestic socio-economic stability also enters the study of geoeconomics as social cohesion is imperative for the state to behave as a unitary actor. The failure to organize society undermines the aptitude to mobilize resources and advance strategic interests in the international system. Socio-economic disruptions, caused by the inability of managing an industrial society in transformation, create a political vacuum that is often filled by radical and disruptive political alternatives. Polanyi (1944) argued in *The Great Social Transformation* that the industrial revolution and introduction of capitalism to organize relations between capital and labour caused a schism in human nature. The reactions to the failure of managing industrial society spurred ideological rivals to capitalism in the form of communism and fascism. International political economy is therefore closely linked to organizing industrial societies and managing the schism in mankind. Ruggie (1982) builds on Polanyi's societal ideas in the political economy by introducing the concept of 'embedded liberalism' to describe the balancing between market efficiency and social responsibilities by the state. Edward Luttwak's (2010) work on American geoeconomics similarly integrates sociology into political economy by, for example, arguing that US efforts to mobilize control over the high-tech sector as a comparative advantage entailed abandoning manufacturing, which caused societal division and political instability.

A deductive approach tests a neoclassical theory stipulating that the international distribution of power will increasingly depend on the technological sovereignty of great powers. The new technologies create greater concentration of power and involvement of states in the market, which makes technology increasingly important to assert autonomy and influence. Furthermore, neoclassical realism positions the decision-makers as an intervening variable between the international distribution of power and foreign policy. Technological sovereignty augments the ability of decision-makers to manage socio-economic and political disruption, which is imperative to successfully mobilize resources in the pursuit of great power interests.

The past three industrial revolutions inform the theory about the significance of the Fourth Industrial Revolution and determine the variables to be explored. The scope and complexity of this research topic present a challenge for the research design. Analysing the impact of industrial revolutions on great power politics is a very broad research topic due to the variety of technologies that affect the multitude of instruments of power utilized for power competition. This complexity poses a dilemma for the research design in terms of either pursuing a specific and narrow approach or a broader and more inclusive approach. More focused research on for example the economic, ideological or military aspect of great power conflicts allows for more detailed measurement of specific variables. Although, neglecting the broader scope of variables impacted by technological innovations undermines those theories' predictive utility, given that the international system is becoming increasingly complex. A key problem in political science is the growing rift between scholars and practitioners because the former focus more on rigour than on relevance. This has led to a growing demand for combining a variety of theories to construct complex theories. Sil and Katzenstein (2010) refer to analytic eclecticism as an intellectual stance that addresses intricate problems by building complex arguments. Combining a variety of theoretical constructs and research traditions to address complex research problems seeks to produce knowledge of value to both scholars and practitioners (Sil and Katzenstein 2010). Walt (1998) similarly argues that 'no single approach can capture all the complexity of contemporary world politics'.

A comparative approach is taken to assess causation, in which industrial revolutions are the independent variable and the geoeconomic policies of great powers are the dependent variable. The Fourth Industrial Revolution differs from the former three industrial revolutions in that it also automates the cognitive. The theory holds that this distinction in the independent variable affects the dependent variable. Geoeconomic power is expected to be vastly different as states become more dependent on technological ecosystems that absorb and integrate most economic activity. The concentration and centralization of power due to new technologies incentivize great powers to repatriate global supply chains and dismantle the international division of labour that is based on comparative advantage. At the same time, the state has strong incentives to take on a more assertive role in response to socio-economic and political disruptions caused by the new technologies.

Neoclassical realist geoeconomic theory

Industrial revolutions influence great power politics by reorganizing the relationship between the individual, industries, the state and foreign powers. First, the tools of power competition include geoeconomics, the military and political communication. Second, from the standpoint of geoeconomics, states must ensure socio-economic and political stability as a prerequisite to act rationally in the international system. Socio-economic and political disruptions affect the ability of the state to behave as a rational and unitary actor that can mobilize its resources to advance its foreign policy objectives. Last, global governance is imperative to managing radical changes in the international system, and yet technological change disrupts international institutions, laws and norms.

Neoclassical realism explores the cohesion of decision-makers as an intervening variable between the international distribution of power and foreign policy. A domestic rivalry due to political polarization, an adversarial oligarchy, a deficit of political legitimacy or other divisive issues that prevent the state from behaving as a unitary actor will undermine the ability of decision-makers to pursue foreign policies that maximize security. Internal power rivalry brought down the Soviet Union, is challenging the solidarity of the EU, and the current political polarization in the United States is influencing its foreign policy. Neorealist theory does not address domestic issues adequately because the theory merely posits that the international distribution of power creates systemic pressures (incentives and constraints and incentives) for states. Similarly, geoeconomics can be too preoccupied with the international distribution of economic power and thereby neglect domestic issues that diminish the ability of the state to exercise economic statecraft, such as an irrational commitment to laissez-faire capitalism or the influence of corporate elites with economic interests that are not aligned with state interests or even contravene them.

Neoclassical realism addresses this weakness in neorealist and geoeconomic theory. Neoclassical realism builds on the foundations of neorealism, which postulates that relative power is the principal variable to understanding why states act as they do (Smith 2018). The international distribution of power creates systemic pressures, incentives and constraints affecting how states should behave to maximize their security. According to realist theory, rational behaviour – defined as maximizing security – is defined as acting according to the logic of the balance of power. Waltz (1979) argued, however, that neorealism is not a foreign policy theory because decision-makers do not always act in accordance with the balance of power logic. Waltz subsequently challenged the neorealist assumption that states always behave rationally. Transcending realism is impossible, but failing to respond to the systemic pressures caused by the balance of power undermines security because 'the system punishes' those players (Mearsheimer 2009: 242). Neoclassical realism addresses the rationality gap in neorealism by exploring the extent to which decision-makers act 'rationally' by acting in accordance with the balance of power logic (Diesen 2016: 14). Decision-makers do not always react to systemic pressures because rationality depends on the 'the decision-makers' perceptions and state structure' (Rose 1998: 152). In any strategy, decision-makers must have the capacity to make carefully thought out calculations in pursuance of accurately defined security interests (Schelling 1980: 5).

Robotics and automation will likely cause creative destruction on an unprecedented scale. The concept of creative destruction recognizes the revolutionary aspect of technology as innovations constantly sweep away the old, making entire professions and industries obsolete. Creation is the 'process of industrial mutation that incessantly revolutionises the economic structure from within, incessantly destroying the old one, incessantly creating a new one' (Schumpeter 1942). Robotics and automation may cause permanent mass unemployment as the connection between capital and labour breaks down. The failure of states to address growing economic inequality and the fragmentation of traditional societal structures and institutions creates a demand for new and often radical ideologies that promise to reorganize society. At the same time, new technologies for political communication and organization suggest that governments will compete with social networks and foreign powers to establish narratives that can attract, persuade and unify. Technological developments have enabled individuals, corporations, non-governmental organizations and foreign powers to wield influence previously exercised only by states. Unlike liberal theory, neoclassical realist theory suggests that this imperils the ability of the state to mobilize resources in pursuit of its foreign policy objectives.

Case studies of great powers

Great powers are characterized by their ability to wield influence at a global level, and act independently even in defiance of the hegemon. The five defining criteria for achieving this great power influence are population and territory, economic capability, resources, political stability, and military strength (Waltz 1993). Technology influences the relevance of these great power criteria.

This book will focus primarily on the United States, China and Russia as the three main great powers. They are, respectively, the incumbent, the challenger and an 'unknown quantity'. Great powers are capable of acting independently and exert military, economic and diplomatic influence on a global scale, with the ability to protect that influence from other great powers in the international system. The United States is the incumbent: its technological leadership makes it the principal geoeconomic and military power with substantial cultural and communication primacy. Other Western states cannot act with full independence from Washington and therefore receive less attention here. Although great powers are inherently suspicious of each other, the solidarity among Western powers is made possible by a United States-led hierarchical power structure. The number of great powers, however, could increase due to the rise of non-aligned India and because Germany is establishing leadership in an EU that strives towards greater autonomy and technological sovereignty (Diesen 2020).

China has emerged as the principal challenger to the United States due to its ability and intention to assert technological leadership, its control over the geoeconomic levers of power, and its drive to develop its military force. China was the largest power in the world for centuries. This ended with its defeat by the British in the Opium Wars of the 1850s. China has recovered rapidly in recent decades is seemingly determined to re-establish its global economic and military leadership. Chinese economic nationalism resembles the three-pillared American System that linked nation-building to a manufacturing base, transportation corridors, and a national bank. The ambitious *Made in China 2025* initiative is an industrial strategy to establish technological leadership in the world's innovative industries by 2025. The Belt and Road Initiative (BRI) is a trillion-dollar project to construct transportation and energy corridors physically linking China with the world. Beijing supplements the BRI with the Digital Silk Road, a project for spreading Chinese standards and legislation. In a growing number of countries around the world, trade and new infrastructure projects are increasingly financed by Chinese-led investment banks using the yuan as their international currency.

Russia is a peculiar case and an uncertain quantity. Although it has lost the superpower status the Soviet Union held, Russia has demonstrated over the last decade that it remains a great power capable of acting independently and even against the hegemon. Still, debates continue as to whether Russia is a rising or declining power. The West's failure in the 1990s to develop a Greater Europe that accommodates Russia has pushed Moscow to reassert its great power status – that is, to act independently and strike a balance against what it perceives as an expansionist and hostile West. By replacing Greater Europe with the Greater Eurasia Initiative, Moscow has become the principal supporter of China's ambitions to challenge US leadership by laying the geoeconomic foundations for multipolarity (Lukin 2018). Russia has historically fallen behind on technological developments at the expense of its economic and military performance – only to catch up rapidly later. Russia's potential in the Fourth Industrial Revolution lies in its autonomous digital ecosystem. Russia has the resources for 'technological preparedness', the ability to replicate foreign innovations and develop domestic spin-offs. Furthermore, Russia can take the lead in markets where it is already strong, taking advantage of its current position as an agriculture superpower, of its high-end military technology, expertise in space and other technological infrastructure inherited from the Soviet Union and of a variety of digital platforms that have now caught up to leading standards. However, Russia might either fall behind and lose its great power status or leapfrog technologies and remain one of the world's leading powers.

The geoeconomics of the Fourth Industrial Revolution

Chapter 1 outlines how disruptive technologies influence great power politics. AI, robotics, automation, self-driving cars, the Internet of Things, blockchain, 3D-printing, nanotechnology, neurotechnology and biotechnology are developing simultaneously and at incredible speed. The strategic implications are immense because states must balance the struggle for competitive advantage in the international sphere with economic, social and ethical issues. However, technology is developing faster than the political bureaucracy. The emergence of national strategies provides a glimpse into how great powers envision adapting to the innovative technologies that will serve as the basis for future geoeconomic and military leadership.

   Chapter 2 presents a theory on the geoeconomics of technological sovereignty. Geoeconomics is primarily about shifting the 'balance of dependence' by reducing one's own economic dependence on others and increasing the reliance of others, while the subsequent asymmetries in economic relations are used to leverage political power. High-tech strategic industries create dependencies and are crucial to maximizing autonomy over domestic affairs and influence over other states. As high-tech industries dominate a growing share of economic activity, great powers must develop technological competencies and infrastructure. Geoeconomics is therefore largely focused on supporting the acquisition and diffusion of technologies. Governments support the acquisition of technology through innovation or imitation, and the industrial application of those technologies. Furthermore, governments can slow down the diffusion of technologies through various means to extend the first-mover advantage. The innovator and follower both have advantages and weaknesses in the pursuit of technological sovereignty and dominance.

   Chapter 3 assesses why techno-nationalism disrupts the international division of labour that has characterized cooperation and competition between states.

Free market theory correctly recognizes that developing comparative advantage in specific industries and engaging in international trade maximizes efficiency and absolute gain. However, governments also intervene in the market to climb the ladder of global value chains, developing strategic industries or high-tech activities that have high value and create dependencies. A clearly delineated division of labour tends to produce stability if it is supported by a hegemon that administers a fair and open international economic system. From the British repealing the Corn Laws in 1843 to the United States leading construction of global value chains during the digital revolution, technological leaders have used trade agreements to cement their dominance and formalize core–periphery asymmetrical interdependence. In simple terms, the United States invented new technologies such as the smartphone and China assembled them. The immense scope of automation will fragment global supply chains. Major technological powers can reshore their manufacturing as automated labour outcompetes low-wage manufacturing states. Furthermore, with increased rivalry between great powers, vital supply chains are repatriated under domestic control. China and Russia are pursuing a bottom-up strategy of developing the leading technologies of the Fourth Industrial Revolution while the United States is seeking a top-down strategy, by reshoring manufacturing with the assistance of automation. Developing states with export-based development strategies must adapt to these new realities.

Chapter 4 examines who will seize the means of production in the era of tech giants. Market power is becoming increasingly concentrated in the hands of tech giants due to the favourable conditions they offer and incentives to build monopolies. New technological platforms produce *economies of scope* because leadership in one industry provides a competitive advantage in seemingly unrelated industries. David Ricardo advocated comparative advantage, although market advantage in the Fourth Industrial Revolution lies in 'doing everything'. For example, advanced search engines have an advantage in taking over the transportation industry with automated vehicles; the transportation industry has a competitive advantage for e-commerce, automated logistics and delivery, which provide a technological platform for dominating payment systems, manufacturing and automated food preparation. The capital-intensive investments required to compete with the tech monopolies discourage competitors. Governments face a dilemma in that powerful tech giants capable of competing in international markets wield enough market power to have extensive influence in domestic politics. If the state does not assert control over industry, industry will increasingly assert its influence over the state. This dilemma is solved by using regulation to transform tech giants into national champions aligned with state interests, a tactic that resembles the fascist political economy.

Chapter 5 explores disruptions to political communication. Great power competition includes the ability to construct narratives, build identities and give legitimacy to authority. From the printing press to the Internet, it is evident that technologies for political communication influence the relationship between the people and the state. Initially, the decentralization of communication was expected to strengthen the individual vis-à-vis the state and to usher in an era of democracy and freedom. However, the chaos of unregulated social networks and the intrusion of foreign powers into the domestic discourse incentivized the state to reassert its control over communication technologies. The counteraction to restore control tends to be excessive and fuels the authoritarian impulses of the state. From Snowden to Assange, individuals are fighting to restore a healthy balance of power with the state in the new technological environment. The Fourth Industrial Revolution further disrupts political communication because the ability to extract data is essential for geoeconomic competitiveness and there is an increased need to control the public narrative. Great powers respond to rivalry in the international domain by nationalizing and territorializing the Internet and creating a 'sovereign Internet'.

Chapter 6 addresses the future of geoeconomics as contemporary capitalism comes to an end. Automation and robotics decouple capital from labour, challenging the viability of capitalism. 'Creative destruction' refers to how new technologies can eliminate jobs and entire professions. Historically, creative destruction led to 'up-skilling' as repetitive and dangerous work was replaced with more highly skilled and higher-paying jobs. However, capital and labour have been decoupling since the 1980s because capital owners have mostly been pocketing the growing profits resulting from the greater productivity of machines. During the decline of manufacturing jobs in the 1990s, workers transitioned into lower-skilled and lower-wage jobs. The Fourth Industrial Revolution intensifies this development due to the speed and scope of automation that also targets highly skilled professions. Furthermore, the loss of old jobs is not sufficiently offset by the creation of new jobs. Although communism was a failure, Marx recognized correctly that free market capitalism was a transitional phase in human development because technological advances concentrate wealth in monopolies. Capitalism must undergo reforms to shift the tax burden from labour to capital owners and to redistribute wealth. Furthermore, the disruption to economic liberalism will have wider implications because it has provided a foundation for political liberalism.

Chapter 7 assesses the great societal transformation to come. Creative destruction was initially presented by Friedrich Nietzsche as a societal process of updating values that provide human beings with meaning. When the structures and institutions of the past are no longer capable of delivering values and purpose, destructive nihilism arises and society decays. The First Industrial Revolution produced a rich philosophy about the struggle of mankind to live in industrialized society. The human condition, positioned between primitive impulses and rational decision-making, is disrupted by technological innovation. It has been known since the First Industrial Revolution that the duality of Man manifests itself in contradictory impulses, embracing laissez-faire economics for their efficiency on the one hand, while simultaneously resisting market forces and the disruptions they cause to traditional communities on the other hand. The Fourth Industrial Revolution presents new challenges and opportunities. What happens to the value of human beings when they become uncompetitive in an economically deterministic society in which all value is measured in dollar terms? Should new technologies only reduce labour, increase efficiency and cater to hedonistic urges, or should it also be directed towards reinforcing our humanity? The Fourth Industrial Revolution might have the instruments needed to bridge Gemeinschaft and Gesellschaft – that have grown farther apart ever since the First Industrial Revolution. A guiding philosophy is required to channel the use of new technologies and thus prevent the means from taking precedence over the ends.

Chapter 8 explores the disruption that killer military robots cause to great power politics. Destructive technologies incentivized the shift from militarized geopolitics to geoeconomics, but weapon technologies of the Fourth Industrial Revolution can return military power to the forefront of great power politics. The Fourth Industrial Revolution has the potential to undermine nuclear détente by converting what were originally defensive nuclear arms into offensive weapons. Cyberspace becomes weaponized as the digital world integrates with the physical world, space becomes a contested and militarized domain, and drone technology revolutionizes warfare when, for example, swarm technology can use a centralized digital brain to control millions of small, lethal drones. Governments are faced with the dilemma of whether to automate weapons, targeting and the decision to engage targets, sacrificing human control for the sake of greater speed and efficiency. Challengers to the world's leading military power face pressure to automate more battlefield functions in an effort to establish a balance of power. Miscalculations will also grow as the rules of war and deterrence become obscured by differing views on, for example, when it is acceptable to attack an unmanned drone and what the repercussions should be. The race to develop increasingly 'smart' robots runs the risk of undermining the potential of 'dumb' robots that cannot discriminate clearly between targets.

Chapter 9 explores global governance in the Fourth Industrial Revolution. The first two industrial revolutions enhanced the productive powers and economic activities of industrial societies that did not fit into the cultural and political confines of the nation state. The failure of global governance to manage the expansion of capital and competing geoeconomic infrastructure led to two world wars. The Fourth Industrial Revolution is complicated by the antagonistic transition from a unipolar to multipolar world order. Our present challenges bear great similarity to the world of the late nineteenth century as it moved towards the First World War. The first-mover advantage of Britain's industrial hegemony was waning and governance of an industrial Europe with ever-increasing productive power was lacking. Today, the relative decline of the United States and the emergence of a multipolar order present similar challenges. A system of global governance ensuring strategic stability has not materialized because efforts by the West to cement its unipolar dominance marginalized both China and Russia, and both have since begun decoupling from the United States-led liberal hegemonic order. As a result, global governance is fragmenting into regional constructs, with inter-regionalism the new hope for building a future system of future global governance. While China and Russia seek to integrate various regional formats and harmonize interests under the Greater Eurasia Initiative, Western-led institutions aim to marginalize such alternative structures in an effort to extend their hegemony. Anarchy is growing as the old system perishes and no new system has yet been born. The disintegration of global governance is occurring at a time when new technologies disrupt economic, political and military relations between the great powers.

This book will reach the conclusion that the Fourth Industrial Revolution makes technological sovereignty a key requirement in great power rivalry, which demands a more intrusive role for the state in the economy. New technologies have the transformative potential to overcome humanity's economic, societal and environmental problems. However, they can also exacerbate conflicts in great power politics. The status quo will no longer be tenable, and with uncertainty growing in the world, great powers are likely to pursue security primarily by maximizing their power. Although the United States and China are now the main rivals for technological leadership, Russia's historical aptitude for making a strong finish appears to repeat itself. Russia is carving out a great power position for itself with technological sovereignty to prevent the emergence of a United States–China bipolar international distribution of power. The EU will similarly need to develop technological sovereignty to preserve its internal cohesion.

1

Technologies of the Fourth Industrial Revolution: Towards national strategies

Introduction

Technologies have always granted power to states that could master them for economic, military and political purposes. The status quo in the international system is constantly disrupted as technological innovations create new instruments that shift the international distribution of power. This chapter explores the technologies of the Fourth Industrial Revolution and how great powers gradually adapt with new national strategies.

Western societies made a grand discovery in the First Industrial Revolution – that machinery could increase productivity and prosperity as a positive-sum game, making it possible to attain wealth without war, plunder and extortion. Almost the entirety of the world's population had lived in poverty throughout history. This changed in the mid-eighteenth century when the First Industrial Revolution unleashed unprecedented productivity and wealth creation. Furthermore, the incentives for embracing liberal economic ideas to organize the new economy translated into political liberalism and the elevation of human freedoms.

A second grand discovery from the Industrial Revolution was that advances in innovation and productivity follow an exponential growth curve rather than a gradual growth curve. With the amplified efficiency of each new technology, the path to the next technological breakthrough becomes shorter. Consequently, the technological evolution curve has become increasingly steep and shows no indication of levelling out. States must therefore prepare for an impending technological and intelligence explosion. The exponential growth of digital technologies unlocks a variety of new technologies. Only a few years ago, for example, the technology needed to produce self-driving cars was deemed to be an excessively complex cognitive task for machines to manage, but today, that technology has already been tested and commercialized. The socio-political implications of these technologies, however, and their influence on the economic and military competition among great powers remain unclear.

This chapter will first assess how the characteristics of great powers have changed with successive industrial revolutions. Second, it argues that the development of AI is perhaps the most important component of the Fourth Industrial Revolution, and that states must develop AI if they hope to maintain their great power status. Although previous technologies created tools to automate physical labour, AI is unique in automating cognitive tasks. AI improves all other technologies and is already outperforming humans in certain areas of research and development. Third, this chapter explores technologies that disrupt industrial capabilities. These include robotics, automation, self-driving cars, 3D printing, nanotechnology, the Internet of Things, blockchain, cryptocurrencies, neurotechnology and biotechnology. Last, it assesses the emerging strategies of great powers in the Fourth Industrial Revolution. It concludes that the variables defining great power status are undergoing fundamental changes as the industries that have traditionally underpinned industrial society become obsolete. National strategies indicate that rivalry between great powers will be prioritized above other considerations.

Great powers and industrial revolutions

Great powers are defined by their ability to act independently and to exert their influence on a global scale with economic, military and diplomatic power. Mearsheimer (1990: 7) defines a pole in the global system as having a 'reasonable prospect of defending itself against the leading state in the system by its own efforts'. By this definition, the international system has very few great powers at a time when the world is transitioning away from unipolarity. The end of the military and ideological rivalry that defined the Cold War and the turn towards a global capitalist system mark a shift in great power politics. Whereas, in the era of geopolitics, power was measured almost exclusively in terms of military strength and territory, in the current era of geoeconomics, it is measured more by influence over global markets.

The First Industrial Revolution in the mid-eighteenth century was characterized by the mechanization of agriculture and by steam-powered machines replacing human labour in industry. Britain took the lead for a variety of reasons. Britain's geography as an island state produced favourable conditions for Parliament to legislate land ownership and enclosures, and this sparked an agricultural revolution (Quigley 1979). Britain also had an abundance of cheap and easily extractable coal that replaced wood to fuel steam-powered machines. The First Industrial Revolution was itself a product of great power politics because the growing demand for weaponry put pressures on production efficiency, and the resulting mass production of weapons altered the strategies and tactics of warfare. The amount of wealth the British amassed from favourable trade with its colonies increased demand for high-end products for the affluent. Britain was also under pressure to improve its own efficiency in the textile industry to compete with textile products from India.

The Second Industrial Revolution in the mid-nineteenth century was largely defined by mass production. Electricity replaced steam power, and the development of the combustion engine generated demand for oil and gas. The Bessemer Process enabled the rapid and cheap production of steel, giving rise to the vast expansion of railroads and factories. The improved efficiency of production in factories, transportation by rail, and communication by telegraph led to the greatest economic growth of human history. Occurring between the 1870s and 1890s, it is also commonly characterized as the first wave of globalization. The emergence of steel as a strategic industry also sparked a competition for leadership in steel production between the United States, Britain, Germany, France and Japan. The US embrace of the Second Industrial Revolution laid the foundation for a technological rise that it has sustained ever since. The utility of the telegraph and railroads during the US Civil War was later converted into tools to serve commerce. Railroads also became America's first modern corporation due to their large size, national reach, mass employment, and highly developed organizational methods. Large corporations and supporting bureaucracies emerged, giving rise to a consumer society and more complex relations between the state and corporations.

Germany's use of the railway to integrate German lands also augmented war-fighting capabilities by enhancing mobility for troops that could be despatched to both Western and Eastern fronts. Russia reduced rail connectivity with Europe by using a different track gauge as an obstacle to invading armies. The railway in Pacific Russia was similarly designed for military purposes, away from the frontline, thus reducing its ability to advance economic connectivity. The growth of British industry fuelled a modern system of banking and finance that became dominant in the world and developed financial dependencies abroad as international trade surged. Furthermore, harnessing the world's financial power enabled Britain to construct the most powerful navy in the world to dominate the seas and establish control over maritime commerce. The global rivalry through the nineteenth century between Britain as a maritime power and Russia as a land power soon gave way to the rise of new powers that had industrialized rapidly – primarily the United States, Germany and Japan. The combination of economic developments, societal disruptions and new and powerful weaponry unleashed destructive warfare that ended the primacy Western European powers had enjoyed since the early 1500s. Industrialization through import substitution in interwar Central and Eastern Europe failed due to its focus on old technologies and sectors that were already in decline in more developed states (Berend 2000: 318).

The Third Industrial Revolution in the mid-twentieth century was a digital revolution. Microprocessors and transistors revolutionized the industry, and nuclear technology became crucial in this period. Nuclear weapons became a key condition for great power status, which was subsequently acquired by all permanent members of the UN Security Council – the United States, the Soviet Union, the UK, France and China. US leadership leapt forward during this period, with rapid technological advances cementing its geoeconomic dominance and military superiority. The space race produced unexpected synergy among technologies such as satellite communication with GPS for the Americans and GLONASS for the Soviets (Skolnikoff 1994). The Soviet Union harnessed nuclear power and other technologies, but its ability to compete in the digital revolution was limited as the decentralized function of digital technologies could not be applied optimally in a centralized and authoritarian system. Furthermore, the communists' detachment from international markets meant that the technologies could not easily be converted into economic statecraft and geoeconomic power.

Increasingly large and complex global value chains and a new wave of globalization emerged due to the combination of reduced transportation costs, liberal economics, the clear international division of labour, and a unique international distribution of power. The exponential growth of digital technologies took a major leap in the 1990s with the personal computer, Microsoft's operating system and the rapid expansion of the Internet. The digital revolution focused on communication technologies, intensifying the state's competition for information dissemination vis-à-vis the people and foreign actors. The fossil fuels that have degraded the environment and biodiversity are gradually beginning to give way to renewable green energy. The digital revolution made information and technology intangible commodities on the market. Unlike other commodities, their value does not degrade when consumed.

Defining the Fourth Industrial Revolution

The Fourth Industrial Revolution – a term coined by Klaus Schwab (2016) – is now underway and was conceptualized as the shift away from simple digital innovations associated with communications technology. It represents major progress and builds upon the introduction of the computer chip and superconductor from the Third Industrial Revolution.

The principal distinction and break from the previous digital revolution is the 'velocity, scope, and systems impact' (Schwab 2016: 3). Because the Fourth Industrial Revolution builds upon the digital revolution, it has elicited fair criticism as a mere continuation of the Third Industrial Revolution (Rifkin 2016). Nevertheless, this book refers to *the Fourth Industrial Revolution* as the combination of new disruptive technologies that are making previous technologies obsolete. A key distinction from the Third Industrial Revolution is that the digital world is merging with the physical world. The dawn of a distinctively new period in human history was expressed succinctly by Bill Gates (2007), who argued: 'we may be on the verge of a new era, when the PC will get up off the desktop and allow us to see, hear, touch and manipulate objects in places where we are not physically present'. Indeed, a new era does seem to be emerging, as new technologies disrupt the labour market, capitalism, political liberalism, military competition, the social fabric, and, as a result, great power politics.

Paradoxically, the Fourth Industrial Revolution might mark the end of the industrial era that lasted two centuries. The technological innovations that created the conditions for a mass labour force, liberal economics and industrial thinking that is still with us today might soon become obsolete. The Fourth Industrial Revolution might also be the first environmentally sustainable revolution by making the transition away from fossil fuels. Industrial revolutions involve not only the acquisition and implementation of technology, but also the need to manage the disruptions caused by those technologies. Schwab (2016: 7) argues:

> Ultimately, the ability of government systems and public authorities to adapt will determine their survival. If they prove capable of embracing a world of disruptive change, subjecting their structures to the levels of transparency and efficiency that will enable them to maintain their competitive edge, they will endure. If they cannot evolve, they will face increasing trouble.

The Fourth Industrial Revolution is set to drastically accelerate the speed of changes and disruptions to the international system as technologies advance rapidly and simultaneously. Exponential growth accelerates as digital technologies amass an unprecedented amount of information that is then processed rapidly – which is instrumental in advancing all other technologies. Machine learning, or the ability of computers to learn and improve their own algorithms and become more intelligent, is on the path to an intellectual explosion in the automation of the cognitive. AI unlocks and intensifies technological advances across the spectrum of automation, robotics, nanotechnology, neurotechnology, biotechnology and digital systems such as the Internet of Things, digital ledger technology, cloud computing and related technologies.

A distinctively new era is evident as mankind's relationship with machines undergoes a reversal in terms of the acquisition of knowledge. Past industrial revolutions consisted of scientists developing technologies or products, with machines then replicating and automating the process. The Fourth Industrial Revolution is making machines the innovators. AI involves self-learning through the discovery of patterns and the hypothesizing of causal relationships, leaving human scientists to make sense of the algorithms generated and to attempt to replicate the best solutions produced by the machines.

The unpredictability of technological development is largely due to its exponential growth, also known as accelerating speed. A common misconception about digital technology is the belief that it develops along a linear trajectory with the gradual development of existing technologies. Instead, the speed of development and subsequent application of computer technologies is accelerating exponentially. Moore's Law, the observation that the number of transistors successfully placed on a computer chip doubles approximately every 18 to 24 months, has been valid for the past four decades. For example, Intel launched a computer chip with 2,300 transistors in 1971, 29,000 transistors in 1978, 250,000 in 1988, 9.5 million in 1999, 1.16 billion in 2011, 8 billion in 2016 and 50 billion most recently. With components now approaching the size of atoms, we are approaching the physical limits of Moore's Law as it applies to the manufacture of computer chips. Nevertheless, the development of quantum computers will seemingly be the next step in the development of information technology and would radically increase computing speed.

The race to develop the most powerful supercomputers has followed a similar path and will have a major influence on the international distribution of power in the future. Supercomputers were developed to achieve technological progress, economic competitiveness and military security. In 2009, the US-made Cray supercomputer had the most powerful processing capacity in the world at 1.76 petaflops. By 2016, China's Sunway TaihuLight supercomputer with 93 petaflops was on top, and the United States only re-established its leadership in mid-2018 with the launch of its Summit supercomputer boasting 122 petaflops. The latest US victory could be short-lived, however, because China is planning to release its Tianhe-3 by 2020, a new supercomputer that measures processing speed in exaflops (1,000 petaflops). Although China and the United States hold the lead with such tech areas as Silicon Valley (Palo Alto) and Shenzhen, other large powers such as Russia, Japan, South Korea, India, Germany, France and the UK are also developing supercomputers – a result of the new international distribution of power.

Artificial intelligence

The world's six largest companies in 2018 were all tech corporations that are also among the main developers of AI – Apple, Amazon, Alphabet (Google), Microsoft, Facebook and Alibaba. AI is a reference to intelligent machines. More specifically, AI is the cognitive function of machines that includes the ability to recognize patterns, solve problems and perhaps one day even achieve self-awareness. AI is comparable to electricity for its nearly universal application and as a tool for advancing other technologies – making it the most important feature of the Fourth Industrial Revolution.

In machine learning, computers devise algorithms themselves. Before AI, human programmers developed algorithms by which computers would calculate or solve problems. By contrast, the neural network approach does not teach computers the rules of games and imitate human strategies to win. Rather, the system is self-learning, imitating the human brain by making connections through experience. Vast amounts of data must be fed into the computer and then the computer must be given specific inputs regarding that date. This allows the computer to discover patterns that it expresses as algorithms. For example, a computer can be fed a million images of mammograms and then told which show evidence of breast cancer and which do not. Using AI, the computer then identifies patterns that even scientists might not have discovered and records them as algorithms for identifying breast cancer. Similarly, AI software for extending credit has been developed by entering the computer data of people who borrowed money and then informing the computer which people were able and unable to repay their loans. The strength and utility of such AI programs are their ability to continuously develop and train software to identify breast cancer or assess a loan application with superhuman speed and accuracy. Data is commonly called 'the new oil'. This analogy can be misleading, however, because not all data is the same (Varian 2018). The main limitation of AI is that it only works within a single domain, and AI software developed for detecting breast cancer cannot be used to drive cars.

Artificial intelligence research focuses extensively on board games and video games as narrowly defined tasks in controlled environments where all possible variables and outcomes can be observed and measured. After years of failing to live up to exaggerated expectations, AI now performs beyond expectations by defeating leading human minds in increasingly complex contests of skill. In 1979, the world champion in backgammon was the first to lose to a machine. Two decades later, in 1997, world chess champion Gary Kasparov lost to IBM's Deep Blue software. The development of IBM's Watson program went another major step forward by managing to win the game show Jeopardy. This was a formidable achievement because the machine had to acquire knowledge in a wide range of fields and decipher intricate and often opaque phrases and statements. Watson's impressive achievements were then topped by Google's AlphaGo program that was developed to play Go – a board game that is more complex than chess and that was believed to lie beyond the cognitive functioning abilities of machines. AlphaGo defeated the first professional Go player in October 2015, and through self-learning, went on to defeat the Go world champion in 2017. Leading AI experts had thought that the AlphaGo victory was still a decade away. The moment signified the triumph of machine over Man and mobilized interest in AI by the Chinese public (Lee 2018). The cognitive development of AI was also demonstrated by Libratus, a poker-playing program that defeated leading poker players in a poker tournament. This victory was particularly astounding because poker involves a major psychological component – for example, in choosing when to bluff, determining when other players are bluffing and deciding when and how much to raise or when to fold.

AI requires two key components – processing power and data. Quantity is quality in the age of AI because machine learning depends on greater computing power to analyse ever-greater amounts of data. Both these criteria are now being met. The operation of Moore's Law has radically elevated the processing power of supercomputers, and it has recently become possible to capture huge amounts of data. AI has great significance in terms of first-mover advantage, but it remains a portfolio technology with a variety of limited applications. Moore's Law might also apply to AI in that an intelligent computer capable of teaching itself will become progressively more intelligent at an accelerating rate. The speed and future path of AI remain unpredictable due to the potential for an 'intelligence explosion' that could unlock both the 'known unknowns' and the 'unknown unknowns'. This exponential growth in AI capabilities makes it difficult to predict whether computers will replicate human intelligence by 2025 or 2050. However, once human intelligence has been replicated, we would be left far behind within a very short time. Machines possessing self-awareness could also begin communicating with each other and establish their own objectives.

The obvious risk of AI is in developing something that we would not be able to understand, predict or control, eclipsing humans as the drivers of change. Henry Kissinger (2018) took an interest in AI due to its unpredictable influence on great power politics. Kissinger cautioned that AI could elevate data above human cognition. This would spell the end of the Enlightenment because human rationality would no longer organize society. The AI victory in AlphaGo was significant because of the machine-made strategic moves that humans had never attempted and did not even understand. The relationship between man and machine had moved from the computer replicating human behaviour to humans attempting to understand the superior logic of the computer. Similarly, the use of AI to improve bacteria fermentation has already resulted in effective suggestions, although scientists cannot theorize or comprehend why they work.

The future might bring an 'AI alignment problem' in which a superintelligent machine begins acting independently and in ways that undermine the interests of humanity (Ford 2018). Stephen Hawking cautioned: 'AI could spell the end of the human race. It would take off on its own and redesign itself at an ever-increasing rate. Humans, who are limited by slow biological evolution, couldn't compete, and would be superseded' (Cellan-Jones 2014). Elon Musk worries that AI development has almost reached exponential growth and is sceptical about AI companies that 'believe that they can shape and control the digital superintelligence and prevent bad ones from escaping into the Internet' (Moyer 2014).

Artificial intelligence continuously creates and re-writes its own algorithms and the solutions are often beyond the control of human programmers. An experiment in which an AI machine played the game 'Coast Runners Boat' revealed that the internal logic of digital intelligence could be difficult to predict. Rather than racing its opponents as the game proposes, the computer merely began spinning its player in circles to push adversaries out of the game, eliminating them from play and enabling the machine's player to cross the finish line first (Metz 2017). A robot programmed to win a game of chess might determine that the simplest path to success would be to murder the opponent. Nonetheless, any arguments for limiting AI must take into account the race by corporations and states to reap the benefits of first-mover advantage. The risk of AI slipping out of our control must be weighed against the risk of adversaries with no such limitations developing more powerful AI capabilities.

Robotics, automation and self-driving cars

Driverless vehicles and drones can be considered a category of their own due to the huge market for these products and the important role transportation plays as a catalyst of the Fourth Industrial Revolution. Driverless vehicles are set to transform the transportation industry and will likely cause a restructuring of delivery services, restaurants, payment services, e-commerce, renewable energy and even other industries that are only remotely related to transportation.[1]

There are different definitions of what constitutes a robot, but all refer to the 'three functions'. First is the ability to receive information through a data feed, cameras, lasers or sensors. Second is the ability to process and analyse that information. And third is the ability to make a decision that has some influence on the physical world. Russel and Norvig (1995: 773) define a robot as 'as an active, artificial agent whose environment is the physical world ... whose environment consists of computer file systems, databases and networks'. The first industrial robots, the Unimate series, were developed in 1961 and consisted of a robot arm that performed various functions in the car manufacturing industry. This technology took half a century to mature: it was not until the 2010s, in what can be called the decade of industrial robotics, did robots move out of the factories.

AI possesses a vast potential for automation and robotics that could have unpredictable consequences for global supply chains. On one hand, as low-wage labour becomes less of comparative advantage and developed states with more sophisticated infrastructure repatriate manufacturing, automation and robotics will shorten and simplify the long and complex supply chains that have characterized global commerce. The stakes are high because countries with the most advanced robot workforce – and not those with the lowest labour costs – will have the greatest manufacturing power. The future of manufacturing and distribution has been exemplified by innovators such as Amazon, which has automated its warehouses. What's more, robotics can reduce the costs of transportation infrastructure as automated machines take over control of warehouses, ports and transportation. Most innovations in robotics have

---

[1] Discussed in details in Chapter 4.

industrial applications, but the invention of automated lawnmowers and vacuum cleaners indicates a possible future market in personal robotics as well.

The number of industrial robots is growing rapidly, replacing less efficient human labour and altering global value chains. A total of 115,000 industrial robots were sold in 2008, with that number expected to surpass 500,000 by 2020. Robot density, the number of robots per 10,000 employees in manufacturing, is becoming a measurement for economic competitiveness. South Korea leads the world in robot density, followed by Singapore, Germany and other European states (IFR 2018). Learning from the South Korean experience, Japan established its 'Robot Revolution Council' in 2015 to support the development of technologies and their implementation by Japanese industries. In Europe, Germany has taken the lead in robotics and Switzerland has earned the name of 'the Silicon Valley of robotics'. Despite this, China represents the world's largest potential market for industrial robots. As wages rise and it becomes the driving force for world consumption, China must automate manufacturing to remain the factory of the world.

3D printing and nanotechnology

3D printing or additive manufacturing is a technology that builds layers of material such as metals or plastic to make finished products. Much like a regular paper printer, the 3D printer receives information from software about what to produce. Instead of applying ink to paper, however, 3D printers add successive layers of materials to develop three-dimensional products. Value chains are simplified because customers and producers pay only for raw materials for the printers and the intellectual property rights for printing the product, although many designs are shared for free. Much as the digitalization of music and movies altered the entertainment industry because files could be shared online – whether legally or illegally – so can sharing product designs for everything from footballs to bicycles alter every consumer industry.

Advanced products requiring complex materials or moving parts can be printed at local production plants, while smaller 3D printers that use less complex materials are already available for the home for a few hundred dollars. Faster adaptation can be expected as the technology matures, which is defined by the increase in quality and efficiency, and the reduction in price. Although 3D printers were initially limited in speed, new algorithms are making them faster all the time. 3D printing is cheaper, cleaner, simpler and more effective than traditional manufacturing that is both complex and labour-intensive. Traditional manufacturing requires large supply chains and extensive logistics to bring together mass-produced components requiring such specialized skills as cutting, welding, moulding and other techniques for their creation. The production process is followed by inspections and testing, then packaging, shipping and storage before reaching the consumer. 3D printing bypasses almost all of these steps.

As technology advances and prices decrease, more and more industries will assimilate 3D printing and change global markets radically. The initial competitive advantage of 3D printing lies in its ability to customize, which is why the technology was first used to construct prototypes and complex high-value products. It also offers a competitive advantage for low-volume products because 3D printing can nullify economies of scale as a key economic principle. Large corporations tend to be more competitive because large volumes reduce per-unit costs, resulting in a tendency in capitalism towards the concentration of wealth and the formation of monopolies. By contrast, 3D printing makes it possible to produce each item with identical quality and at the same per-unit cost, regardless of quantity. In a shift away from mass production, the possibilities provided by 3D printing suggest that markets in the future will be defined by unlimited customization and creativity, enabling people to design and produce almost anything on demand.

3D printing is commonly associated with consumer goods such as clothing, toys and home equipment. However, 3D printing can also be used for large products such as entire houses and complex components with moving parts such as jet and rocket engines. Bioprinting involves the production of biological matter such as food or even body parts. At Northwestern University in the United States, working ovaries were printed for infertile mice (Burns 2016). An obvious problem is that this decentralization also applies to criminal activity. Free designs for printing handguns are already proliferating on the Internet through decentralized networks, with the creators often acting on libertarian political convictions.

One key competitive advantage of 3D printing is the reduced need for transportation and storage. Complex supply chain management with expensive logistics and billions spent on transportation and warehousing could be radically reduced as manufacturing is brought closer to the consumer. Cost savings are also achieved in other aspects of production by minimizing labour material wastage. Government subsidies to incentivize adoption can be justified from a mere environmental perspective due to the environmental footprint from traditional manufacturing, which is produced more waste from cutting material, packaging and transportation. The need for raw materials instead of produced goods could also make discarded plastic in the oceans valuable. Shorter delivery time is also why several American delivery companies such as UPS have already integrated 3D printing into their services. Eliminating complex supply chains makes it possible to produce goods faster and closer to the end consumer (Lipson and Kurman 2013).

Ultimately, the future of 3D printing depends on its ability to compete with mass-produced goods. Although increasingly effective algorithms and technology make 3D printing more competitive for mass production, it will still have to compete against modern manufacturing facilities benefitting from automation and robotics. In the same way, companies already exist that 3D-print food, and these could become competitors to automated food preparation plants. The range of materials it can employ and the scale of objects it can produce remain two major limitations of 3D printing.

Nanotechnology is merging with 3D printing to produce advanced materials. Nanotechnology manipulates material at the atomic and molecular level to create new materials to advance technologies. Nanotechnology can, therefore, be applied to develop computing power, medicine, biotechnology, energy and other industries. For example, limitations on batteries are dictated by the materials used to make them: altering the material can improve battery performance. Russian scientists solved the problem of the low resolution and low speed of 3D printing by using nanoparticles to print three-dimensional structures at higher speeds.

The Internet of Things

The Internet of Things (IoT) is a reference to the use of the Internet to link computers with everyday objects. The popular and mundane application of the technology includes using a phone to operate the coffee machine, thermostat, automated lawnmower, or alternatively receive information from objects such as the fridge when particular products are running low. The IoT market is poised for rapid growth. The common case study is that of elevator maintenance, where regular maintenance checks are replaced with digital notifications when repairs are needed. The IoT market is expected to more than double from 2017 to 2021 (Columbus 2018). The launch of fifth-generation (5G) mobile data networks technology radically enhances the speed of the Internet and the ability to extract data. 5G will form the nervous system of emerging technologies ranging from the IoT and AI to self-driving cars, blockchain and other technologies that will restructure the entire global economy and the world. These technologies are further supported by cloud computing – large data centres accessed through the Internet – that is a critical component of the Fourth Industrial Revolution. Cloud computing offers easy and cheap digital infrastructure and is also a source of data (Oracle 2016).

Intelligent wearables such as the smartwatch extract data about your body and offer guidance for improved health. Its functions could expand to include, for example, blood testing for diseases, thus completely revolutionizing the health industry. A smart home extracts data about heating, air conditioning, ventilation and lighting to, for example, make energy consumption more efficient. Similar energy-saving AI initiatives are also applied to offices and industry. For example, Google used DeepMind to cut energy use for cooling its servers by 40 per cent and reduced its total energy consumption at its data centres by 15 per cent (Vaughan 2016). Smart cars can connect to and cooperate with smart homes to, for example, turn on the heat when the car approaches. Smart cars will also communicate with each other, transmitting information from their sensors about the immediate vicinity so that a car approaching from around the corner knows what environment and activity to expect. The military application is also evident because swarm technology enables a centralized brain to operate and coordinate as many as tens of thousands of drones simultaneously. Smart cities use sensors on bridges and other critical physical infrastructure to send alerts in case of dangerous decay. Parking spaces are monitored for efficient use of space, smart waste management detects loads, smart elevators evaluate maintenance needs and smart lighting reduces energy consumption. Smart agriculture and smart greenhouses offer precision farming with sensors that extract data regarding temperature, moisture, light, humidity and other important variables affecting soil fertility. Machines can then increase productivity and reduce waste using automated irrigation systems and ground-based and aerial drones to sow, spray and monitor crops. Similar systems are also used for collecting information on farm animals and performing automated milking.

Blockchain and cryptocurrencies

Distributed ledger technology, also known colloquially as blockchain, has the potential to revolutionize the monetary and financial systems that underpin the international economy by creating banking without banks. Digital banks using virtual currencies are expected to produce a Bank of Things (BoT) that enables direct financial interactions between individuals without banks as intermediaries (Del Giudice, Campanella and Dez 2016).

'Banking without banks' is becoming more attractive as technologies mature using digital peer-to-peer lending platforms to offer both lenders and borrowers improved rates. The domestic and international implications are difficult to predict due to the central role banks have held since the First Industrial Revolution. Banks have already been at the forefront of digitalizing to improve the quality of their services and reduce costs. The next step in digitalizing banking, however, might be to do away with the bank altogether as an unnecessary middleman.

Banking and currencies are at the heart of geoeconomic rivalry, and China and Russia are collectively revolting against US dominance over investment banks and the dollar as a trade and reserve currency. The global financial crisis of 2008–2009 largely discredited fractional banking because it encouraged debt and set the stage for a banking crisis by lending more capital than banks had on their books. The underlying problems of the great financial crisis were never resolved. Instead of restoring fiscal discipline, the leading economies in the West only accrued more debt. In contrast, Russia paid of its debts and China has grown weary of its exposure to the US dollar and treasury.

China uses applications that allow people to make payments and transfer money from one app to another without a bank as an intermediary. A report by the Massachusetts Institute of Technology argues that platforms such as WeChat or Sesame are redefining financial services and are likely to outperform traditional banks (Lipton, Shrier and Pentland 2016: 17). US banks have cause for concern: although the technology has not yet been applied to the banking and financial industry, it has found wide applications in society.

Cryptocurrencies are attracting investors and political leaders as a decentralized alternative to currencies under government control. Alternatively, governments can restore trust in national currencies by using the same technologies to impose fiscal discipline. The willingness to experiment with new technologies will likely grow as the leading developed nations in the West continue to accumulate unsustainable debt and the US dollar comes under greater pressure. Widespread adoption of cryptocurrencies would diminish the economic leverage enjoyed by the United States, that has the advantage of being able to run large deficits and use the dollar as an economic weapon (Smith and Dumieński 2018). While governments have been critical of cryptocurrencies because of the lack of oversight, they are also viewed as a potential instrument for 'de-dollarising', for diminishing what Charles de Gaulle referred to as an 'exorbitant privilege' (Hurrell 1995: 340). Krugman (2018) has been more sceptical about the potential of cryptocurrencies. He cites the fact that, because they are not backed up by anything of value, cryptocurrencies have extreme fiat characteristics and must be mined for liquidity.

Neurotechnology and biotechnology: Improving human beings

Advances in neurotechnology and biotechnology enable the improvement of human beings. The altruistic objective of eliminating diseases will dominate in the early stages of technological development. Yet, like other technologies, they will find other applications and markets. The technology to manipulate human evolution will have unpredictable consequences for the economy, military, society, and relations between governments and individuals. These technologies could also lay the foundation for a new class structure based on the financial ability to 'upgrade' individuals or groups.

Neurotechnology builds on new insights into the human brain. These include advances in detecting brain activity and manipulating the chemical and electrical activity of the brain to improve cognitive abilities. Formerly in the realm of science fiction, abilities such as mindreading are now a reality and could have broad applications. In a successful experiment in 2008, a monkey used brain waves to control its robot arm, and in 2017, Rodrigo Hubner Mendes became the first person to drive a race car using only his mind (Schwab 2018). The possibility of recording dreams might be only a few years away, an advance that could result in a variety of applications. Neuroscientists from the University of Glasgow have already been able to extract memory of human faces from the human brain, which can then be 3D-printed as a physical facial model (Zhan et al. 2019). Neurotechnology is a $150 billion industry that is growing at a rapid pace of 10 per cent annually due to its applications in everything from medicine to the military. Apple, Google and Facebook are reportedly 'raiding' animal research labs and universities for neuroscientists who can link the brain with AI to also advance such technologies as self-driving cars (McBride and Vance 2019). The digitalization of the brain – that is, connecting the brain to digital feeds – could make it possible to share experiences with others in vastly more personal ways than social media. Connecting the brain to the digital space could also work the other way: using computers to manipulate the brain could open the prospect of gaining unprecedented control over human beings.

Biotechnology uses living systems to develop products. To date, it has mainly been applied in simple areas such as in the manipulation and production of bacteria for improving the fermenting process. Genetic modification will become increasingly advanced in the coming years due to its immense commercial potential. Mapping the human genome is a relatively recent achievement that could have profound possibilities for the health industry in terms of both curing diseases and modifying human characteristics. Significant advances have been made in animal testing as well, such as the successful effort in 2017 to grow a baby sheep grown in an artificial womb. The ability to manipulate DNA and make genetic changes has already evoked questions about ethics and where the line should and can be drawn. Although public and political support can be expected for eliminating inheritable diseases, it is unclear where the path of improving human beings will end before it reaches the point of creating designer babies and superhumans.

Advances in human longevity make it possible to slow down and even reverse the ageing process. In 1900, worldwide life expectancy averaged 31 years. By 1950, it was 48, and in 2010 it had reached 70 (Letzter 2016). Although methods promising to slow down symptoms of ageing or even prolong life have already become a billion-dollar industry, most of the products accomplish little, if anything. Most of the industry is driven by vanity and offers nothing more than the chance to appear younger. However, AI is making a huge leap forward in pharmaceutical research by discovering ways to slow down or even reverse biological processes such as ageing (Zhavoronkov et al. 2018). The enormous profits already enjoyed by the beauty industry for superficial and inefficient products provide a glimpse of the even larger potential market for extending human longevity. Putting a price on the holy grail for longer life will doubtlessly take the pharmaceutical industry to unprecedented heights (Mellon and Chalabi 2017).

New technologies can also be used to improve human beings to ensure they can keep pace with the development of machines. Humans have historically worked alongside machines as opposed to being defeated by them. Yet, AI represents a different challenge by surpassing mankind's relatively stagnant intelligence that relies on biological evolution. By linking biological intelligence to digital intelligence, AI would develop rapidly by processing and finding patterns in the complexity of the brain. Furthermore, the same information would allow AI to learn and replicate human thought patterns and effectively digitalize the human brain. In the more distant future, humans could merge with machines to varying degrees. Instead of attempting an unwinnable race against machines, Brynjolfsson and McAfee (2012) argue that we need to 'race with the machines' by using new technologies to advance human capabilities. Elon Musk called for the 'merger of biological intelligence and digital intelligence … for humanity to achieve symbiosis with machines' (Winkler 2017). Musk aims to achieve this objective by developing a connection between the human brain and machines to upload and download thoughts. Musk launched the Neuralink Corporation to develop a direct cortical interface between the brain and computers, to enable humans to reach higher levels of cognition.

Great power strategies in the making

The vast number of disruptive technologies now emerging will unavoidably cause major dislocations to great power politics. The new international distribution of power will be determined by those with the greatest technological capabilities. Because China and the United States already have a strong lead, the race could end in a bipolar international distribution of power. At the same time, Russia, the UK, Germany and others trailing the leaders might either manage to catch-up or else fall even further behind. Digital technologies that underpin AI and big data will lay the foundation for most technologies related to the Fourth Industrial Revolution. AI is itself not a geoeconomic instrument or a military weapon, but a technology that makes other technological changes possible. AI can be compared to electricity or the combustion engine from the Second Industrial Revolution that unleashed a myriad of other technologies that changed societies and the international military–economic rivalry.

The United States has been slow to develop a clear and cohesive national strategy on AI. It has grown comfortable from a decades-long technological leadership that it can no longer take for granted. The White House released an AI policy road map in 2016 that focused on US leadership and the regulatory framework (Felten and Lyons 2016). The former CEO of Google, Eric Schmidt, is adamant that an actual national strategy on AI is required, much like the national strategy on nuclear weapons, due to its immense influence on the international distribution of power (Dougherty and Jay 2018). Washington did eventually come up with an AI strategy in 2018, but it lacked a clear increase in funding for AI other than larger budgets for the military and intelligence agencies (Department of Defence 2019).

The United States has attempted to cover all aspects of AI by assessing its economic, military, societal, and ethical implications. Hegemonic ambitions and efforts to defend the so-called 'liberal international order' are central to Washington's AI ambitions. Having a military strategy that seeks security through dominance (no challengers), the United States can use AI to revive the military superiority it enjoyed in the 1990s but that it has since been losing rapidly. Indirect subsidies for AI are funnelled through Pentagon funding that has historically benefitted private enterprises through the awarding of contracts. Furthermore, it is important for the United States to use AI to restore its economic leadership in the world. The approach it uses to achieve these goals will vary depending on which presidential administration is leading what is becoming an increasingly polarized country. Obama envisioned more state support to develop AI leadership, while Trump, an economic nationalist, ironically has sought to attain that goal using the free-market principle of removing barriers for innovators.

China's approach is best summarized by its national strategy on AI, the *New Generation Artificial Intelligence Development Plan* of 2017, the Three-Year Action Plan for Promoting the Development of Next Generation Artificial Intelligence Industry (2018–2020), and the ambitious industrial policy of *Made in China 2025* (China State Council 2015*)*. The national strategy stipulates the imperative 'to build China's first-mover advantage' as a 'major strategic opportunity' (Webster et al. 2017). The Chinese government indicates that it aims to use AI primarily for commercial innovation to establish the country's economic leadership in the world. Towards this end, Beijing actively partners with national tech corporations to advance China's leading role. The following plan by the Chinese government was more specific and focused on four key tasks: intelligent networked products such as driverless vehicles and identification systems; AI support systems like neural network chips and intelligent sensors; intelligent/robotic manufacturing; and improving the safety and environment for AI with, for example, cybersecurity (MIIT 2017). China's national strategy considers AI an instrument of economic competition as a central domain for great power rivalry, yet also links it closely with military security (Kania 2017). Beijing views technology as the means for restoring China's central place in the world that it enjoyed prior to its defeat by the British in the 1850s and subsequent collapse. The *China 2025* program, announced in 2015, is the world's boldest industrial policy and endeavours to establish Chinese leadership in the key technologies of the Fourth Industrial Revolution.

Russia is a latecomer to the Fourth Industrial Revolution, but it appears intent on catching up. Although its national strategy on AI is still in the making, some indications of the content are becoming evident. President Putin gave a speech on 30 May 2019, calling for Russia to establish 'technological sovereignty' by developing AI infrastructure and existing strengths in STEM (Science, Technology, Engineering and Math), and by protecting intellectual property rights and civil rights. Moscow's objective is to establish a multipolar system because it views the post–Cold War unipolar international distribution of power as detrimental to Russian security as having left it facing a hostile and expansionist West on its borders. Putin translated these political concerns into the language of technology: 'If someone can provide a monopoly in the field of artificial intelligence, then the consequences are clear to all of us: he will rule the world' (Bendett 2019).

Russia has been vocal about the economic and military imperative of developing AI. Russia has traditionally been a military power because of its vast borders, and therefore also seeks to develop AI for military operations. As a major arms exporter and military power, Russia considers the economic and military function of AI to hold major positive synergy potential. Because technological developments in renewable energy could lead to energy diversification and reduce the significance of hydrocarbons, they have the potential to radically alter great power politics. Energy exporting states would face a geoeconomic decline due to the loss of revenue and political influence, upsetting the international balance of power. To prepare for a disruptive and volatile future, Russia and other exporters of hydrocarbons should immediately implement policies for using energy revenues to rapidly modernize and diversify the economy. Technology improves economic development more when it leverages natural or existing capabilities. Agriculture is a key niche market due to Russia's vast geography and proximity to Asian markets. Russia has already established itself as an agricultural superpower and is increasingly employing smart agriculture to exercise greater control over the industry and increase barriers to entry for others. Similarly, Russia is employing nanotechnology in space to advance satellites and other equipment.

Because it is not a technological leader, Russia has little ability to rival the technological ecosystems of the United States and China. The key threats it faces entail falling too far behind on technology accumulation and implementation, thus becoming 'technologically colonized' due to excessive reliance on foreign platforms that would saturate the market and impede domestic alternatives from maturing. The optimal approach for Russia is to establish technological preparedness by integrating spin-offs into a domestic technological ecosystem. Russia's great power characteristics such as its natural resource wealth must be used to fund modernization. Its large population offers provide it with negotiating power to make such demands such as technology transfers in return for access to the Russian market. Its military applications of advanced AI can be transferred to the field of commercial security, and the country's geography carries the imperative of connecting with the large consumer market of Asia. Finally, technological advances in space can be utilized to cooperate on equal terms with powers such as China. Overall, Russia has the necessary tools to assert itself as a great power in the Fourth Industrial Revolution. However, Russia's ability to implement strategies is disadvantaged: economic statecraft suffered from seventy years of communism followed by the liberal economic illusions of the 1990s. Furthermore, Russia must modernize while under economic coercion from the West and trying to cultivate a partnership with a much more powerful China.

2

The geoeconomics of technological sovereignty: Managing diffusion

Introduction

Technology is power. Governments develop technologies out of a desire to establish leadership and the fear of being left behind. Technological leadership has historically been of utmost importance in great power politics, but has traditionally focused on military technology. Since the development of nuclear weapons, military innovations have reached a level of destructiveness that fundamentally alters the cost–benefit calculations of pursuing foreign policy objectives by force. Technology also augments economic power. This has resulted in great power competition shifting from the military to the economic sphere because increased economic connectivity between states heightens the potential for economic statecraft. Geoeconomics means that control over markets becomes the source of power, as opposed to merely exerting control over territory and military power.

Geoeconomics is based on the assumption of realist theory that international anarchy cannot be transcended. In the absence of a world government, states are the highest sovereign force and must compete for power to survive in the international system. Geoeconomics, therefore, rejects the fundamental assumptions of liberal economic theory because trade and broader economic connectivity are conducted primarily to advance relative gain – that is, to elevate one's own economic power above others. Economic interdependence does not enable states to overcome international rivalries. Rather, economic interdependence can be used as an instrument of power for competition. Interdependence implies that states lose some autonomy while gaining influence. Economic interdependence is, however, rarely symmetrical and states strive to develop asymmetrical dependence to maximize both their autonomy and influence. For example, Laos is economically very dependent on China and therefore loses much of its autonomy to Beijing, whereas the reverse is to at all the case.

Innovative technology is imperative for geoeconomics and a necessity for any advanced economy. Advanced technologies lay the foundation for strategic industries, which are defined as having the ability to preserve autonomy and create dependence by others. Furthermore, high-tech industries enjoy higher profits because they face less competition. Domestically, high-tech industries create opportunities in the form of high-skilled and high-wage jobs. In contrast, low-tech industries do not create dependencies and are usually less profitable due to greater competition.

This chapter theorizes why technological sovereignty increasingly defines geoeconomic power, and why great powers require technological sovereignty. It first explores the realist theoretical assumptions of geoeconomics as the traditional balance of power is translated into a balance of dependence. Geoeconomic power advances by cultivating asymmetrical economic dependencies with other states to maximize both autonomy and influence. Technology lays the foundation for most strategic industries because 'natural' advantages tend to be eclipsed by innovative technologies. Second, due to the greater market power of new technologies, geoeconomic power is largely determined by the ability of governments to slow down or speed up the diffusion of technology to either extend or reduce the first-mover advantage of innovative states. Technological leaders and followers adopt different strategies to support the acquisition of technology through innovation or imitation, and assist with implementation to increase commercial value. Last, neoclassical realist theory opens up the 'black box' of decision-making in geoeconomics, which recognizes that competitiveness in the international system also depends on domestic socio-economic and political stability as a precondition for mobilizing internal resources in pursuit of foreign policy objectives. This chapter reaches the conclusion that technologies can magnify or reduce global inequalities, depending on the extent to which those technologies are diffused.

Geoeconomics and the balance of dependence

Geoeconomics is the political economy of realist theory. The term geoeconomics is often used as an ambiguous catchphrase referring to economic competition. The term can, however, be assigned a clear definition supported by established theoretical assumptions. The fundamental assumption of geoeconomics is that states compete for relative economic gain to survive in an anarchic world.

Geoeconomic theory repudiates the liberal theoretical assumptions of trade and economic integration. Huntington (1993: 72) criticized liberal assumptions, writing: '[T]he idea that economics is primarily a non-zero sum game is a favourite conceit of tenured academics'. Trade at the international level functions differently than at the domestic level due to anarchy – defined by the absence of a supreme sovereign or world government capable of asserting order. States are the highest sovereign and must, therefore, compete for relative military and economic power to survive. Friedrich List, Alexander Hamilton, Gustav Schmoller, Sergei Witte and other neo-mercantilists in the nineteenth century did not reject Adam Smith's arguments about the benefits of free trade: they merely sought to harmonize liberal economics with realist theoretical assumptions about politics. Neo-mercantilism is largely about nation-building as a development strategy that recognizes the central role of the state in the international system (Schmoller 1897; Heckscher 1955). Friedrich List (1827: 30), who established much of the theoretical foundation of geoeconomics, postulated that liberal economics cannot be applied to international relations due to the rivalry between states:

> As long as the division of the human race into independent nations exists, political economy will as often be at variance with cosmopolitan principles ... a nation would act unwisely to endeavour to promote the welfare of the whole human race at the expense of its particular strength, welfare and independence.

In geoeconomics, the realist concept of a balance of power translates into a 'balance of dependence' (Diesen 2017a). In any economic relationship between a rich and a poor person or country, the richer side has less of a stake in the relationship compared to the poorer counterpart. Asymmetrical economic interdependence enables the more powerful side to extract economic and political concessions (Hirschman 1945). States intervene in the market to develop favourable symmetry, establish a privileged or even monopolistic position for domestic corporations and to maintain the dependence of others and concurrently diversify away from excessive reliance on others to deny them similar advantages.

Realists recognize that peace and stability can exist only when there is a balance of power because states do not voluntarily constrain themselves. Geoeconomic stability similarly manifests when there is a balance of dependence because neither side can exact excessive political concessions from the others. By contrast, excessive reliance on an asymmetrical economic partnership enables the stronger side, which is less dependent, to maintain its autonomy and exert political influence. Geoeconomic theory, much like realist theory, argues that the world will gravitate naturally towards equilibrium because excessive reliance on an asymmetrical partnership is destructive and, therefore, temporary. The weaker side is motivated to reduce its economic dependence due to the adverse influence it has on sovereignty. The weaker state will intervene in the market to develop strategic industries and/or diversify economic connectivity to reduce its reliance on the more powerful economy.

Geoeconomics represents the convergence of economics and security, with economic instruments of power used to advance security interests. Geoeconomics is the economics of geopolitics because, in an economically interdependent world, 'economics is the continuation of war by other means' (Bell 2008: 330). Tasking the state with 'harnessing economic power to foreign policy goals presents formidable obstacles ... Yet if war is too important to be left to the generals, surely commerce is, in this context, too salient to be left to bankers and businessmen' (Huntington 1978: 71). Geoeconomics is consistent with fundamental realist tenets because 'interdependence' is really the search for relative gain that powerful states can use to exert influence over weaker states (Waltz 1970: 214). States and markets are often at odds over their conflicting economic interests. Markets seek to maximize absolute gain even as the state operates in an anarchic international order in which relative power is imperative for survival. Exploring the political economy of great power competition, Gilpin stipulates that 'realism today necessarily means neo-mercantilism' (Guzzini 1997: 134).

Geoeconomic policies are offensive when they are used to obtain influence and defensive when they protect autonomy. Much of the original literature defined geoeconomics as actions designed to reduce excessive reliance on other states. Schmoller (1897: 76) defined defensive neo-mercantilism as 'shaking off commercial dependence on foreigners which was continually becoming more oppressive' and cultivating economic autarky (Schmoller 1897: 76). Hirschman (1945: 16) similarly cautioned that

> The power to interrupt commercial or financial regulations with any country, considered as an attribute of national sovereignty, is the root cause of the influence or power position which a country acquires in other countries, just as it is the root cause of the 'dependence on trade'.

The belief that the liberal international order that followed the Second World War somehow 'transcended' the past was merely a temporary phenomenon. The Cold War masked geoeconomic policies because the main US rivals were communist states that were largely decoupled from international markets and economic statecraft. The ideological and military confrontation of the Cold War had a mitigating effect on the geoeconomic rivalry among capitalist allies. Nevertheless, by the 1980s, geoeconomic competition between the United States and its allies in Western Europe and Japan was already exposing the fragile underpinnings of liberal economics.

By the end of the Cold War, Luttwak (1990: 17) recognized the return of geoeconomics: 'Everyone, it appears, now agrees that the methods of commerce are displacing military methods – with disposable capital in lieu of firepower, civilian innovation in lieu of military-technical advancement, and market penetration in lieu of garrisons and bases'. Rather than amassing large armies for influence, the instruments of power entail 'productive efficiency, market control, trade surplus, strong currency, foreign exchange reserves, ownership of foreign companies, factories and technology' (Huntington 1993: 73). Lorot (1999) similarly argued that the global economic connectivity following the Cold War has caused a return to economic nationalism and geoeconomics:

> Nations are engaged – alongside their national companies – in offensive policies to conquer external markets and to take control of sectors of activity considered to be strategic. For nations today, the quest for power and assertion of their rank on the world stage depends more and more on their economic health, the competitiveness of their companies and the place that they occupy in world trade.

Technology and geoeconomic levers of power

The First Industrial Revolution elevated the significance of geoeconomic power, which falls into three categories: strategic industries, physical transportation corridors and financial instruments. Industries such as textiles, iron, steel, mining and chemicals shaped an international division of labour and economic dependencies. Steamboats, railways and canals produced new transportation corridors to advance physical connectivity. Financial instruments, primarily banks, flourished as the English sought to organize the financing of industries and transportation. Taken together, these three categories of geoeconomic power are instrumental in establishing monopolistic power in industries with limited opportunities for diversification.

Strategic industries are defined by their ability to skew the balance of dependence. Strategic industries consolidate monopolies and create high dependencies due to the limited possibility of diversification. Geoeconomic power is obtained by 'develop[ing] exports in articles enjoying a monopolistic position in other countries and direct trade to such countries' (Hirschman 1945: 34). John Rockefeller famously argued that monopolies are where the money is made because the alternative, competitive markets drive prices down to the benefit of the consumer. Furthermore, monopolies allow economic power to be converted into political power. Fruits, for example, are not a strategic industry because any disruption to supply can be resolved by merely finding another supplier, by growing one's own fruit as a low-skilled industry, or by substituting fruits with another food group. By contrast, industries defined by natural scarcity offer fewer opportunities to diversify and more political power for the supplier. Dependence on imports from strategic industries has the potential to become a 'commercial fifth column' by causing economic elites in the importing country to develop higher loyalties to a rival foreign power (Hirschman 1945: 29).

Strategic industries usually fall within one of two categories: man-made monopolies of high-tech industries and natural monopolies such as natural resources or when competitiveness is augmented by geographical proximity. High-tech industries enjoy a temporary monopolistic position due to the first-mover advantage – that can be prolonged by slowing down the diffusion of technology. A technological rivalry between the United States and China will reduce their ability to establish a monopolistic position and to slow down the diffusion of technology. Natural resources are divided into different categories based on the ability to accrue a monopolistic position. Oil is transported relatively easily and therefore exposes suppliers to competition from suppliers around the globe. In contrast, exporters of natural gas benefit from geographic proximity because gas has traditionally been transported through pipelines. Technological advances enable gas to be liquefied for transportation, yet liquefied natural gas (LNG) requires complex and expensive infrastructure and processes that render pipelines more competitive. Nuclear energy required a combination of scarce resources and technological competences to harness the power. Former industrial revolutions sparked a race to control the sources of coal, oil, gas and uranium. The Fourth Industrial Revolution will increasingly elevate the strategic industries of man-made technologies above natural resources by unlocking the potential of renewable energies or by possibly even mining asteroids.

Transportation corridors are strategic because they are limited by geography and have varying degrees of reliability and commercial competitiveness. States controlling transportation corridors can risk a greater reliance on trade and can extract political influence by providing favourable access to allies or denying the right of use to adversaries. Technologies ranging from maritime transportation, railways and the Internet have drastically altered physical connectivity between states. Efforts by European powers to establish maritime routes to China in the early 1500s led to them controlling the world's strategic waterways and ports as the arteries of global trade. The ability to control access to resources and markets for manufactured goods transformed European powers into mighty empires and laid the foundation for five centuries of their global dominance. Steam power and the Suez Canal provided European maritime powers with greater control over international commerce, but this was threatened by Russia developing intercontinental railroads in the late nineteenth century to connect the vast Eurasian landmass (Mackinder 1904: 434). The radical reduction of transportation and telecommunication costs between 1950 and 1980 diminished geographic proximity as a competitive advantage for manufacturing. More recently, the Belt and Road Initiative that China launched in 2013, coupled with its Digital Silk Road, indicated that Beijing is tearing away at US control over maritime transportation corridors as an important pillar of geoeconomic power. The Fourth Industrial Revolution will increasingly make digital connectivity the new arteries of the global economy. There are, however, few new technologies that will further reduce the cost of transportation of physical goods, other than automated ports, driverless vehicles and technologies enabling and supporting an Arctic trade corridor.

Financial instruments establishing favourable conditions for cooperation and competition, financial and economic instruments are vital sources of geoeconomic power. Banks and currencies have become an indispensable source of power for geoeconomic hegemons, from the British Empire to the Bretton Woods system under US control. China is challenging US financial instruments by creating new trade regimes and development banks, and by internationalizing its own currency as a rival to the US dollar. The Fourth Industrial Revolution opens entirely new fronts in the geoeconomic struggles, with digital solutions offering 'banking without banks' and cryptocurrencies circumventing national currencies. Mechanisms for financial and economic cooperation also include standards and regulations outlined in trade regimes that are imperative when developing rival technologies. Economic blocs that provide collective bargaining power have become more important and will increasingly be instrumental in establishing regional technological sovereignty supported by collective technological platforms and legislative space.

Technology acquisition and implementation

Diffusion of technology is a major factor in shaping the international distribution of power. States promote technological innovation 'to maximize benefits within their own boundaries' (Luttwak 1990: 18). In the Fourth Industrial Revolution, great powers seek to establish technological sovereignty to obtain a favourable balance of dependence. As innovative technologies lay new foundations for almost all industries and services, technological sovereignty ensures that the state does not lose autonomy by becoming excessively reliant on foreign technologies and increases influence by creating technological dependencies among smaller and weaker states.

Innovators attempt to slow down the diffusion of technology to extend their first-mover advantage, while followers strive to reduce the advantage of the innovator by speeding up diffusion. Ideally, the follower achieves 'technological preparedness' – the ability to develop spin-offs of foreign technologies and to introduce them rapidly in the domestic technological ecosystem. Because only a relatively few countries develop the overwhelming majority of disruptive technologies, other countries must depend on imitations and spin-offs to avoid falling too far behind or become excessively reliant on an adversarial power (Keller 2010). Technologically advanced countries are capable of either educating or attracting talented individuals to work in a culturally and legislative environment that encourages innovation.

As the current leader in this regard, the United States enjoys an extensive first-mover advantage that lays the foundation for future competitiveness. For example, Apple's smartphone provides billions of dollars in profits that are directed towards further research and development. Also, technologically advanced states can 'naturally' sustain their leadership by more easily attracting a skilled workforce from abroad with the promise of work at the cutting age of technology and offering the most competitive remuneration. China has become a major innovator in the Fourth Industrial Revolution. Although the United States has most of the top AI talent, China has a larger pool of highly skilled AI professionals. Neither is China disadvantaged in this regard because breakthroughs in AI can be replicated quickly by others and, therefore, provides few first-mover advantages (Lee 2018). China's advances in AI research are narrowing the scope of US leadership in the field. Domestic control over AI platforms is imperative because it provides a great competitive advantage in developing all other industries. In fact, most new business ideas boil down to *Product/service 'X' + AI*.

Imitation is essential because it is unnecessary for every company and country to reinvent the wheel. Instead, countries can acquire the technological know-how, put in place the requisite domestic technological ecosystems, develop the pertinent industries, train the workers and provide the government support required to rapidly adopt new technologies and implement spin-offs. Achieving technological preparedness does not require having the 'best of the best' in terms of technology or skills. Although innovative leaders enjoy various degrees of first-mover advantage that they seek to extend, followers with high technological preparedness can establish a preferential position. If the technology diffuses rapidly, the follower need not bear the heavy research and development cost of the innovator (Gerschenkron 1963). Followers can even establish leadership if they can quickly imitate and implement new technologies and direct funds normally devoted to research and development into capital-intensive investments instead, also developing complex hardware as a barrier to entry. Achieving technological preparedness is a prudent strategy for follower states such as Russia that might only be capable of leading in a few niche technologies and industries. Although Russia is not a leading innovator in digital technologies, it is one of the very few countries in the world with the potential for achieving technological sovereignty. Domestic companies lead most of Russia's digital infrastructure, such as the most-used search engine, email provider, social media, mapping services, ride-hailing app, e-commerce provider, etc. By contrast, American digital platforms such as Google, Amazon and Facebook reign supreme across the rest of Europe.

Acquisition

States aspiring to technological leadership have historically intervened in the market to acquire and implement new technologies. The state supports technology acquisition through direct and indirect subsidies and tariffs that enable companies to either innovate or catch up. Subsidies are an important geoeconomic intervention in the economy because 'the provision of state funds for domestic technological development is inherently discriminatory against unassisted foreign competitors' (Luttwak 1990: 19).

States subsidize technological developments directly by providing support for their industries. This is especially important for major national projects such as the space race or new environmentally friendly technologies. Although acquisitions can assist in catching up, staying ahead requires extensive and continuous investments in education, infrastructure and engineering. Governments also provide indirect subsidies by funding specific elements of infrastructure for education and public use. States attempt to cultivate innovation domestically by developing creative and global cities that facilitate innovation centres and ecosystems, special economic zones, technopoles of high-tech manufacturing, higher education and similar stimuli for innovative hubs (Moisio 2018: 28).

Indirect subsidies commonly take the form of physical infrastructure that also serves the public interest. In the United States, the railways and Route 66 were projects that used public funding to develop the economy and enhance industrial competitiveness. In the Fourth Industrial Revolution, the Chinese government similarly builds entire cities capable of accommodating innovative technologies. The Chinese government cooperates with Baidu, the 'Google of China', to develop the special economic zone of Xiongan as an AI city. It will serve as a prototype for future cities whose infrastructure will fully accommodate autonomous vehicles (Lee 2018: 134). China also plans to invest more than \$2 billion in an AI development park in Beijing's Mentougou district.

Implementing reforms to social services and law enforcement can also function as an indirect subsidy. For example, China's 'smart cities' increasingly use facial recognition technology in conjunction with CCTV cameras to enhance the surveillance capabilities of law enforcement. China subsidizes the development of solar panels, which are linked to its electric vehicle industry. Indirect subsidies for innovation also include facilitating formal and informal social networks between scientists, entrepreneurs, companies, investors and government (Taylor 2016). Governments intervene in the market by supporting and subsidizing such initiatives, and concurrently enhance market efficiency by reducing the obstructive presence of the state through the elimination of red tape and constrictive legislation.

Technology transfer from the military is a leading form of indirect subsidy. The military is typically a leading recipient of public funds for research and development. Although states have traditionally been concerned about rival powers using civilian technologies for military purposes, in the era of geoeconomics, governments also transfer military technology to commercial industries as an indirect subsidy (Luttwak 2010: 65). Russia – a country with advanced military and space technology but a less competitive commercial sector – could take a geoeconomic leap forward by improving cooperation between its military, government and commercial entities. Russia's military is making impressive advances in AI and robotics that have civilian commercial applications.

Space exploration is likely to develop as a new form of indirect subsidy for technological development. The publicly funded space and arms race of the Cold War produced innovative technologies for both the United States and the Soviet Union. One example is the US Global Positioning System (GPS), a satellite-based radio navigation system with sophisticated hardware that presents a high-entry barrier because few states have equivalent technological capabilities. Furthermore, the GPS platform used its first-mover advantage to cement itself in technological platforms across the world and is thus attractive due to its universality. The Soviet Union developed an independent system because of its adversarial relationship with the United States. The result is that the Russian GLONASS system has been the only strategic alternative to GPS for many years. GLONASS achieved full global coverage in 2011 and the Russian government has protected it as a component of the domestic technological ecosystem by placing high taxes on devices sold in Russia that support GPS but not GLONASS. Space is the natural area of application for the technologies of the Fourth Industrial Revolution that makes it possible to overcome previous constraints and barriers. Furthermore, space can mitigate societal disruptions with an endless frontier that instils meaning and common purpose, and that signifies status among great powers. Commercial industries will likely make a growing contribution as the barriers to entry in space are reduced.

Tariffs and non-tariff barriers are also used to protect domestic industries to give them breathing space to mature in the domestic market. Non-tariff barriers traditionally involve the imposition of excessive regulations for environmental and health reasons (Raza 2007; Cwik 2011). For example, Russia and Iran frequently cited environmental concerns to block the West from constructing pipelines under the Caspian Sea to access Central Asian energy resources. Technology transfer can also be restricted by citing national security concerns (Gilpin 2011: 139). Early Cold War, the Truman administration attempted to restrict the proliferation of technologies to the Soviet Union by establishing the Advisory Committee on Requirements and the Technical Steering Committee. The Export Control Act of 1949 similarly authorized the Department of Commerce to control exports of goods to the Eastern Bloc.

Currently, the United States uses national security as a pretext for restricting Huawei's 5G networks and banning the use of Russia's Kaspersky antivirus program for the government's computer networks. Similarly, Russia restricts foreign digital providers such as LinkedIn by requiring that they store their user data on Russian territory. Mapping in China is subject to state secrecy restrictions, thus limiting Google's first-mover advantage and giving primacy to the Chinese version of Google Earth. Restrictions on street mapping for foreign corporations give Chinese developers a pivotal competitive advantage for controlling the world's largest market for automated vehicles. In Russia, the national provider, Yandex, also has superior domestic mapping services compared to Google.

As China's leadership in electric vehicles continues to grow, Beijing will most likely introduce environmental legislation that cements the competitive advantage of its own electric vehicles in what is the world's largest market for automobiles. There are also natural barriers that give domestic corporations an advantage. For example, although the Google search engine generally dominated around the world, it did not enjoy the same competitive advantage in countries that use different alphabets. For example, Google's limited penetration into the Russian market was largely due to the language, indirectly helping the domestic provider, Yandex, to establish leadership. The Snowden revelations in 2013 about extensive spying by the NSA for commercial and political purposes demonstrate that digital ecosystems are critical infrastructure that great powers should keep under domestic control.

Education has traditionally played an important role in preparing the general population to cope with an economy and society undergoing radical changes. High-quality education, generous public investment in science, easy access to investments and an entrepreneurial culture are strong assets for technological leaders. Governments can also facilitate greater cooperation between universities and businesses for the transfer of technology and skills. A growing share of all professions will begin to resemble the IT industry whose workers must continually update their education because the work environment and technology change so rapidly. The era of being prepared for a lifelong career after finishing education in one's early 20s is coming to an end. The United States is home to many of the world's best universities, although sustaining that position is challenged by the diminishing quality of its infrastructure, education, public research and development (Engelke and Manning 2017). University education in the United States is also becoming too expensive and crippling student loan presents barriers to upskilling. With a low chance of return on their investment and a weak social safety net, young people will be less likely to risk obtaining higher education at such high cost. Much of the problem the United States faces stems from investing more heavily in militarized geopolitics than in developing its geoeconomic power.

Attracting technologically advanced workers is becoming increasingly important. States might begin competing for the top talents in unconventional ways. For example, ambassadors might be tasked with identifying and recruiting desirable candidates in the country in which they are stationed as part of a proactive immigration competition. If it were to relinquish its technological leadership, the United States would begin losing many of the skilled workers from around the world that had flooded to the country to work for the technological leaders. A decline in the United States' university leadership would similarly slow down the brain drain towards that country. Also, the demographic changes and cultural disruptions caused by mass immigration to the United States and Europe have caused growing resistance to immigration.

Developing a strong work culture is crucial for technological advancement. Max Weber (1958) famously credited the Protestant work ethic with imbuing capitalism with the spirit of hard work and progress. Unlike most religions that condemn material affluence, the Reformation made a strong moral argument for the work ethic and worldly success. In 1986, a Reformation of communism arrived in China when Deng Xiaoping declared that 'to get rich is glorious'. Deng Xiaoping explained his approval of materialism:

> According to Marxism, communist society is based on material abundance. Only when there is material abundance can the principle of a communist society – that is, 'from each according to his ability, to each according to his needs' – be applied.
>
> (Whiteley 2007)

China has achieved an important competitive advantage by establishing the culture and demand of its tech workers to labour '9-9-6' – from 9 am until 9 pm 6 days per week. The one-child policy is also part of the country's unique work culture: it puts immense pressure on the one child to perform, while the parents can also devote more time and resources to their sole child.

Implementation

To implement new technologies in commercial and military applications, it is vital that the necessary funding for research and development be put in place. The invention of the smartphone offers a key example of a product that reaches a broad spectrum of consumers and generates huge profits. This, in turn, produces a vast amount of data that must be compiled for the technology and its applications to develop further.

The implementation of technology into commercial industries has both advantages and disadvantages for developed states. Those with primarily high-wage workers have greater incentives to adopt new technologies that automate labour and enhance efficiency. By contrast, developed states with a primarily low-wage workforce will find that their industries have fewer economic incentives to adopt new technologies. By the time these technologies become more efficient and less costly, the technological infrastructure of low-wage states will already have fallen far behind.

Governments can manipulate the incentives for private industries by subsidizing the implementation of new technologies. Legislation can be passed that allows corporations to write off the costs of technology upgrades, and that provides support for the training and management that is especially important in encouraging small businesses to adopt new technologies. One case in point: labour costs do not correlate with salary levels as expected because China outperforms most Western states in the implementation of robotics. This is largely because China provides its companies with massive subsidies to implement robotics in an effort to offset the lack of incentives stemming from low-wage labour. States can also support new technological innovations with 'predatory financing of their sales during their embryonic stage' (Luttwak 1990: 23).

Implementing disruptive technologies can be more challenging for leading developed states when it requires the abandonment of technologies that had sustained their leadership. What had been short- to medium-term advantages for the incumbent leader can become disadvantages in the long term. The technological leader might have made major economic, political, social and cultural investments in maintaining and updating existing technologies. The ability to abandon existing technological platforms depends on the extent to which they have become entrenched in the bureaucracy, culture, skilled workforce and power hierarchy. Cultures also differ in terms of their ability to adopt new technologies. Japan, for example, is renowned for its strong cultural openness to embracing new technologies (Goldman 2006). Developing states that have fallen behind can even leapfrog the existing technologies. A technological revolution can give less developed states an advantage in terms of adopting the newest technology as it does not disrupt the existing and entrenched technological infrastructure, business and political interests.

To date, the United States has been the lead innovator, but China has been more successful with implementation in terms of using AI to develop products and services across a variety of industries. US geoeconomic leadership largely relies on preserving and maintaining the existing system of trade, currency, commercial banks and development banks. This makes US legislators hesitant to provide governmental and legal support for implementing technologies that upset the existing financial and economic order. By comparison, China has leapfrogged credit cards by going from cash directly to QR codes. Similarly, developing nations are already starting to make changes required for adopting digital currencies and embracing the concept of banking without banks. In barely a decade, China's position in the e-commerce market has grown from obscurity to global leadership, now accounting for more than 40 per cent of e-commerce transactions worldwide (McKinsey 2018). The value of China's mobile payments is eleven times greater than those in the United States. Payment apps are not easily implemented in the United States due to the immense inertia of the existing banking and financial system.

Cultural and organizational opposition to implementing new technologies is exemplified by military history. Military hierarchies often seek stability, and the strong bureaucracy in leading military powers makes them more resistant to adopting disruptive technologies, despite leading in their development (Gilpin 1983). The US Navy resisted making the transition from wood to iron in the late nineteenth century despite the latter's proven capabilities during the Civil War. The Navy brass and its professional engineers even attempted to undermine the new technologies. The existing power hierarchy is predicated on culture and people with specialized skill sets. The steam engines 'challenged the idealized postwar cultural, social, and technical self-image of the naval profession' (McBridge 2000: 4). Consequently, technologies that disrupt stability and displace the existing guard are adopted only hesitantly.

The implementation of modern technologies such as military drones encounters similar resistance because drones displace pilots, a gateway profession to high-ranking military and political positions. The United States, as a heavily militarized country, devotes much of its military budget to maintaining and upgrading existing technologies that underpin its leadership – but that could also soon become outdated. For example, aircraft carriers are major investments that are intended to serve for decades, but that could become extremely vulnerable to missiles or inexpensive airborne or submarine drones in only a few years' time (Hammes 2018). In democracies, the state's desire to implement existing technologies in commerce and the military must also be reconciled with broader society's vested interest in the status quo. By comparison, China's more centralized decision-making process enables it to allocate more of its booming military budgets to the implementation of new technologies rather than to maintaining old and soon-to-be-obsolete technologies.

Extending the first-mover advantage

Technological leaders strive to slow down the diffusion of technologies to extend their first-mover advantage (Lieberman and Montgomery 1988). In contrast, followers with technological preparedness have a great incentive to encourage technologies to diffuse faster (Rogers 2010). Historically, states have employed economic and military coercion to prevent the proliferation of their technologies and to preserve their leadership in the existing balance of power.

Advanced states with complex hardware are able to consolidate power due to the inherent entry barrier that slows down diffusion to less developed states and non-state actors. For example, nuclear weapons require sophisticated know-how and technologies that are fuelled with scarce and expensive resources and fissionable material. The space race also had great barriers to entry in that only technologically advanced powers that placed ideological victory and world leadership above economic gain had the necessary funding and motivation. In contrast, software is diffused with greater ease because it need only be copied. In the economic realm, simple digital apps such as Uber are copied cheaply, so corporations and states have an incentive to build up an infrastructure around the innovation. For example, a business based on taxi-hailing apps can exert control over drivers and car ownership, and develop self-driving vehicles, battery-charging facilitates and other value-added infrastructure as barriers to entry.

Technologies in the Fourth Industrial Revolution can be implemented with complex hardware and infrastructure to establish a first-mover advantage in a market. AI consists of software, yet it often requires supercomputers as complex hardware to develop or 'train' machine-learning algorithms (Murphy 2017). The race for supercomputers will, therefore, continue to be led by China and the United States. The collection of an enormous amount of data is also an entry barrier. However, AI has broad application and does not cross domains. For example, AI for shortlisting job applicants cannot be used for driving a car. Experience with the commercial application of AI suggests that it will spread rapidly, thus limiting first-mover advantage.

States face a dilemma between innovation and slowing down diffusion due to their reliance on foreign direct investments. For example, restricting Chinese investments in US high-tech industries weakens the innovativeness of US corporations, yet accepting Chinese investment risks the faster spread of technologies. Technologies developed for commercial use spread more rapidly due to the profit-seeking nature of private enterprises, while technologies developed for the military diffuse much more slowly (Rogers 2010; Horowitz 2018). Access to the global market has shortened China's learning curve. For example, its BeiDou Navigation Satellite System was developed largely due to China's participation in Europe's Galileo global navigation satellite system. Furthermore, China conditioned foreign access to its large domestic market on technological transfers and joint ventures.

Great powers are able to curb several factors that accelerate technology proliferation. Google's development of AI facilities in China fits within its profit-seeking model and is supported by Google's identity as a global company, rather than merely a US company. Researchers are more likely to publish their findings openly if they idealistically seek to advance humanity. Tesla offered its technology to spur the transition to electric cars, citing environmental preservation as motivation. The company might also have an economic motive, hoping to take advantage of the synergy effects of its advances in battery technology as it seeks to broaden its market.

Governments have some ability to restrict private corporations from selling to specific countries. Governments can also prevent other states from establishing a first-mover advantage, as demonstrated by Washington's pressuring of its allies to ban Huawei's 5G technologies and instead wait for the United States to catch up and offer the same technology. Predatory pricing can saturate foreign markets and discourage the development of rival technologies. Unlike commercial technologies, government-owned and military technologies have greater protection and consequently diffuse more slowly. Intellectual property rights are a means of extending first-mover advantage by providing the innovator with a greater return on investment. Diffusion is also slowed by trade agreements that further extend and enforce intellectual property rights, or by non-proliferation agreements in the military sphere. In Silicon Valley, corporations spend billions of dollars to purchase patents from companies holding technologies that might advance their own products, or file disruptive lawsuits against rival companies to slow them down. The spread of technologies can also be slowed by establishing an international division of labour, when, for example, an exporter of industrial goods establishes economic interdependence with an exporter of natural resources.

In the military sphere, there is natural segregation of technological systems because their mingling can lead to 'technological leakage'. For example, the technologies of the F-35 could be compromised by Turkey's purchase of the Russian S-400 missile defence system. Furthermore, military and economic alliances often lead to expectations of purchases as well as efforts to avoid the supply chains of adversaries. The need for technological compatibility, therefore, dictates future purchases.

Conclusion

Geoeconomics suggests that power derives from control over markets rather than military power and territory. Geoeconomics has traditionally focused on controlling strategic industries, transportation corridors and instruments for financial and economic cooperation. Asymmetrical interdependence enables states to wield political power, which creates systemic pressures for rival powers to restore the balance of dependence. Governments can skew the balance of dependence by developing geoeconomic instruments of power and diversifying their economic partnerships to avoid excessively reliance on a more powerful actor. Sustainable and mutually beneficial cooperation can only develop when there is a balance of dependence and a desire to maintain the status quo.

The Fourth Industrial Revolution will significantly increase the relevance of technology on all three levers of geoeconomic power. Geoeconomics in the current industrial revolution primarily involves states influencing the acquisition and implementation of new technologies through innovation and imitation. States strive to slow down technological diffusion to extend their first-mover advantage, or else to speed up proliferation to catch up. As innovative technologies increasingly define the power of states, technological sovereignty becomes a requirement for great power status.

The following chapters will assess technological developments in accordance with the geoeconomic principles outlined in this chapter. The fragmentation of the international division of labour, as great powers repatriate supply chains, will fundamentally reorganize economic connectivity as the foundational requirement to the exercise of economic statecraft. The ability of states to act rationally in accordance with strategic interests is undermined as new technologies unravel the balance between capital and labour and uproot societal structures and institutions.

Techno-nationalism and reshoring: Fragmentation of the international division of labour

Introduction

Under pressure from the US government, Google suspended its Android licence agreements with Chinese telecom giant Huawei in May 2019. It represented another salvo by the United States in its geoeconomic warfare against China, with US tech companies already banned from selling computer chips to Huawei. Bankrupting Huawei would be a momentous geoeconomic victory because the company is the world leader in 5G technology, a stepping stone to leadership in the Internet of Things and AI. The US actions communicated an unequivocal message: technology is a tool of the great power rivalry, and not merely of business.

China received the message and responded in the only responsible way, by withdrawing from supply chains that rely on technologies from the United States and its obedient allies. Repatriating supply chains requires that China develop its own technologies to replace those it previously imported – everything ranging from semiconductors to operating systems. China will need to develop technological sovereignty to safeguard its power and security and, possibly, to ensure its survival. Beijing also needs to retaliate and discourage future aggression by imposing costs on economic coercion against its strategic industries. This can be limited to industry and accomplished by cutting off Chinese-made supplies and by further restricting rare earth exports used in electronic equipment. Alternatively, China could punish the United States with other geoeconomic levers of power. In the financial domain, it could abandon the use of the US dollar, or in trade and military matters, it could expand its reach in the South China Sea, thus limiting US control over maritime corridors. The breakdown of the international division of labour in an integrated global economy is not just a story about the communist authorities in Beijing or the nationalist government in Washington; rather, it represents a predictable development that accords with geoeconomic theory and the experience of past industrial revolutions.

At first glance, world history since the First Industrial Revolution appears to have followed a linear path towards an increasingly integrated global economy. The liberal economic system is based on an international division of labour in which each country focuses on its particular comparative advantage and then trade with the rest of the world for absolute gain. The so-called 'liberal international economic order' spread throughout the West in the years since the Second World War, while the demise of the Soviet Union and opening of China gave rise to a truly global free-market economic system characterized by ever-more complex global value chains. After three decades of developing a common global market governed by the rules of the World Trade Organization (WTO), it appeared that the world had transcended its past and moved into the era predicted by liberal theory. In China alone, several hundred millions of people have been lifted out of poverty by committing to this liberal international economic system based on comparative advantage. It is, therefore, a puzzle as to why the world's leading powers have become so uncomfortable with the international division of labour and have intervened in the market to advance autarky.

This chapter will explore why the international division of labour is fragmenting and giving way to techno-nationalism. It first argues that the international division of labour is a reflection of the international distribution of power. A liberal economic system in which each state advances its comparative advantage is contingent upon the existence of a geoeconomic hegemon, while reducing the concentration of economic power fragments the international division of labour.

Second, the chapter compares the first three industrial revolutions. The First Industrial Revolution developed under the technological and geoeconomic leadership of Britain, which advocated open markets and comparative advantage as soon as it achieved the leadership position. Repealing the Corn Laws was instrumental in forming an international division of labour that would cement asymmetrical dependence. Similarly, during the Third Industrial Revolution, the US government provided formidable support for its digital industries before seeking a clear international division of labour. The United States announced a 'repeal of the Corn Laws 2.0' in the form of extending its intellectual property rights for digital industries in return for opening its manufacturing industry to low-wage competitors.

Now, the Fourth Industrial Revolution is emerging at a time when US geoeconomic leadership is challenged by China. The end of the Cold War enabled

China, Russia and other former communist adversaries of Washington to engage in economic statecraft, while its allies became more willing to augment their autonomy and defy the United States. Beijing used the final years of the Third Industrial Revolution to climb global value chains and is now in a position to challenge US technological leadership. The United States, meanwhile, has been unable to convert its geopolitical and military alliances into geoeconomic loyalty.

Finally, technologies themselves are undermining an international division of labour. Finding an arrangement akin to 'repealing the Corn Laws 3.0' is problematic because technologically advanced states will no longer need the states that compete with low-wage labour. Automation and robotics are prompting states to reshore their industries. However, reshoring disrupts the balance between capital and labour that serves as the basis of the international division of labour.

It is concluded that the Fourth Industrial Revolution will be defined by coercive geoeconomics between technological leaders pursuing primacy, thereby undermining the conditions for free trade and economic liberalism. Great powers endowed with high-tech will increasingly seek to bring supply chains under domestic control and less developed states will see their comparative advantage decline in the international economy.

Power and the international division of labour

The international division of labour is a reflection of the international distribution of power. A clearly delineated international division of labour is cultivated by the geoeconomic hegemon, and in the absence of a hegemon, the division of labour breaks down.

After a state intervenes in the market to establish technological leadership, the hegemon advocates laissez-faire capitalism to cement its comparative advantage and bring the international economic system under its leadership. A system of comparative advantage opens the hegemon's low-skilled and low-tech markets to foreign competition in return for establishing technological leadership in the markets of less developed states. An international division of labour is an important tool for slowing the diffusion of technology because it enables the leader to saturate the high-tech markets of less developed states. Under an economic hegemon, there is a natural drive towards market liberalization and a clear international division of labour:

> If economic capabilities are so concentrated that a hegemon exists, as in the case of Great Britain in the late 19th century and the USA after World War II,

an "open" or "liberal" international economic order will come into being. In the organisation of a liberal order, pride of place is given to market rationality. This is not to say that authority is absent from such an order. It is to say that authority relations are constructed in such a way as to give maximum scope to market forces rather than to constrain them.

(Ruggie 1982: 381)

Cooperation and competition are often juxtaposed, yet the international division of labour facilitates both. States are partners by cooperating in the production of products, and are concurrently rivals by competing for the high-skilled and high-value-added economic activities with the global value chain. The market system creates a hierarchical division of labour in terms of the distribution of wealth at both the domestic and international level. Each labour function in domestic and international society is divided and compartmentalized into specialized functions. The division of labour forms a dynamic and wealthy core and a weaker and dependent periphery. The high-value economic activities and power of the core stem from technological and economic development, whereas the periphery relies on the core to which it exports natural resources or low-skill manufactured goods. Geoeconomic power of the hegemon subsequently derives from sustaining asymmetrical dependence between the advanced core and the underdeveloped periphery. The core continues to grow in power by expanding the periphery to create greater asymmetrical dependencies. However, the diffusion of productive technologies tends to result in the emergence of new poles of power that can eventually challenge the core (Gilpin 2001: 57).

Realist theory and geoeconomic theory recognize that hegemony is temporary. Hegemonic stability theory postulates that international anarchy diminishes when the dominant state establishes itself as the higher sovereign capable of mitigating power competition (Kindleberger 1986). At the same time, the hegemon itself is an entity competing for power. The hegemon must balance its role as an administrator of the international system against its role as a state actor using its administrator position to accrue power and maintain hegemony. When its efforts to maintain hegemony undermine its ability to administer the international economic system, the system unravels. Translated into geoeconomics, the dominant power can successfully act as an administrator by keeping the international economic system open. The technological hegemon has strong incentives not to misuse its authority over the international economy to advance narrow national interests, because such behaviour breeds distrust and encourages others to break away from the division of labour to avoid becoming overly vulnerable and dependent on the hegemon. However, when the leading power is in relative decline and contested by a rival power, it has more incentives to use its administrative role in the international economy for coercion and thereby undermines trust in complex supply chains.

When the concentration of economic power diminishes, 'the liberal order is expected to unravel and its regimes to become weaker, ultimately being replaced by mercantilist arrangements' where national authority is established above market forces (Ruggie 1982: 381). When new poles of power emerge in the periphery, the hegemon is faced with the dilemma of either accepting that its primacy is withering away or of weakening the rising power by restricting its access to markets, industries, technologies, transportation corridors, financial institutions and the international trade currency. If the hegemon opts to shore up its position in the international system by denying access to rivals, the new challengers will develop alternative geoeconomic instruments of power and reject the former international division of labour.

The Fourth Industrial Revolution is occurring in a fragmented international economy that is less committed to free trade, a significant development that will make economic statecraft more blatant and coercive. It elevates the techno-nationalist cause above the market forces that incentivized global value chains.

Globalization, fuelled by economic liberalism, is destined to fragment for two key reasons. First, economic liberalism is dependent on a geoeconomic hegemon. The relative decline of the United States is compelling Washington to depend more on economic coercion, and this continues to erode its ability to act as an administrator of the international system. Second, the Fourth Industrial Revolution is undermining the foundation of interdependence between a capital-intensive core and low-tech human labour at the periphery. Innovative technologies automating cognitive functions continue to concentrate power in capital, while low-tech human labour becomes less valuable. The technologically advanced core only has an interest in low-wage states at the periphery for access to their domestic market. However, without an export-based development strategy, economic growth by states at the periphery becomes dependent on supplying their domestic demand with import substitution.

The first and second industrial revolutions

Ever since the First Industrial Revolution, the international distribution of power has increasingly defined the relationship between states. Trade and other international economic connectivity developed under the administration of an economic hegemon that controlled the geoeconomic levers of power – the key technologies for advanced and strategic industry, the transportation corridors for commerce and mechanisms for financial and economic cooperation such as banks and the principal trade currency.

With significant government intervention to support its industries, Britain positioned itself as a technological leader during the First Industrial Revolution. The industrial policy of Britain was supported by James Steuart (1770) as a 'scientific form of mercantilism'. The British state utilized protectionism, regulations and subsidies to support Britain's manufacturing base from its infancy to international leadership (Ashworth 2017). Manipulation of tariffs to assist British exports, guaranteed rates of interest and railway construction ensured industrial output, while the government also used its maritime power to control foreign markets for extracting resources and selling manufactured goods.

Once in a leadership position, Britain had incentives to embrace free-market principles because an international division of labour would cement its technological leadership. Britain's repeal of the Corn Laws in 1843 signified the transition to the free market. This decision was largely motivated by the need to open up foreign markets and construct an international division of labour in which Britain would export manufactured goods and continental Europe would, in return, export agricultural produce to Britain. Without free trade, it was feared that states such as Germany and the United States would develop their own manufacturing industries and thus erode Britain's comparative advantage of technological leadership (Hilton 1977: 280; McKeown 1989; Irwin 1989). Opening up the low-skilled agricultural market to other powers made it possible for Britain to dominate the market for manufactured goods. Britain's industrial strength and its high-value activities in the international market were strengthened by creating incentives for potential rivals to, instead, specialize in exports of raw materials. Free trade served a geoeconomic purpose inasmuch as 'the agricultural nations of the world might be given a stake in England's Empire of Free Trade' (Semmel 1970: 205). In parliamentary debate, it was argued that free trade for Britain as a technological leader implied that 'foreign nations would become valuable Colonies to us, without imposing on us the responsibility of governing them' (Semmel 1970: 8).

David Ricardo's liberal economic theory about comparative advantage – that is, the structuring of an international division of labour based on merit – was largely inspired by the technologically advanced position Britain had created for itself in such a system. Irrespective of the realist systemic incentives to advocate free trade as a tool to cement technological leadership and asymmetrical dependence, Ricardo's theory was clothed in the liberal language of absolute gain:

> Under a system of perfectly free trade each country naturally devotes its capital and labour to such employments as are most beneficial to each. This pursuit of individual advantage is admirably connected with the universal good of the whole. By stimulating industry, by rewarding ingenuity, and by using most efficaciously the peculiar powers bestowed by nature, it distributes labour most effectively and most economically; while, by increasing the general mass of productions, it diffuses general benefit, and binds together, by one common tie of interest and inter course, the universal society of nations throughout the civilised world. It is this principle which determines that wine shall be made in France and Portugal, that corn shall be grown in America and Poland, and that hardware and other goods shall be manufactured in England.
>
> (Ricardo 1821: 139)

Great power politics in Europe subsequently became increasingly defined by political economy. The Industrial Revolution had made Britain the dominant manufacturing and industrial centre in Europe and gave it significant trading power and financial clout. The first-mover advantage in industries was extended by pursuing industrial expansion in the underdeveloped world. The limited economic power in the underdeveloped world enabled Britain to position itself as the dominant world trader, shipper and banker (Hobsbawm 1968). Military power remained instrumental to extend first-mover advantage. British Prime Minister, William Pitt, argued in Parliament: 'If the Americans should manufacture a lock of wool or a horseshoe, I would fill their ports with ships and their towns with troops' (Van Tyne 1927: 33).

The ideology of free trade subsequently played an important role in slowing the diffusion of technologies. German economist Friedrich List (1827) argued that developing states could intervene favourably in the economy by using temporary subsidies and tariffs to develop infant industries until they became competitive in international markets. List advocated national isolation only as a development strategy to enable late developers to attain a more favourable position in the international system. At the crux of List's ideas was the notion that, in a world divided into states, the state must ensure that the economy serves national interests. The fear was that free trade would only preserve asymmetrical dependencies between the core and periphery and that colonization would gradually erode the sovereignty of those states. Thus, List (1885: 295–6) scorned British ideological advocacy of free trade as a mere hegemonic strategy to 'kick away the ladder':

> It is a very common clever device that when anyone has attained the summit of greatness, he kicks away the ladder by which he has climbed up, in order to deprive others of the means of climbing up after him. In this lies the secret of the cosmopolitical doctrine of Adam Smith, and of the cosmopolitical tendencies of his great contemporary William Pitt, and of all his successors in the British Government administrations.

Henry Clay, a prominent US statesman, similarly warned in 1832 that 'free trade' equated to succumbing to British colonial power:

> What was meant by free trade, was nothing more nor less than, by means of the great advantages we enjoyed, to get the monopoly of all their markets for our manufacturers, and to prevent them, one and all, from ever becoming manufacturing nations.
>
> (Williams 2011: 221)

The ideas of Henry Clay translated into the American System, which became the main instrument for subsidizing its industrialization. The American System was based on the three pillars of geoeconomics: the development of a domestic manufacturing base, the construction of railways and transportation infrastructure, and the establishment of a national bank. List defined American economic nationalism as anti-hegemonic, arguing that the

> English national economy has for its object to manufacture for the whole world, to monopolise all manufacturing power, even at the expense of the lives of the citizens, to keep the world and especially her colonies in a state of infancy and vassalage by political management as well as by the superiority of her capital, her skill and her navy. American economy has for its object to bring into harmony the three branches of industry, without which no national industry can attain perfection ... It has for its objects lastly to be free and independent and powerful ... English national economy is predominant; American national economy aspires only to become independent.
>
> (List 1885: 167–8)

Similarly, Alexander Hamilton argued that the United States could not rely on free trade if it was to develop its own domestic industrial base. Hamilton viewed economic self-sufficiency as essential for nation-building and felt it was necessary for the country to shed its excessive technological and economic dependence on Britain to maintain its political independence (Mott 1997: 22). The subsequent strong industrialization of the United States, supported by tariffs, thwarted British efforts to convert the American Mid-West and Central America into informal dependencies (Gallagher and Robinson 1953: 10). By protecting domestic industrial power with high tariffs from 1865 to 1932, the United States grew into a technological and industrial leader.

Following the Second World War, the country's manufacturing capabilities and the emergence of 'big business' as an organizational structure enabled new US corporations to dominate the technology sector. America's technological leadership rested on being the centre of innovation, capital and skilled labour. For a time, this leadership was self-sustaining due to the 'brain drain' suffered by potential rival states. The best and the brightest from around the world came to work for leading US tech companies where they contributed to ground-breaking innovations and enjoyed generous remuneration.

Even seemingly rudimentary innovations such as the intermodal shipping container helped spur economic integration after the Second World War. In 1956, Malcolm McLean invented container shipping when he converted a US tanker from the Second World War to carry fifty-eight trailer units. Today, a single freighter can carry up to 20,000 individual containers. McLean's invention brought about one of the most significant changes to global value chains. For centuries, items had been loaded onto ships separately. The shipping container cut both the time and price of shipping radically, making it possible for exporters to become competitive in markets of non-complex items such as clothing. Furthermore, the use of a standardized intermodal shipping container deepened the connection between markets around the world. Unlike cars driving on different sides of the road or variations in rail gages, the standardized container fits on trucks and ships around the world. Because a broader variety of items could be shipped from increasingly distant destinations, cities with suitable ports grew rapidly in economic significance and came to occupy an important place in global value chains.

The Digital Revolution

Early on in the Third Industrial Revolution, the United States established a hegemonic position as a high-tech innovator in global value chains. The technology of the electronics industry spearheaded a shift towards increasingly complex global value chains. This process began in the 1960s when companies first began outsourcing the production and assembly of semiconductors to East Asia, where low-wage workers were abundant (Lazonick 2009).

The economic stagnation of the West in the 1970s further incentivized corporations and governments to collectively construct global value chains that would maximize efficiency for corporations and enable the most advanced states to retain their geoeconomic leadership. Bell (1973) predicted in *The Coming of Post-Industrial Society* that the economics of goods would shift to the economics of information as manufacturing societies gave way to service industries ruled by technical–professional elites. Such a post-industrial society or 'knowledge economy' would depend more on technological advances than material goods. This increases pressure on governments to embrace 'developmentalist' policies that support the development of new technologies and their transfer to domestic corporations. This leads to more intense development of intellectual institutions and competition for research and intellectual property.

The East Asian powers tasked with manufacturing and assembling electronic components began to develop more educated populations as individuals' incomes and skills increased. The absence of challenging and high-wage domestic jobs, however, led to an economically harmful brain drain to the United States in the 1960s and 1970s. States managed to reverse this trend only by intervening to 'climb the ladder' in global value chains. Formidable government support and collaboration with such major conglomerates as South Korean Chaebol and Japanese Zaibatsu focused on investment in high-value activities and the establishment of domestic corporations and technological platforms (Lazonick 2009: 166).

Similarly, Western Europe used significant subsidies to climb the technological ladder and global value chains. For example, Western European airlines received extensive subsidies and virtually interest-free loans from their governments, which allowed them to operate at a loss until they became competitive vis-à-vis their US counterparts. Airbus Industrie penetrated and rose in the US market by running deficits at the expense of their taxpayers, at one point leasing out twenty-three of its A300 airliners to US Eastern Air Lines at a price of $1 a year: 'Just as in the past when young men were put in uniform to be marched off in pursuit of schemes of territorial conquest, today taxpayers are persuaded to subsidize schemes of industrial conquest' (Luttwak 2010: 34). Western European airliners soon became world leaders, while US airlines without government support were pushed towards bankruptcy. Germany then used this approach to boost its automobile, communications, superconductor and other strategic industries (Luttwak 2010: 34).

The United States also strengthened its own position by further subsidizing its technology sector and pursuing initiatives to slow down the diffusion of its digital technologies. In the 1980s, corporations and governments increased their cooperation, applying economic liberalism to overcome the stagnation of the 1970s. The international division of labour began changing in the 1980s as low-profit activities in the supply chain were outsourced to low-wage countries. High-tech multinational corporations with their base in the United States, Western Europe and Japan began to restructure their supply chains and business operations by absorbing and consolidating control over research, development, marketing and intellectual property rights (Pretchel 2000). Governments began supporting global value chains in the 1980s, with Reaganism and Thatcherism providing the ideological and legal framework required for liberalizing their respective economies and forming the necessary trade agreements to open trade. Furthermore, companies and governments cooperated to develop financial networks that could establish economic connectivity between the various participants in the supply chain (Serfati 2008). Subsequently, global value chains were created through a combination of political and economic power.

Direct and indirect subsidies contributed to the emergence of large-scale tech corporations capable of asserting global dominance. Key industries in the new industrial revolution such as high-tech, pharmaceuticals, chemicals and biotech are especially well funded through public spending. Large mergers and acquisitions were permitted with the goal of developing tech leaders capable of dominating global value chains (Hopkins and Lazonick 2014).

The myth of Silicon Valley as an organic technology hub arising solely out of American entrepreneurial spirit and free-market forces conceals a geoeconomic tactic of using military technology to augment commercial competitiveness. After the Second World War, the US government devoted billions of dollars to developing high-tech leadership to outcompete the Soviet Union economically, militarily and ideologically. Silicon Valley became a key beneficiary. The costs were socialized, while the profits were privatized in the form of patents. In the era of geoeconomics, military spending can become a source of indirect subsidies as public funds are directed to corporations. Many military technologies were developed by contractors in Silicon Valley, which then acquired patents and also used the technology also for commercial industry (Benner 2002: 70). While patent laws are intended to create a return on investment for research and development, patent wars are used to develop monopolies. Patents are obtained simply to obstruct rivals, and larger corporations with armies of lawyers can use patent laws to entangle smaller companies in litigation they cannot afford and lack time to wait out.

Washington placed its full weight behind its leading international corporations to cement their global dominance, abandoning free-market capitalism in favour of becoming what can be called a 'hidden developmental state' (Block 2008). Corporations lobbied heavily in the United States, Western Europe and Japan for changes in laws and taxation policies and for foreign direct investment to construct their optimal global value chains. In the United States, the Congressional Package and the US Economic Recovery Act of 1986 enabled domestic corporations to sell and outsource segments of their value chains to low-wage states with more relaxed labour laws. US corporations instead focused their capital in the more profitable upper tiers of global value chains (Prechel 1997). The European Union was likewise formed in the early 1990s to increase foreign direct investment and to restructure domestic businesses at the higher end of supply chains akin to their US counterparts (Lawton 1999). The EU has since openly discussed its policies to support industries such as the EU2020 Strategy.

By increasing their focus on intangible assets such as intellectual property rights and reducing the share of less valuable tangible assets, United States, European and Japanese companies grew rapidly throughout the 1980s and 1990s (Baruch 2001). This period was characterized by the transitioning from manufacturing to service industries. Between 1991 and 2010, manufactured goods from low- to middle-income countries (LMIC) increased in the United States from 20 to 50 per cent, in the UK from 9 to 22 per cent, in Germany from 8 to 23 per cent and in Japan from 21 to 52 per cent (Milberg and Winkler 2013: 38).

Competition for patents has been instrumental in the new technological competition. The United States provided indirect subsidies for its tech corporations by selling technological innovations and patents from publicly funded institutions to private enterprises at low cost (Perelman 2003; May and Sell 2005). Legislation such as the Bayh-Dole Act of 1980 enabled publicly funded universities to patent their innovations (Ward 2012). Subsequently, public funding of research intended for broader use within society was placed in private corporations to restrict its use and limit competition. The United States, EU and Japan strengthened domestic patent laws from the 1980s and 1990s and sought to expand them globally by pursuing trade-related intellectual property rights (TRIPS). These efforts produced results in the Uruguay Round of GATT and were institutionalized in the World Trade Organization (Sell 2003). The diffusion of technologies was subsequently slowed down by extending the time required for obtaining patent protection, thereby strengthening first-mover advantage (Shadlen 2005).

The end of the Cold War for Allies

The end of the Cold War produced a renaissance of geostrategic thinking, with the significance of ideology and military conflict giving way to geoeconomics as the focus of great power competition. US corporations equipped with superior technology and economic dominance began to absorb a greatly expanded periphery around their core in the form of US-led global value chains. Geoeconomic tensions, however, began to flare up. Previously, the Cold War had mitigated tensions from the geoeconomic rivalry between Western allies. The United States had faced a dilemma between tolerating a loss of market share to European and East Asian allies for the sake of presenting a collective Western front against communism and the desire to maintain its economic and technological primacy within the Western alliance.

By the end of the Cold War, the United States had already become more reluctant to accept the industrial policies of the Europeans and East Asian allies. The United States had a more severe reaction to Japan because of its ability to dominate in digital technologies. Japanese conglomerates received both overt and covert support by their government. Funds were channelled from the government and favourable loans provided, while various means were used to keep foreign competitors out of the domestic market. At the same time, subsidies were provided for an export-based development strategy. As Japan climbed the technological ladder and value chains, the United States used the power of the state to counter the threat to its technological and economic leadership. Japan mounted a challenge to US textiles in the 1950s and to steel and synthetic fibres in the 1960s, and competed fiercely in electric consumables, cars and semiconductors from the 1970s to 1990s. The United States stoked economic patriotism with the slogan 'Made in America' as a comparative advantage in the automobile industry. Nevertheless, Japan's ability to become the world leader in the supply of microchips had even greater importance because the Third Industrial Revolution had shown that digital technologies were key to achieving leadership in future industries.

Washington subsequently accused Tokyo of unfair trade practices and technology theft, resulting in the punishment of Japan to restore US technological leadership. Washington also managed to translate Japan's excessive security dependencies into geoeconomic leverage. In 1985, the United States imposed 100 per cent tariffs on Japanese semiconductors. In 1987, Toshiba products were banned for three years in the United States. In 1989, Japan was required to share semiconductor technologies by opening its patents to the United States. In 1991, Japan had to agree to double the US share in the Japanese semiconductor market to 20 per cent. Even as it crushed Japan's semiconductor industry on the pretext of unfair trade practices, the United States provided formidable support to domestic producers to reassert its international leadership.

The Western Europeans had also become concerned about the United States and Japan establishing leadership in the digital era. As digital technologies became increasingly prominent in the economy, Western European states sought to reduce their excessive reliance on US and Japanese technologies. They feared 'technological colonisation' because the direct investments made by American and Japanese multinational corporations in Europe produced only low-skilled and low-paid jobs, diminished the EU's attractiveness for local and international talent and reduced Europe's ability to produce spin-offs (Keller 1992: 112). In other words, the investments and division of labour demonstrated striking similarities with the repeal of the Corn Laws. The EU was subsequently leaning towards embracing industrial policies similar to that of Japan in support of strategic high-tech industries. Ironically, the Western Europeans were, at the same time, preaching the virtues of laissez-faire capitalism to Russia as its market opened up to European corporations and technologies.

The end of the Cold War between adversaries

The Cold War had been devoid of significant geoeconomic tensions with large Eurasian adversaries because communist states were largely decoupled from international markets. With the demise of communism, great powers capable of counterbalancing the United States began adopting the use of economic statecraft.

China had initially pursued an industrial strategy committed to 'catching up' by encouraging the diffusion of technologies and climbing global value chains. Wage suppression and currency manipulation were employed effectively to shift global manufacturing to China (Cwik 2011). Concurrently, China demanded that foreign companies set up joint ventures with domestic companies to transfer technology and know-how. In more covert fashion, China also reverse-engineered foreign technologies and products, and set up cyber espionage units with the main purpose of stealing technologies from the West (Mandiant 2013). Beijing also pursued technology transfers through legal means by acquiring large corporations (Le Corre and Sepulchre 2016: 54). Beijing began to establish its own 'American System' based on the three pillars of geoeconomic power – manufacturing, transportation corridors and financial instruments – with the goal of restructuring global value chains around China.

The most important component of China's version of the American System, however, has been its development of the high-tech industry. The *Made in China 2025* initiative is pushing to establish Chinese leadership in the key technologies of the Fourth Industrial Revolution. China has complemented the Belt and Road Initiative with a Digital Silk Road that includes AI, quantum computing, big data, cloud technology, nanotechnology and other digital technologies. With approximately $200 billion invested in the Digital Silk Road, China is enhancing its digital infrastructure with undersea cables and by installing broadband in countries with insufficient digital infrastructure. The digital enhancements also include a major expansion of its BeiDou satellite network from 17 to 35 to achieve coverage of the entire world.

The Belt and Road Initiative launched in 2013 develops large infrastructure projects and places land and sea transportation corridors under Chinese influence. These infrastructure projects improve economic connectivity between China and Europe, and connect China more closely with developing states that can supply needed resources and serve as markets for Chinese exports. Furthermore, these infrastructure projects have become instrumental in developing Chinese financial instruments such as investment banks, in internationalizing the Yuan as a trade currency and in establishing favourable technical standards and trade regimes. China had earlier earned a reputation as a 'copycat' that could only imitate and steal but not innovate. That soon changed once China had caught up.

Russia fell into the 'liberal division of labour trap' by embracing free-market principles, and by exporting energy resources and importing manufactured goods, Russia embarked the path towards deindustrialization. Furthermore, Russia developed an excessive reliance on an asymmetrical economic partnership with the West that contributed to marginalizing Russia in Europe. The West even aimed to further skew the balance of dependence in its favour by reducing Europe's reliance on Russian energy resources, Russia's sole strategic industry in relations with the Europeans. Gradually, Moscow sought to diversify its economic ties to reduce that excessive dependence on the West and to instead pursue a geoeconomic strategy of integrating Greater Eurasia in concert with

China. Russia is also embracing the economic development policies advocated by List and Hamilton by following the Chinese development model (Diesen 2021).

The dual decoupling of the Fourth Industrial Revolution

The Fourth Industrial Revolution is causing a dual decoupling in the international division of labour. States are incentivized to repatriate global value chains due to the availability of new technologies and because of the competition for technological and geoeconomic leadership. A split is occurring between developed and developing states, as well as between developed states.

Technological innovations have traditionally encouraged ever-more complex supply chains by reducing the significance of geography. Innovations in maritime transportation from the 1950s and in international finance since the 1970s further enabled multinational corporations to dominate and establish global strategies. The increasingly intertwined global trading system appears to be the inevitable result of technological advances. However, the technologies of the Fourth Industrial Revolution improve local production. This facilitates flexibility and convenience and harnesses the economic nationalist appeal of producing goods domestically (Fratocchi et al. 2016).

Technological innovations incentivize the repatriation of global supply chains. After decades of offshoring production and other value chain activities to low-wage and low-cost states as a competitive advantage, this trend appears to be slowing and even reversing. 'Reshoring' increasingly enters the English vocabulary as robots are becoming more competitive than low-wage workers in developing states. 'Industry 4.0' refers to a high-tech approach to production that includes robotics, 3D printing, the Internet of Things, the Internet of Goods and other technologies associated with the Fourth Industrial Revolution. Developed states with sophisticated technology and infrastructure are increasingly attaining an advantage in manufacturing over states whose only strength is in low-wage labour. The practice of offshoring, however, will not come to an end because it provides a means for establishing proximity and access to large markets abroad (De Backer et al. 2016).

The main change in infrastructure is the shift to regional production closer to the end market. The use of software for 3D printing as a replacement for the traditional technical skills needed in product design tends to simplify global supply chains. For example, the automobile industry is recognized as having one of the most complex supply chains in the world, with each vehicle containing more than 20,000 parts originating from several thousand suppliers. By contrast, Local Motors unveiled a 3D-printed autonomous vehicle in 2016 that was produced in a single location. A Chinese company, Pix Moving, uses AI to design vehicles that are uploaded to a cloud and transmit instructions to 3D printers that can print the vehicle at any location. Legislation can support the process of reshoring with economic inducements as a response to a working class that has suffered from stagnating salaries and loss of jobs due to offshoring. Most of those repatriated jobs, however, would go to robots rather than human workers.

Reshoring disrupts the foundation of the international division of labour established after the First Industrial Revolution. The former development model used by the Asian Tigers and China will no longer be available to countries such as Vietnam or Bangladesh to the same extent. As many as 137 million workers in Indonesia, the Philippines, Thailand, Vietnam and Cambodia, or approximately 56 per cent of their entire workforce, are threatened by technological unemployment due to their excessive reliance on low-skilled professions such as those in the garment industry that are especially vulnerable to automated manufacturing (Chang, Rynhart and Huynh 2016).

The inequality between developed and developing states could grow and reverse the process of evening out differences that had continued since decolonization. Power will concentrate in developed states with sophisticated technology, while the developing world will have less to gain from committing to free trade and preserving intellectual property rights. Furthermore, a reduced need for unskilled labour will decrease the demand for foreign workers and subsequently diminish remittances. Reduced remittances from Central Americans working in the United States, Central Asians working in Russia and the vast pool of labourers that flocked in from the countryside and fuelled China's manufacturing boom will cause major disruptions. Tajikistan relies more on remittance than any state in the world. Money sent home by Tajikistani nationals working in Russia accounted for 29 per cent of the country's entire GDP in 2018.

However, AI and robotics also offer developing states a historical opportunity to leapfrog and transition away from their former economic model of relying excessively on their position at the lower end of global value chains. For example, mobile phones enabled underdeveloped regions to leapfrog costly investment in landline infrastructure, the Internet improved financial services in regions without bank branches and made online education available for the development of a skill-based economy, smart agriculture technology helped inefficient agricultural communities become competitive. However, what will low-wage states that previously relied on an export-based development strategy contribute to the global economy?

Outside Asia, the significance of exports in GDP has been declining, which will likely continue due to the automation of manufacturing (Rodrik 2018). The export-based development strategy must be replaced by developing technological platforms to supply domestic or regional demand. The main constraint is access to capital and the development of a skilled workforce. With diminishing benefits from access to markets in developed states, developing economies must restrict their markets and encourage import substitution and techno-nationalism. Growth in Africa has largely been fuelled by domestic demand as opposed to export (Diao, McMillan and Rodrik 2017). Thus, low-wage states can gain from protecting their domestic markets from being saturated by imports. Temporary subsidies and tariffs for selected strategic industries and financial infrastructure are imperative for developing states, which should seek collective bargaining power and economic integration with similar economies in their regions.

Contested technological leadership and the splinternet

The digital leadership the United States had established by developing AI and building exportable technological platforms initially appeared to pave the way for a comfortable lead in the Fourth Industrial Revolution as well. Unlike the Digital Revolution in which the US government provided temporary support for Silicon Valley before pulling back, the Fourth Industrial Revolution will require even greater intervention into the market to support domestic industries. This will inevitably challenge the international division of labour. It is becoming increasingly apparent that for the United States to stay competitive with China, Washington will need to commit to prolonged large-scale support for domestic industries. Direct and indirect support for US industries and the coercing of the rest of the world to link itself to US supply chains will contribute to the further unravelling of global supply chains.

The term 'splinternet' implies the Balkanization of the internet. In September 2018, former Google Chief Executive Eric Schmidt predicted 'bifurcation of the Internet' resulting in one Internet led by the United States and another by China. For some time, Beijing has sought to establish Chinese digital technology standards around the world to circumvent US-dominated cyberinfrastructure and make Chinese companies less reliant on foreign patents and licences

(Heilman et al. 2014). Russia is making advances in the development of domestic digital ecosystems and a national Internet, or 'RuNet' that would ensure all connections pass through government nodes. It also seems likely that the EU will develop some technological autonomy if it survives its internal problems. The EU's federalist ambitions, to become the United States of Europe, will be aided by developing common technological ecosystems in the format of techno-nationalism or techno-regionalism as the modern foundation for nation-building.

Global value chains will be repatriated as governments increasingly define key technologies as critical infrastructure. AI creates powerful incentives for technological sovereignty as it requires the collection of large quantities of data, which becomes an issue of privacy and national security. Even Adam Smith and John Stuart Mill advocated restrictions on international trade when it was warranted by national security interests (Baldwin 1985: 85). Parallel digital infrastructures are costly and inefficient, yet rivalry between states can cause major technological and economic setbacks as each side seeks to sabotage the other. However, this could lead states to stop the practice of sharing technologies. China is preparing contingency plans in case the United States severs its supply chains. China must diversify its trade corridors and energy suppliers, and similarly cannot rely on US technologies for strategic industries. China is transitioning from its former development strategy by establishing a competitive advantage based on its huge market, access to data and massive capital. China is also investing its vast trade surpluses made from manufacturer into subsidies for high-tech industries.

China is highly dependent on the import of semiconductors as an important component for its digital products. The United States sees its leadership in this industry as a national security asset. The US Army was the initial large customer of chips, which gave rise to Silicon Valley. In 2018, the United States banned domestic companies from selling chips and intellectual property to ZTE, a Chinese producer of smartphones and other telecommunications equipment. This would have doomed the company to go bankrupt overnight had not Trump decided later to repeal the ban. This was a clear message to China that dependence on US components would enable the United States to crush leading Chinese corporations if necessary.

It is therefore evident that for China to overtake the United States as a tech leader, it must reduce its reliance on US-made components. It is similarly crucial that the United States ensure that such allies as Japan, South Korea and Taiwan – that have highly developed semiconductor industries – do not assist China in developing its own. A non-aggressive approach by the United States would involve simply relying on market forces to stay ahead of China in research and development. However, this is no longer possible. The United States can promote free trade agreements and intellectual property rights to ensure that China does not imitate or use unfair trade practices, yet the United States would have to use its own unfair trade practices and economic coercion to blunt the rise of China as an innovator.

A technological security dilemma becomes evident as US actions further incentivize China to reduce its reliance on US components. The attack on Huawei is a prime example of using a trade war to prevent Chinese companies from taking the lead. Huawei's 5G technologies are about one year ahead of those developed by US corporations, and this gap could grow. The United States began by arresting the Chief Financial Officer of Huawei and then followed by banning Huawei products and demanding that allies fall in line. China's response of rapidly repatriating supply chains, however, had already been in the making. The *China 2025* initiative explicitly sets out to establish greater technological autonomy by increasing the share of domestically produced core components and materials to 40 per cent by 2020 and to 70 per cent by 2025. Excessive reliance on processing and memory chips from Intel, Broadcom, Qualcomm, Micron, Western Digital and ARM is rightly considered an intolerable vulnerability that must be mitigated. Similarly, Beijing will reduce its dependence on Google's Android system by replacing it with China's own HongMeng operating system and/or by cooperating with Russia's Aurora operating system as part of a collective technological platform for Eurasian integration. Discussions about selling Huawei smartphones in Russia with the Russian-owned Aurora operating system indicate a tech alliance forming to reduce reliance on the United States. Huawei also partners with Russian universities to ensure opportunities for the top talent and thus prevent a brain drain to the West.

Throughout the political and, at times, military confrontation of the Cold War, the United States was able to leverage the considerable asymmetry in power that it enjoyed with allies to secure their loyalty. Efforts to convert geopolitical solidarity into geoeconomic solidarity, however, became problematic when they undermined the ability of weaker states to establish their own economic power and relegated them to the condition of permanent protectorates. The EU can be expected to distance itself from the United States and assert its autonomy. Otherwise, by simply continuing to play junior partner to the United States, Europe would return to its Cold War status and remain a near vassal of the United States. Germany and the EU are also becoming alienated by Washington's excessively militaristic policies (Szabo 2015). Furthermore, as German and EU trade shifts towards the East, the definition of national interests will change and alter foreign policy (Szabo 2015: 69).

To date, the United States has largely failed to obtain support from allies in preserving its geoeconomic levers of power. US Vice President Mike Pence argued at the Munich Security Conference that 'we cannot ensure the defence of the West if our allies grow dependent on the East' (White House 2019). The speech alluded to the Europeans forming dependencies on Chinese telecom giants, primarily Huawei, to implement their 5G network. This development is significant because the 5G network will form the nervous system of the Internet of Things, self-driving cars and other technologies of the Fourth Industrial Revolution. Furthermore, the supplier of the network would have access to an unprecedented volume of data that it could use to develop artificial intelligence or pass on to security services and spy agencies. It is highly likely that the Chinese government works directly with the country's tech companies, even as the Edward Snowden leaks confirmed that US tech companies have created backdoor channels for their government. European powers are defiantly ignoring US warnings and continuing with plans to implement the Chinese 5G network. Similar developments had already arisen. In 2015, the United States placed immense pressure on all its allies to rebuke China's invitation to join the Asian Infrastructure Investment Bank (AIIB) as an alternative to the IMF and World Bank. Most US major allies instead rebuked Washington by signing up. Former US Secretary of State Madeleine Albright argued that Washington 'screwed it up' because 'all of a sudden everybody was in' and the United States was left isolated. Later, Italy decided to participate in the Chinese Belt and Road Initiative. Despite enormous opposition and threats of sanctions by the United States, Germany and the EU pushed ahead with the Northstream pipeline, while Turkey and other states have committed to buying Russian weaponry such as the S-400 missile system despite threats of sanctions by the United States. Faced with US threats for continuing to trade with Iran, the EU has begun developing its own payment system to ensure it is not held hostage to US extraterritorial sanctions.

Conclusion

After the collapse of the Soviet Union and the victory of capitalism, liberal theories predicted that the United States would lead the continued integration of the global economy. Fast forward to January 2017, President Xi Jinping of Communist China delivers a speech at the World Economic Forum in Davos in which he defends the virtues of the free market and globalization – in stark contrast to growing US protectionism. The current state of international affairs demonstrates that ideologies supporting free trade and an international division of labour are merely a reflection of power. Liberal international economic systems emerge when there is a geoeconomic hegemon because the international division of labour cements its control over geoeconomic levers of power such as strategic industries, transportation corridors and financial instruments. The Fourth Industrial Revolution is occurring as the United States and China compete on technologies that will determine who becomes the geoeconomic leader of the future. Furthermore, the increased importance of technology as an instrument of geoeconomic power makes technological sovereignty a prerequisite for great power stature.

An open and unified global market under a single system of governance will soon become a thing of the past. As the two leading rival powers, the United States and China will largely drive the repatriation of supply chains in an effort to limit their vulnerability and technological dependence on each other. The subsequent disruption to the global economy will have broader consequences as both the United States and China seek to coerce the rest of the world into operating under their technologies and levers of geoeconomic power. A Cold Warlike bipolar distribution of power is unlikely to develop, however, because obtaining geoeconomic loyalty differs from securing the geopolitical loyalty of weaker states through military might. Large powers such as Russia will seek to negotiate partnerships, primarily with China, that gives Chinese technologies preference if they form partnerships with Russian domestic technological platforms in Moscow's effort to maintain technological sovereignty. The international division of labour will, therefore, not be influenced solely by market forces.

Great powers will aim to capture more of the high-value economic activities in the global economy, employ their own workers, have the best technologies and avoid unfavourable asymmetrical dependence. The trade rules of the current liberal economic system will continue to break down as sanctions, theft, subsidies and protectionism are applied arbitrarily. Without a clear framework for the rules of competition, mutually beneficial cooperation will also unravel.

4

The rise of the tech giants and the authoritarian state: Seizing the means of production

Introduction

Who will seize the means of production as large technological ecosystems replace former industries? The digital domain is conquering the physical world as the industrial Internet transforms traditional industries. Over the next few years, digital platforms will absorb the products and services of corporations across all industries. Those corporations that provide search engines, social media, e-commerce and other digital platforms will increasingly conquer transportation, logistics, renewable energy, delivery services, financial services, payment services, news, agriculture, food preparation, retail, grocery stores, construction, space exploration, manufacturing and other seemingly unrelated industries.

Whoever controls AI and big data will control the industries of the future and other geoeconomic instruments of power. Tech giants with high processing power and access to an abundance of data are laying the foundations for unprecedented capital-intensive monopolies. Digital technologies that replace human labour operate on high fixed costs as an entry barrier and minuscule variable costs as an incentive for economies of scale. Markets based on high fixed costs and low variable costs, much like the railways of the nineteenth century, diminish competition and unleash the monopolistic impulses embedded in capitalism. In previous epochs of industrial capitalism, monopolies aimed to become more efficient and close off competition with horizontal mergers between companies that were in direct competition and vertical mergers within the same supply chains. In the era of digital industrialism, products and services from all industries are merged under digital platforms due to the *economies of scope*. The concentration of productive power makes it vital for great powers to develop their own technological ecosystems to preserve their sovereignty and great power standing.

This chapter will first argue that technological advancements increase the market power and political power of large corporations to the extent they can challenge the authority of the state. The overwhelming market power of tech giants will increasingly make them ungovernable unless they are broken up or brought under the control of the state. Breaking up tech giants will reduce their competitiveness in international markets while nationalizing them can give birth to a corrupt and authoritarian government. Second, it is argued that the concentration of power will amplify due to the concept of 'economies of scope', which explains why digital platforms absorb seemingly unrelated industries. The technological platform for one industry can be used to conquer what had previously been an unrelated industry. Last, it is argued that the transportation industry will likely be a key catalyst enabling tech giants to integrate technological ecosystems under their control. It is concluded that governments are moving towards converting tech giants into national champions aligned with the state. A more authoritarian state asserts itself by using extensive regulation to control private industry, using private industry to assert increasing influence over the population and using more forceful geoeconomic instruments of power to wield influence internationally.

The market power and political power of tech giants

The rise of tech giants as the hub of capital reintroduces an old question about capitalism: When are corporations too large? States face a dilemma regarding large and influential corporations: they can be more efficient and are necessary for influence and power in international markets and politics, yet large corporations also wield greater influence in domestic politics and can even challenge the authority of the state.

If large corporations are no longer constrained by the state, what ensures their loyalty to national interests? How can governments ensure that *What is good for Silicon Valley is good for the US, and what is good for Shenzhen is good for China?* In the past, governments often took the lead in new technologies such as nuclear power and space exploration. Now, private corporations are in the driver's seat and have an ambiguous relationship with and loyalty towards the state. Corporations operating globally can undermine the state as they 'have little need for national loyalty, view national boundaries as obstacles that thankfully are vanishing, and see national governments as residues from the past whose only useful function is to facilitate the elite's global operations' (Huntington

2004: 8). In many cases, tech giants developed with significant public funding and state support, helping them to achieve immense influence. How can it be ensured that what is good for the tech giants is also good for the country and its people? Should governments prevent the proliferation of key technologies? Is the world gravitating towards the US model of a corporate state or the Chinese model of strict government control? Either way, efforts to achieve geoeconomic power necessitate cooperation between government and industry.

The transition to petroleum in the nineteenth century and its implications are comparable to the current transition to digital technologies. As a strategic industry with monopolistic potential due to the limited possibility for diversification, the concentration of wealth and control over assets, petroleum companies were able to expand and control the market by controlling the entire supply chain. As a case in point, John D. Rockefeller became the richest man in US history through oil and related industries. Rockefeller acquired the entire business process ranging from extraction, transportation, refining, and retail and wholesaling. This business model then spurred the Rockefeller family to absorb mining as an alternative natural resource, railroads, shipping, pipelines and oil terminals for transportation of energy, refineries, banking for financing the industries, and other industries with favourable synergy effects. Controlling the entire supply chain enhanced efficiency and was instrumental in creating a barrier to competitors.

Monopolies

Competition drives prices down to the benefit of the consumer and compels companies to innovate and enhance efficiency to reduce costs. Historically, monopolies have therefore concentrated wealth, corrupted politics and reduced innovation.

A key critique of capitalism has been that free-market competition is only a temporary and transitory stage (Marx 1867 [1887]). The concentration of capital over time reduces the negotiation power of workers. The concentration of capital was expected to create cartels that would compete on the international stage for dominance (Hilferding 1910 [1985]). Lenin thus concluded that imperialism was the final monopolistic stage of capitalism. The trend in the late nineteenth century towards large corporations displacing smaller companies lent credence to theories about the temporary nature of the free market. In the inter-war period, Keynes (2016: 272) published his essay, *The end of laissez-faire,* that argued from a technological and economic point of view that the units of production were becoming too large, that economies tended towards the aggregation of production, and that monopolies were asserting themselves. Similarly, Rüstow (1949 [2009]: 51) advocated nationalization of industries where monopolies are formed due to technical or natural causes.

Corporations with high fixed costs and low variable costs are more susceptible to becoming monopolies. The mass expansion of railroads in the Second Industrial Revolution created a disruption to the liberal economic theories that had emerged after the First Industrial Revolution. Leading economists recognized that market forces were tearing industry apart and recommended the formation of monopolies. During the late nineteenth century, leading US economists studied the development of the railroad industry closely. Competition among railroad companies created havoc rather than making the industry healthy. By 1893, a third of all railroad companies had already fallen into receivership. Economists began to fear the disruptive effects of market forces. Critics argued that these large corporations should be allowed to protect themselves from the excessive competition by forming monopolies, trusts, or cartels that would be regulated by the state (Perelman 2006).

By the late nineteenth century, it had become evident that large corporations had accrued enough power to challenge the state and infringe on individual freedoms. Henry Adams (1956: 189) cautioned that the concentration of private capital undermined democracy and the sovereignty of the state:

> The belief is common in America that the day is at hand when corporations far greater than the Erie – swaying such power as has never in the world's history been trusted in the hands of mere private citizens ... after having created a system of quiet but irresistible corruption – will ultimately succeed in directing government itself. Under the American form of society, no authority exists capable of effective resistance. The national government, in order to deal with the corporations, must assume powers refused to it by its fundamental law, – and even then is exposed to the chance of forming an absolute central government which sooner or later is likely to fall into the hands it is struggling to escape, and destroy the limits of its power only in order to make corruption omnipotent.

Brook Adams (1900: 80) believed that the answer was for the state to exercise economic statecraft to protect the individual and compete in international affairs, because the state would, in the future, become 'a gigantic corporation whose business is to materially benefit its members'. A powerful administrative capability of the state was deemed necessary to harmonize state interests with the market (Adams 1900). Standard Oil became a prime case study illustrating the dilemma between smaller and less competitive companies versus larger and more corrupt companies. Standard Oil was broken up in 1911 in accordance with the US Supreme Court ruling on antitrust law.

Following the First World War, a new economic system appeared to be in the making. The 'Rationalisation Movement' developed in inflation-ridden Weimar Germany as the economy was becoming an instrument of state power (Du Bois 1941). The middle class had been destroyed due to the loss of personal incomes, savings and property values, while corporations had been empowered to repay their debts and renew equipment using the inflated currency. Furthermore, corporations were organized into large and specialized units capable of making Germany a leading technological and manufacturing powerhouse in the world. Subsequently, the relationship between the people, corporations and the state was restructured. The all-powerful industrial sector was brought under control of the state to ensure that it served the interests of the public and could be used in the international competition for power. The fascists hijacked the political economy that reflected the reality of new technologies. Du Bois (1941: 383) warned that 'unless England and the United States follow the footsteps of Germany, they can never expect to rival her in technical production and distribution'.

Tech giants have accrued unprecedented market power. Google dominates Internet searches in the United States with almost 90 per cent of the market share, while Facebook controls an almost 80 per cent market share of social networks (Tepper 2018). As Mark Zuckerberg essentially admitted during testimony to the US Congress in 2018, there is no real alternative for Facebook in terms of social media. Apple's iPhone and Google's Android control the mobile app market, while Google and Facebook effectively set up a duopoly in online advertising, enabling them to dictate conditions for the market. Amazon is similarly replacing traditional 'brick and mortar' retailers, with the result that approximately one-third of malls in the United States will close down over the next few years. Rather than shrinking, the scope of businesses these mega-companies are involved in is only increasing and thus cementing their monopolistic position. Joseph Stiglitz, Nobel Prize winner in Economic Sciences, cautioned about the growing market power of tech giants:

> The potential consequences of the market power held by the new technology giants are greater and more pernicious than anything we saw at the turn of the twentieth century. Then, the market power of companies like Swift, Standard Oil, American Tobacco, the American Sugar Refining Company or US Steel allowed them to raise the price they charged for food, steel, tobacco, sugar or oil. Now it's about more than just price. The existence of the new technology

giant's market power is seen most dramatically every time Facebook changes its algorithms, the way it determines what individuals see and in what order. A new algorithm can bring on the quick decline of a media outlet, or can create, and then possibly end, new ways of reaching large audiences.

(Stiglitz 2019: 124)

Challenging the authority of the state

High-tech and natural resources are very similar in creating high dependencies due to the limited diversification they allow. Yet, the high-tech industry is more capable of usurping political power because it can claim legitimate political influence beyond simply representing critical infrastructure. High-tech is a complex industry led by experts who have more knowledge about the digital industry than democratic institutions. More precisely, the tech industry can easily justify writing its own legislation. Silicon Valley corporations are able to capture more of the legislative space as they represent an ever-increasing share of the economy. This influence is further augmented by the growing power of Silicon Valley to co-opt bureaucrats. As Jack Ma, the former CEO of Alibaba argued: 'Innovation always develops much faster and I think future laws should not be driven only by governments; they should be driven by the private sector and all stakeholders together' (Schaake 2019). While the premise that only the high-tech companies themselves have the skills to fully understand the market is undoubtedly true, the solution of granting them control over legislation allows the fox to guard the henhouse. And yet, governments are shifting the responsibility for regulating the Internet, for example, hate speech, to the tech companies. When powerful tech companies are empowered with rule making and governance, democracy inevitably suffers. Governance is thereby privatized by entrusting private industry with public interests.

The tech giants also have questionable loyalties. The US status as a unitary actor is challenged as a gap grows between Washington and Silicon Valley. The high-tech community tends to consider the government an obstacle that should get out of the way to let the innovators freely change the world, while the government wants to ensure that what benefits Silicon Valley also benefits the United States as a whole. Furthermore, the government must cooperate with the tech giants for the sake of the innovation they achieve because the US government cannot offer the same salaries as private industries.

Surveillance technology can be turned against one's own population and weapons technologies raise obvious ethical issues. For better or worse, these ethical concerns are often addressed in corporate boardrooms rather than by the US military or elected officials. Similarly, the political–technological gap was evident when the FBI attempted to force Apple to unlock a phone. A common cosmopolitan mindset in Silicon Valley holds that they are global rather than US companies. The disconnect between Washington and Silicon Valley can be bridged through increased funding and contracts that skew interdependency in favour of the government.

The Snowden revelations made high-tech corporations more cautious about government contracts. Google even announced it would not renew its contract for the US Pentagon known as Project Maven that would use AI to analyse drone footage. A leaked email revealed that a Google employee recommended: 'If the government wants a company to build some software for unethical purposes, we should volunteer to do it … I promise the deadlines will slip for decades and we'll never produce anything remotely functional' (Fox 2018). Google cites ethical reasons for its reluctance to work for the Pentagon, and yet the company is developing a search engine that censors at the behest of the Chinese government especially for that country. Microsoft is similarly cooperating with a Chinese military university to develop AI systems that could potentially be used against the Chinese population or the United States (Murgia and Yang 2019). A key challenge for the US government is to ensure that its companies align themselves closely with national interests. DARPA's growing budget puts pressures on Google because its funding could go to a competitor such as Amazon. Alternatively, Washington might develop stronger legislation to constrain market forces and impose control over US tech giants.

Towards national champions

A few large corporations receiving state support will dictate the direction and health of the economy. Tech giants are headed towards becoming so-called 'national champions' in various forms. This is an attempt to solve the dilemma of ensuring that large corporations wield influence internationally while remaining loyal domestically. National champions are large and powerful corporations that are expected to both seek profit and advance the interests of the nation. Beyond the potential for private industry to gain unacceptable market power, there are also ethical reasons to restrict its development in other spheres. It is unlikely that the free market can be trusted with technologies that enable the altering of human beings through biotech and genetic manipulation, or that experiment with the planet through geoengineering.

Russia had a crash course on the important relationship between the state and strategic industries. Its radical US-backed 'shock therapy' reforms for the transition from communism to free-market capitalism turned into a criminal revolution. The rapid rise of the oligarchs in the 1990s gave a handful of individuals the power to challenge the authority of the state through their control of natural resources, business, media and politics (Sakwa 2008: 151–2). These oligarchs did not have any incentives to offer Soviet-era energy discounts to foster better relations with neighbouring states (Tsygankov 2006: 120). Instead of using the economic resources of the state to advance public and state interests, the oligarchs used their influence over the state to advance their respective business interests in contravention of Russia's interests. The oligarchs became a national security challenge because foreign powers, especially the United States and the UK, were courting them. It appeared that Russia was headed towards becoming a colony because the country was controlled by oligarchs and the oligarchs were increasingly influenced by foreign powers. It also seemed possible that Russia would slip into political radicalism, with nostalgic communists and radical nationalists emerging as powerful rivals to the discredited government. Others predicted that the country would simply collapse and dissolve as the Soviet Union had done a few years earlier.

Once Putin became president, he immediately addressed these problems by nationalizing the natural resources in the hands of the oligarchs. Moscow responded to the deteriorating situation by announcing that oligarchs who interfered in political life would be held accountable for the crimes they had committed in the 1990s. The richest oligarch in Putin's Russia, Mikhail Khodorkovsky, was arrested in 2003 just as he was preparing to sell a major share of his oil empire to ExxonMobil and Chevron-Texaco (Tsygankov 2009: 146). Putin's views on strategic industries can be traced back to his dissertation at the St. Petersburg Mining Institute, in which he advocated the merger of energy companies into large 'national champions' (Balzer 2005). Large state-owned energy corporations were deemed necessary to compete with large Western multinational energy corporations, and concurrently to prevent them from undermining the authority and interests of the state and the Russian people (Balzer 2005).

Moscow takes a similar approach to digital platforms in the Fourth Industrial Revolution to avoid powerful corporations from acting against state interests, or to fall under the control of foreign powers. Case in point, Yandex as 'Russia's Google' have after negotiations with the Kremlin agreed to form a 'Public Interest Foundation' to ensure that corporate interests are aligned with the people and the state. Subsequently, the state has obtained influence within Yandex to limit foreign ownership. Also, Yandex was pressured to form a partnership with Sberbank, a state-owned bank and a national leader in AI, to bridge Yandex with the state.

Europe now faces the dilemma of either breaking up large tech corporations or nationalizing them. French President Emmanuel Macron argued that tech companies were becoming 'too big to be governed. Which is brand new. So at this point, you may choose to dismantle. That's what happened at the very beginning of the oil sector when you had these big giants. That's a competition issue' (Thompson 2018). Yet, Macron leans towards nationalizing sensitive technologies such as AI:

> I want AI to be totally federalized. Why? Because AI is about disruption and dealing with impacts of disruption. For instance, this kind of disruption can destroy a lot of jobs in some sectors and create a need to retrain people. But AI could also be one of the solutions to better train these people and help them to find new jobs, which is good for my country, and very important. I want my country to be the place where this new perspective on AI is built, on the basis of interdisciplinarity: this means crossing maths, social sciences, technology, and philosophy. That's absolutely critical.
>
> (Thompson 2018)

In the United States, President Trump railed against the tech companies for their censorship and political activism. Conservative personalities such as Laura Ingraham argue that tech companies such as Twitter and Facebook should be run as utilities. Even the co-founder of Facebook, Chris Hughes, called for breaking up and regulating Facebook due to the degree of market power it has amassed and the consequent 'unchecked' power of CEO Mark Zuckerberg (MacCarthy 2019). Similar concerns are growing with regard to Jeff Bezos, who is protecting his technology empire by establishing a firm foothold in the Pentagon and purchasing *The Washington Post* to control publicity.

Others, such as Stiglitz (2019), suggest that strict implementation of the law could limit the market power of tech giants. For example, big data is collected to assess how much individuals are willing to pay and to assign prices accordingly. The market function of AI and big data could be scaled back by, for example, making price discrimination illegal. The same could be done for such predatory practices as identifying people with addictive personalities to promote trips to Las Vegas or other forms of gambling.

The authoritarian state

Technology is power, and the Fourth Industrial Revolution concentrates this power in the hands of only a few due to the economies of scope. Allowing private corporations to control this power undermines both the interests of the state and the people, but transferring some of this power to the state can have its own corrupting effect. Furthermore, the rights of the people would be undermined in a power-sharing arrangement between private corporations. Keeping big data in private corporations rather than with governments makes little sense: the Snowden disclosures demonstrated that the US government would anyway gain access to the date using backdoor channels into the corporations' platforms (Stiglitz 2019).

The challenge for the United States, according to Du Bois (1941), would, therefore, be to develop a benevolent industrial democracy (Du Bois 1941: 386). Developing economic statecraft akin to Germany's after the First World War would have far-reaching implications for the United States. Liberalism and democracy had relied on 'economic anarchy' in which individual economic freedoms were the basis of political freedoms. The need for industries to be 'rationalised' into large specialized segments that cooperate closely with the state would unavoidably conflict with the democratic rights and liberalism that are an intrinsic component of American identity. Trotsky (1934: 398) cautioned that free-market capitalism would come under growing pressures from increasingly productive industrial power. The 'progressive role of competition has led to a monstrous concentration of trusts and syndicates', he wrote, 'and this, in turn, has meant a concentration of economic and social contradiction'. The spectre of fascism looms as 'attempts to save economic life by inoculating it with virus from the corpse of nationalism result in blood poisoning which bears the name of fascism' (Trotsky 1934: 398). Ronald Reagan (1975) famously cautioned that fascism could come through liberalism: 'Fascism is private ownership, private enterprise, but total government control and regulation. Well, isn't this the liberal philosophy?' Ultimately, the growing convergence of government and big business – in an attempt to ensure that the latter serves the national interest – resembles the political economy of fascism.

The competitiveness of open economies has been translated into political liberalism. The Fourth Industrial Revolution, however, appears to give authoritarian states a competitive advantage. Already, great powers from China to the United States have strong systemic incentives to scale back on political liberalism. China's political restrictions open up more economic freedom because the Chinese authorities permit the development of a wider range of technologies, such as stem cell research. China's authoritarianism enables it to experiment more with, for example, new financial instruments, knowing that the authorities could quickly impose regulations if the technological innovations cause problems. China does not need to stop its testing of self-driving cars if they have accidents and it can accrue large amounts of data with fewer concerns for constraining privacy laws.

Although the United States has traditionally to resisted monopolies, China is more comfortable with them due to the authority of the government. Given these strong incentives for developing a more authoritarian state, the United States can be expected to drift in this direction in the future.

Economies of scope

Economies of scope refer to a situation in which it is less costly for a corporation to combine two or more product lines than to produce them separately (Panzer and Willig 1981). Economies of scope 'are based upon the common and recurrent use of proprietary know-how or the common and recurrent use of a specialized and indivisible physical asset' (Teece 1980). Although there were strong economic incentives in the past to outsource components of the supply chain, new technologies create economic incentives for bringing them back into the same platform. Furthermore, the growing use of AI and big data makes it profitable to incorporate a vast variety of industries within a single commercial structure.

Free market principles seem not to apply in modern and high-tech industries because digital platforms have high fixed costs and low variable costs. The 'railroad economics' of the nineteenth century demonstrated that there were high fixed costs to developing and managing railway infrastructure, but that the variable cost of increasing the freight on the railway was minimal (Perelman 2006). There were subsequently great incentives to increase the scope of business. There was also a danger of prices dropping because the marginal costs that influenced pricing did not take into account the fixed costs that had to be paid. As a result, competition among US railroads in the nineteenth century caused disruptive bankruptcies because most of the fixed costs were independent of output, and when competition pushed prices down, companies were unable to cover the high fixed costs required to stay in business.

The railroad economics model is important for modern and high-tech industries because the foundational infrastructure is immensely costly to develop and implement, while the curve for variable costs is flat. Variable costs usually consist of labour, utilities and material. Industries characterized by reliance on manual labour have low fixed costs and high variable costs. As in railway economics, variable costs become increasingly low in the digital and automated world.

Industries with high fixed costs are more susceptible to predatory pricing due to the ease of and payoff from bankrupting competitors. First, larger is always better because fixed costs are not related to the number of goods or services provided. Second, it is easier in such industries to push competitors into bankruptcy simply by lowering the selling price below fixed costs, leaving rivals with no way to adjust. Third, once the adversary is bankrupted, the monopoly can absorb the infrastructure of the competitor and set its own prices because a new entrant to the market is deterred by the huge fixed cost of entry and the need for a significant trade volume to break even. The role of government is therefore not to enforce disruptive competition in industries with high fixed costs, but to manage and regulate monopolies and cartels (Perelman 2006).

Replacing human labour with automation and robotics creates incentives for merging what were previously considered unrelated industries. Software development and training AI with supercomputers require capital-intensive investments, yet delivering the product to one hundred users or one million users has little, if any, bearing on marginal costs. The development of an online search engine has large fixed costs, but the ability to service more customers does not add significant marginal costs beyond upgrading the capacity of servers.

Digital platforms are also naturally inclined towards forming monopolies because the more people that use the platforms, the greater the connectivity they offer and the more valuable they become to the user. For example, social media companies such as Facebook and Twitter are more attractive simply because 'everybody' is using them. Uber becomes more appealing as more users and drivers connect to the platform, ensuring fast access to a passenger or driver. In the era of AI, platforms decrease fixed costs by increasing the number of users, thereby gaining access to more data needed for training algorithms.

The monopolistic impulses of digital platforms are further fuelled by the ability to use the platform of one industry to dominate a previously unrelated industry. For example, online search engines are entering the market of mobile phones, battery-driven vehicles, self-driving vehicles, payment and banking services, real estate, retail, restaurants, and delivery services. As high-tech industries incrementally absorb all industries that can be automated, the entire logic of comparative advantage is turned on its head. Instead of seeking to specialize in one industry, comparative advantage is the development of technology ecosystems to 'do everything'. By consolidating a variety of industries, large digital platforms become increasingly similar and therefore direct competitors.

Platform monopolies and technological ecosystems

The first stage of concentrating various services on a single platform was limited to digital services without a significant presence in the physical world. For example, Google offers a search engine, email, calendars, photo storage, maps and other services largely confined to the digital domain. As the leading search engine, Google's leadership in digital calendars automatically follows. The concentration of services into a single digital platform adds value to the consumer due to convenience, while Google uses the capital-intensive concentration of services to lock out competition. Furthermore, access to large quantities of data produces additional value to all services. The business model is not based on providing cheaper services for the customer because most of these services are free. Rather, revenue derives from the ability to extract as much data as possible to sell and use for advertisers. Open-source programs and software are, therefore, commonly offered at no cost when building a platform.

The second stage of expanding platforms entails mergers and acquisitions of other digital platforms that were not in direct competition. The digital revolution was spearheaded by information technology, initially with the personal computer. As smartphones replaced computers as the most frequently used device for accessing the Internet, the digital domain gradually absorbed digital technologies such as the camera that had previously treated photography as a chemical process. Digital technologies went on to absorb music, movies and a multitude of other industries. The smartphone further incentivized companies such as Google to acquire other companies specializing in mobile software, social networking, advertising, mapping, artificial intelligence, mobile payment, virtual reality, cloud migration, big data. With each acquisition, the monopolistic position strengthens by increasing the amount of capital required to challenge the market leader. Cross-subsidization is a pivotal competitive advantage as more users are drawn to the platform.

The third stage of expanding digital platforms entails conquering services that previously belonged exclusively to the physical world. For example, the Internet of Things prompted Google to invest in Nest to develop smart home devices such as thermostats, smoke detectors, doorbells, locks and security systems that could be controlled digitally through phones or smartwatches. The Internet of Things is revolutionary in terms of extracting data at unprecedented levels. Connecting physical objects to digital infrastructure then extends to smart manufacturing, smart agriculture, smart energy and other areas where digital infrastructure uses sensors to capture live data and AI to enhance efficiency. The Internet of Medical Things will similarly revolutionize the health industry by monitoring people's bodies in real time. Similarly, the Internet of Goods will alter manufacturing because 3D printing, robotics and other instruments of automated manufacturing will instantly produce products ordered through e-commerce and provide rapid and automated delivery. The transportation industry connects most of these industries and becomes the catalyst for cross-subsidization.

Case study of the transportation industry as a catalyst

Over the past decade, the smart phone has led innovations due to the broad adoption, the remarkable revenue and the unprecedented ability to collect data, and the improved online connectivity had great synergy effects with other industries. The transportation industry will likely become a key catalyst for innovations in the coming years due to its ability to expand technological ecosystems.

The transformation of the transportation industry represents a milestone in terms of digital platforms conquering industries that previously belonged solely to the physical world. The automated vehicle market is expected to become a multi-trillion industry, making it a key economic prize of its own as it (Schwartz 2018). Intel predicts that the automated vehicle market could become a $7 trillion 'passenger economy' by 2050. By comparison, the top car companies of today are worth approximately $650 billion (Schwartz 2018). Tech giants taking on the transportation industry is also significant due to the synergy effects in retail, e-ecommerce, manufacturing, renewable energy, payment systems and other seemingly unrelated industries. Even city planning will increasingly fall outside government planning as ride-hailing companies make key decisions about the transportation system for us (Grush and Niles 2018). For governments to reassert control over city planning, they will need greater regulatory control over ride-hailing platforms. More importantly, mastering the technology and controlling the transportation industry will spur the horizontal integration of industries and services. The transportation industry has become the catalyst for advancing technological ecosystems under the monopolistic control of a handful of tech giants. Search engines and social media are using their existing technologies as a competitive advantage in the transportation industry.

United States: The leader

The five largest corporations in the world in 2018 were all American tech giants – Apple, Amazon, Alphabet (Google), Microsoft and Facebook. US tech giants and individual entrepreneurs are developing and integrating large technological ecosystems with monopolistic powers. Amazon aggressively acquires rising companies. But when firms are unwilling to sell, Amazon draws on its massive revenues to employ predatory pricing that bankrupts rivals with smaller reserves of capital. After several such examples, the smaller companies learn the lesson and dutifully sell when Amazon, in Godfather-like fashion, makes them an offer they cannot refuse. Google similarly buys up AI start-ups and various digital platforms to enhance its own capabilities and eliminate competitors.

United States tech giants recognize that future growth and dominance will depend on their ability to absorb the transportation industry. Google, Apple and Microsoft are developing self-driving cars, and Amazon began investing in Aurora in 2019 to also acquire technologies for automated vehicles. Investing and merging with ride-hailing businesses such as Uber and Lyft is imperative to obtaining a competitive advantage in transportation. Apple has invested in the Chinese ride-hailing app Didi, Google has invested in Lyft, Microsoft in Uber and Facebook in Uber and Lyft (Babones 2018a). Traditional car manufacturers such as General Motors and Ford are attempting to defend their market position by acquiring the technologies for self-driving cars and investing in ride-hailing services.

Ride-hailing apps such as Uber and Lyft use their existing market and technology as a springboard towards the development of autonomous cars and other industries. Uber has established Uber Eats as a basic food delivery app with delivery by human labour, a service that could increase efficiency and economies of scale by utilizing autonomous cars. The economies of scope can be extended further by also moving into automated restaurants and shifting to delivery with automated Uber vehicles and drones. Google and other tech companies are investing in a variety of companies that are developing a network of kitchens, storage facilities and pickup counters that prepare food (Bradshaw 2019). A network of kitchens placed in strategic low-cost areas will supply food to Uber

Eats, Deliveroo, Doordash and other delivery services to reduce their reliance on securing food from more expensive restaurants. By concentrating kitchens in specific locations, it also creates stronger economic incentives for automating food preparation. This, in turn, requires breaking into the automation and robotics industries similar to those found in manufacturing.

Google is taking it a step further by also pursuing the possibility of growing food itself. Google is investing in AI technologies for agriculture that will revolutionize farming and grow fresh fruits and vegetables geographically closer to where they are consumed (Terazono 2018). The ambitions go beyond fruit and vegetables by also using AI to develop meat without animals. Sergey Brin, a co-founder of Google, funded the development of meat in a petri dish that did not require the killing of animals. The experiment cost approximately 384,000 US dollars, but it is projected that the price can be brought down to 50 US dollars in the coming years, and then plummet still further due to the economies of scale and the maturation of the technology.

Jeff Bezos provides a prime case study on expanding digital platforms. His e-commerce giant Amazon uses its growing dominance in the retail industry to become the world's largest provider of cloud infrastructure services. With its advanced cloud computing, Amazon is also fulfilling contracts with the Pentagon for the development of military technology and a secret cloud for the CIA. Bezos then used the resultant technologies to develop the robotics that automates the warehouses used by the Amazon e-commerce platform. Those same robotic warehouses were quickly transferable to grocery stores, freeing them of human workers as robots order, restock shelves and deliver goods. Amazon opened its first supermarket without human staff in Seattle in 2016. Furthermore, Amazon's experience with home delivery provided the company with competitive advantages over traditional grocery stores.

Replacing human labour with automated delivery further advances Amazon and heightens the entry barrier. It is estimated that Amazon's delivery costs could be cut by 40 per cent by taking the driver out of the equation (Muller and Pandey 2019). Amazon has already begun testing delivery with smaller automated vehicles that can deliver to a customer's front door. Amazon Prime Air was launched to deliver packages with aerial drones. Amazon then patented a system for a security service: its delivery drones can also film the houses they fly over, using AI to detect irregularities as a service to residents. Amazon has followed the Chinese model by launching Amazon Pay that provides retailers with discounts for adopting its payment system. The technological ecosystem could then spread in other unpredictable directions. For example, Facebook announced its intention to launch its own currency – the Libra. In this way, tech companies can strengthen their position within the financial services sector.

Leveraging his enormous wealth, Bezos has also become engaged in various other industries. Bezos purchased *The Washington Post* in 2013, giving him influence over the media. The technological ecosystem could develop further as Bezos invests heavily in Blue Origin, his space travel company. Blue Origin has developed a reusable rocket, the New Shepard that will drastically reduce the cost of space travel. The company intends to generate its initial profit from space tourism. Bezos even has ambitions to send a manned mission to the Moon in 2024 to establish a self-sustaining lunar colony. Colonists will mine the Moon for platinum, titanium, thorium, magnesium, silicon, aluminium, iron and ice before expanding further into space to tap as yet unimaginable technological and economic opportunities.

Elon Musk's success is similarly based on his ability to use economies of scope to bring together a variety of industries. Musk initially established himself by co-founding the online payment system PayPal. He then co-founded Tesla, an energy and automotive company, to develop electric cars. The battery technology developed by Tesla led to the establishment of a subsidiary, Solar City that provides solar power services. Tesla's competitive advantage in electric cars also provided an opening for the company to expand into self-driving cars. Musk's ambitions and expertise in the transportation industry led to the development of Hyperloop, a high-speed underground transportation system. Musk's Boring Company similarly works towards developing a system of underground tunnels for transportation. Musk's *Neuralink* Corporation aims to upgrade the cognitive functions of human beings by developing an interface between the brain and a computer.

The transportation industry has even extended into space with the founding of SpaceX, whose corporate mission is to reduce the cost of space travel. SpaceX has also developed reusable rockets and has set the objective of colonizing Mars, which suggests that private corporations will lead a revival of the space race in the Fourth Industrial Revolution. The space market is currently valued at an estimated USD 350 billion today. Bank of America Merrill Lynch predicts that this figure could balloon to approximately USD 2.7 trillion over the next three decades, and far more if asteroid mining proves feasible. States and corporations endeavouring to conquer space will need to integrate a broad technological ecosystem of Fourth Industrial Revolution technologies. AI will make space exploration more efficient and affordable; robotics will reduce reliance on frail human beings; 3D printing in space will reduce reliance on supplies from earth, and many construction materials can even be mined in space; nanotechnology and advanced materials will be necessary to protect against radiation and other challenges in space; advanced bioengineering will develop smart farming in space, and so on.

China: The challenger

China is also developing technological ecosystems. Its tech giants are acquiring monopolistic powers through economies of scope, with key corporations such as Baidu, Alibaba and Tencent taking the lead. Baidu can be referred to as China's Google; Alibaba, JD and Taobao as China's Amazon; and Tencent as China's Facebook. China has become most successful at bringing together various industries by taking advantage of the economies of scope. Baidu and Tencent launched the WeChat app that has the comparative advantage of doing 'everything'. WeChat combines functions of calls, messaging, social media, shopping, paying bills, accessing government services, playing games, hailing taxis and interacting with a digital assistant. Alibaba began, much like Amazon, with e-commerce that replaces traditional retail. However, its supplementary services now also include the functions of FedEx, eBay, PayPal, Google and cloud service. The e-commerce companies Alibaba, JD and Taobao have become so powerful that Amazon had to admit defeat by announcing in 2019 that it was closing down its e-commerce business in China. Tencent launched WeChat Pay and Alibaba launched Alipay, now China's two main QR code payment systems replacing cash. This has placed China far ahead of any other country in terms of developing a cashless society that cuts into the revenues of banks. This impressive transition was achieved by using subsidies to encourage both the driver of the technologies and the end customers to adopt the system (Lee 2018: 76). The Chinese technological ecosystems function much like South Korean and Japanese conglomerates, structured to provide superior service through synergy effects and to prevent foreign tech corporations from penetrating the domestic market.

China is also taking the lead in transforming the autonomous car market. Baidu, Didi, Tencent, Alibaba and JD have all commenced their self-driving car projects. China's largest search engine, Baidu, first began developing autonomous vehicles in 2013 and remains the leader in the field. Baidu launched its Apollo project, an open-source platform for autonomous driving software. Didi, the taxi-hailing app, has the advantage of volume by already controlling an extensive fleet of taxis. Although originally a spin-off of Uber, Didi eventually absorbed Uber China and also took over the cars and drivers, turning the physical infrastructure into a competitive advantage. Once in control of the main taxi fleet, Didi moved to develop electric cars to establish an entire fleet of all-electric cars. This enabled Didi to take the lead in battery technologies as well. In 2017, the city of Shenzhen converted its entire fleet of more than 16,000 buses to electric in a project that is expected to be emulated by other cities (Babones 2018b). The scale is crucial due to the huge fixed cost of developing and installing charging piles throughout China. Public and private charging piles are sprouting up across China, and the government has set a goal of installing 500,000 public charging piles by 2020 (Babones 2018b). The ability of tech giants to make further advances in renewable energy is supported by government investment in infrastructure. One example is the Jinan Expressway, a solar highway that will soon be able to charge electric cars as they drive over the solar panels in the road. In 2014, electric car sales in the United States surpassed those in China, but by 2018, US sales had grown to just 361,000 units whereas Chinese sales had reached 1,225,000 vehicles (Richter 2019). Tech giants in both China and the United States are also becoming leading investors in other renewable energy sources such as wind and solar power.

Didi will merge its self-driving cars with its existing taxis to create the world's largest fleet of robot taxis. Such a major fleet of robot taxis will also expand the market for battery-powered electric vehicles: private demand for such cars is limited by their short battery life and the time required for refuelling at charging piles. Electric robot taxis would selectively respond to fares based on their remaining battery charge, while other robot taxis would be temporarily removed from service to recharge. Combining these industries under one technological ecosystem has also enabled China to launch the world's first solar panelled highway. Located in Jinan, the highway's solar panels can melt the fallen snow and recharge autonomous electric cars as they drive. With China's restrictions on foreign corporations mapping its streets, domestic companies will have immense advantages as the country's car industry changes beyond recognition.

E-commerce retailers such as JD are also developing self-driving cars to reduce their delivery costs. Much like their American counterparts, Chinese tech giants such as JD have also developed smart warehouses that are already completely automated. Food delivery services are also absorbed into the transportation technological ecosystem. China currently has a duopoly on food delivery between Alibaba's Ele.me and Tencent-backed MeituanDianping.

China is also making headway in terms of automating the restaurant industry, which could incentivize the tech giants to further expand the linkage between food delivery and automated kitchens.

China's ability to expand the transportation industry into space falls behind US efforts in this area. China still relies heavily on the government space program to catch up with Russia and the United States. However, the co-founder of Chinese search giant Baidu, Robin Li, has expressed his passion for space and begun investing in China's growing private space industry. The Chinese government's lack of competitiveness has prompted it to reach out to Russia that has more experience in space.

Russia: The follower

Russia's development of independent technological ecosystems resembles the Chinese approach, albeit at a smaller scale. Most power is concentrated in Yandex, the countries largest search engine and email provider. VKontakte is Russia's main social media platform. Unlike the other European countries, Russia has the foundation for developing a largely independent domestic digital ecosystem, and yet Russia is still far behind in terms of the share of its economy that is linked to the digital economy (World Bank 2018). Russia has also fallen behind on automating its retail and does not yet have a domestic equivalent to Amazon that dominates in e-commerce.

Ozon, Russia's first online retailer, benefits from a growing infrastructure of warehouses. Other Russian e-commerce companies in the market include Wildberries and Ulmart. There is great potential, however, for a tech giant to consolidate control over the market and attain the advantages of superior infrastructure and economies of scale. The search for a joint venture with a global leader has brought Russia closer to China, as aggressive anti-Russian sanctions by the United States have made it an unreliable partner. Three Russian companies – the Mail.ru social network, the Russian Direct Investment Fund and the Megafon mobile operator – are cooperating with China's Alibaba to develop an e-commerce platform in which the latter has a 48 per cent stake. Also, China's new Alipay and WeChat payment systems have established themselves in Russia. Russia's state-owned Sberbank, the largest bank in Russia, stands out internationally with its objective to 'compete with global technology companies'. It does this by developing and implementing AI, blockchain, cloud technology, virtual reality, the Internet of Things and robotics (Sberbank 2018).

Yandex is Russia's most successful corporation in developing a technological ecosystem. It is the leading search engine and email provider, making Russia one of the few countries in the world where Google is not the principal provider. Yandex has built upon this foundation by launching a broad ecosystem of online services that are essential to the Fourth Industrial Revolution. They include cloud services, artificial intelligence to develop recommendations, a virtual assistant named Alice, online payment services, a real estate app, online shopping, music streaming, cloud service and other disruptive technologies. Yandex is challenging the leadership of AliExpress in Russia's e-commerce market by forming a partnership with Sberbank. Yandex and Sberbank collectively created two e-commerce platforms, Beru and Bringly. These platforms build on and convert the Yandex price comparison site into a competitive online retailer, thus opening up prospects for building automated warehouses. The Yandex–Sberbank partnership could harmonize commercial and state interests by bringing together Russia's largest private tech giant with a powerful state-owned entity. Copying Microsoft's strategy, in 2014 Yandex developed firmware to replace Google's Android apps with Yandex apps and then worked with smartphone producers to end their cooperation with Google. By mid-2018, Yandex had replaced Google as Russia's top search engine on Android-based phones. In late 2018, Yandex also released the first of its own Android smartphones.

Russia's technological restructuring of its transportation industry will be the key means for expanding its technological ecosystem. Yandex moved into the taxi industry in 2011 using the competitive advantage of its online dominance and supplementing such applications as Yandex Maps and Yandex Navigator with a ride-hailing application, Yandex Taxi. Although Russia was a late comer to the industry, Moscow is now the No. 1 European city and No. 2 city in the world for car sharing. Because the majority of Russia's taxi drivers signed on with Yandex, the service also established itself in other former Soviet Republics. In late 2017, Yandex and Uber formed a joint venture to establish uncontested leadership in Russia and neighbouring countries. Yandex then tested its first self-driving car in 2017, drawing on its combination of sophisticated technologies, artificial intelligence, advanced algorithms and taxi fleet to establish a unique position in the driverless car market. Russia has permitted self-driving cars on public roads since 2018, and Yandex has also been driving its unmanned taxis on public roads in Israel (Ermolaeva 2018). In 2019, Yandex announced trials of the Yandex Rover, a delivery robot similar to the model of Amazon. Russian truck manufacturer KAMAZ has also developed an automated electric bus in cooperation with the Central Scientific Research Automobile and Automotive Engines Institute (NAMI). Although the driverless KAMAZ electric bus navigates using digital maps and sensors, it relies on simpler technology by having planned routes and stops prepared.

Yandex has also followed the Chinese model by using its platform to develop a food delivery app to gain a foothold in the restaurant industry. Already, hordes of young men with large thermal backpacks delivering food from restaurants to private homes and companies have appeared throughout Russia's major cities. Restaurants are finding that they must cooperate with Yandex if they want to stay in business. In the future, linking the platform to Yandex automated cars could reduce costs and delivery time, enhancing the platform. Yandex would then be able to replace the restaurant industry by developing automated kitchens.

Conclusion

The principle of comparative advantage is losing force as the strength of corporations and states becomes the ability to 'do everything' through the establishment of independent technological ecosystems. Between technology incrementally replacing human labour and the synergy effects among dominating markets, the logic of comparative advantage has been turned on its head. Technological ecosystems include mutually reinforcing technology platforms. These technological platforms are monopolistic in nature because quantity tends to equal quality and the dominant corporations gradually absorb the entire value chain. Furthermore, there is an incentive to develop physical infrastructure that raises fixed costs as a deterrent to new entrants on the market. When the technological and economic advantages to maintaining monopolistic tech giants outweigh the incentives to break them up, the state will assert its influence over private industries to ensure that they develop as national champions.

Digital ecosystems have given rise to large monopolies wielding unprecedented market power. Large digital platforms are establishing a dominant position in all areas of the economy. They strive to close off their markets to competitors and to develop corporate independence from the technologies of rival companies. As digital platforms absorb more economic activities, they become increasingly similar and thus preserve direct competition in the marketplace. Technological sovereignty of great powers serves an important function of decentralizing the market power of large tech giants. Digital ecosystems will become central to maintaining the balance of power between great powers. This incentivizes governments to territorialize digital ecosystems to avoid the concentration of market power in adversaries and the subsequent excessive reliance on foreign companies. Technological sovereignty is achieved by developing domestic technological ecosystems.

5

Political communication: The state, the individual and foreign powers

Introduction

In geoeconomics, governments intervene to establish a favourable position for the country in international markets and then use the resulting market power to extract political autonomy and influence. Because communication technologies are controlled by market forces, geoeconomics also includes information technology as a strategic industry. Will these market forces serve the interests of the state, the individual or foreign powers?

In the Fourth Industrial Revolution, the ability to control communication technologies is critical because market power increasingly derives from the ability to collect data. Large corporations amassing, monitoring and analysing data exchanges have greater surveillance capabilities and influence than many countries do. If governments harness the market power of these corporations they can protect their autonomy from rival powers, assert influence over foreign states and subdue their populations. Ceding this market power to industry could undermine the state accidentally causing divisiveness and chaos. Alternatively, ceding market power over communication technologies to hostile foreign powers could lead to the deliberate undermining of the state. As new technologies disrupt the former balance of power between the state and citizens, a struggle for control over these technologies ensues.

In 1839, Edward Bulwer-Lytton coined the famous phrase: 'The pen is mightier than the sword'. This implies that power does not derive primarily from coercion, but from the ability to control the dissemination of information and communication. States and other political entities are constructed using narratives that underscore the similarities between people within shared borders and how they are distinct from peoples outside these borders. Democracy also requires the construction of *demos*, a common people believed to share a common fate. Controlling the formulation and proliferation of narratives is instrumental to develop identities, harnessing loyalties and mobilizing the public to confront adversaries. Foreign policy is largely about promoting 'a favourable image to allies, opponents, neutrals, and last but not least, one's own domestic audience' (Herz 1981: 187). Political communication is essential to great power politics because it organizes the relationship between the individual, the state and the wider world.

Society is managed by two distinct organizational forces: the centralized hierarchy of the state and social networks of the people (Ferguson 2019). The state cultivates a common narrative and shared identity for unity, while social networks balance the excesses of the state by organizing independent voices. An excessive concentration of communication power enables authoritarian governance and undermines the liberty of the people, but undue decentralization produces chaos as the collective and unifying narratives erode. Civil society tends to thrive under conditions of high social capital – the interpersonal connectivity of social networks that underpins a collective identity. As social capital (connections within a society) decreases, power shifts towards the hierarchical power structure of the government. The stability, strength and endurance of society depend on the balance of power between the state and social networks. New communication technologies tend to disrupt this balance.

As communication technologies reduce the relevance of geography, the state also engages in competition with rival powers. The decentralized structure of social networks makes them susceptible to chaos, a problem that is exacerbated if they are infiltrated by foreign powers. The term 'public diplomacy' denotes the ability of a government to communicate directly with the population of a foreign state and is commonly associated with propaganda efforts. States can combat this by restoring sovereignty, territorializing technologies and limiting access by foreign powers. The obvious dilemma in forcefully asserting state power to counter foreign powers is that upsets the balance of power between the state and social networks, withering individual liberties.

In this chapter, it is argued that new communication technologies initially tend to shift power from the state to the individual. While the strengthening of social networks promises greater liberty, the weakening of the state's central role leads to a more fragmented population and creates opportunities for intrusion by external powers. The state subsequently responds by asserting control over the technology to restore order. Excesses by the state create totalitarian traits, defined as extremely hierarchal power structures.

This chapter first explores the printing press as a key communications technology that unleashed a power struggle between the people and the authorities. Second, it looks at the digital revolution that demonstrated remarkable similarities to the story of the printing press, also sparking a rivalry between individuals and the state. Third, it considers the Fourth Industrial Revolution that exacerbates all the disruptions and challenges of the digital revolution because control over communication is required to collect data and develop AI. The domestic power balance between the state and individual competition becomes entangled with competition between states and rival powers. This, in turn, prompts states to nationalize and territorialize the digital space. It concludes that effective political power requires finding an equilibrium between corporations seeking to collect all data that has market value, individuals endeavouring to protect their privacy and the government's need to ensure that corporations align their market power with the state's political interests.

The printing press

By making the widespread and rapid dissemination of information possible for the first time in history, the printing press laid the foundation for the First Industrial Revolution. This reoriented cultural and religious learning, helping to unleash the 'rational calculation' that further modernized societies (Eisenstein 1979: 88). The breakthrough in communication technology demonstrated how society transformed by merely transmitting information with greater ease.

The power of the printing press was harnessed by governments to construct larger political entities. Prior to the 1500s, the identities and loyalties of Europeans were focused on a scattering of regions because people had little interaction with those beyond their rural communities. The state's reliance on local feudal lords severely limited its ability to exert influence within or beyond its borders. The printing press made a huge contribution to the rise of the nation state by assisting in the development of a common language and discourse. Human beings are social creatures that instinctively organize themselves into homogenous groups, and in-group loyalty providing the basis for feelings of security, belonging, morality and trust. The ability to harness these instinctive impulses in human nature is imperative to establishing political structures.

The printing press aided in the creation of larger political entities by consolidating geographical areas into 'imagined communities' because the political legitimacy and collective identity of the nation state derived from a shared ethnicity, religion, culture, traditions and foundational myths (Anderson 2006: 43). When Martin Luther translated the Bible into a widely known dialect of the German language, the printing press made it possible to disseminate the work among the population. This contributed to the formation of national identity and, ultimately, to the unification of the German nation state in the nineteenth century. The ability to communicate more broadly enabled German leaders to construct a common identity. Loyalty to the state was represented by the flag, anthem, crests and historical national narratives based on original myths, shared victimhood and victory over outsiders. By facilitating nationalist political movements, the nation state obtained legitimacy and the loyalty of the people, thus creating a large, unified and powerful political entity that could then conquer the world (McLuhan 1969).

At the same time, the people harnessed the power of the printing press to advance liberty. Prior to the printing press, the scarcity of information strengthened hierarchical power structures because knowledge and written communication had largely been confined to the upper echelons of power. The power structures of the religious, political and scientific elite ceded control over the ownership and proliferation of information, thus empowering the people through the emergence of various social networks. The printing press became an equalizer of the classes, with reading and the sharing of ideas no longer the exclusive prerogative of kings and the affluent. The philosopher Thomas Carlyle argued that the printing press 'was disbanding hired armies and cashiering most kings and senates, and creating a whole new democratic world' (Hruschka 2012: 3).

The decentralization of communication and the proliferation of ideas advanced the enlightenment by enhancing science and political participation. The printing press also strengthened the formation of public opinion by facilitating written political discourse and thus enabling political protests in opposition to the government (Dittmar 2011). Socio-political disruptions broke out in the sixteenth and seventeenth century due to the printing press. Eventually, the printing press also steered the world towards the Industrial Revolution and liberal political revolutions such as the American Revolution and the French Revolution.

'People power' also strengthened in the religious sphere. Like others before him, Martin Luther (1483–1546) criticized the Catholic Church for being corrupted by power, arguing that the Bible did not authorize the church to sell pardons to absolve sin. Unlike others before who had rejected the Pope's authority over purgatory, however, Martin Luther became the leading figure of the Reformation as his *Ninety-five Theses or Disputation on the Power of Indulgences* in 1517 spread through social networks. The printing press enabled him to prevent his publication from being filtered through the hierarchical power structures it was meant to challenge (Ferguson 2019). The printing press made it possible to equip each person with their own Bible. This helped establish a direct connection between Man and God and reduced reliance on corruptible middlemen.

Martin Luther rightly understood that the concentration of power corrupts, but he incorrectly expected that the decentralization of power would create a more benevolent future. Justice and order are mutually dependent, yet they can also be contradictory. While centralized and hierarchical power structures that promote conformity are vulnerable to corruption, social networks are decentralized and anarchical and less capable of promoting conformity. Some believed that Martin Luther had not been vigilant enough in his Reformation efforts, and others rejected his views and refuted them with the Counter-Reformation. The decentralization of communication thus led to the fragmentation of the Church and the unleashing of religious conflicts and wars in Europe over the next 130 years.

The nation state asserts itself

Governments largely reasserted order in Europe after the Thirty Years War, signing the Peace of Westphalia in 1648. The Westphalian system granted states full sovereignty over their territories. This was not to be infringed upon by autonomous actors within their borders, such as the Church, or by interference from actors beyond its borders. The peace treaty established the hierarchical power structure of the sovereign state as the highest sovereign and thus the main actor in the international system. The nation state absorbed the overlapping authorities of the Church, kings, barons, trade guilds and other organizational forces that rivalled the state for claiming people's loyalty and defining their identity. The state then established a collective identity by fostering ethnocultural and religious distinctiveness and essentially becoming a large tribe. In France, the state incentivized conformity through conversion to Catholicism and penalized non-conforming individuals with second-class citizenship or even expulsion (Mann 2005: 49). In England, the Civil War came to an end and solidarity was restored only when Protestantism emerged victorious and was established as the dominant religion.

The state's need to exert control to ensure order produced an extensive philosophical debate on human nature and the social contract. Thomas Hobbes (1588–1679), who lived through the political and religious radicalism of the English Civil War, believed that the hierarchical power of the state was necessary to establish order because the natural condition of Man is perpetual war and anarchy. John Locke (1632–1704), whose philosophy was heavily influenced by the Enlightenment and liberal ideals, advocated a limited role for the state because, he believed, human nature is inherently good and the centralization of power undermines liberty. The opposing perspectives of Hobbes and Locke concerning the 'state of nature' have defined the framework for much of Western philosophical debate about the appropriate role of the state.

The telegraph – that came into use in the 1830s and 1840s – was the first communication technology to transmit information faster than the horse, pigeon and railroad. The telegraph immediately raised several concerns. First, governments lost control over the ability to intercept communications and control public opinion. Because the telegraph reduced the relevance of geography, leaders held the valid concern that rebellions could be initiated at various locations simultaneously. Second, it was feared that simple communication over telegraph lines would lead to misunderstandings and erode the art of diplomacy. In 1837, France banned unauthorized use of the telegraph, while Russia similarly feared political communication passing out of government control. Yet, states that attempted to restrict the technology to maintain domestic stability found themselves less equipped to compete against rival powers. By contrast, Germany immediately implemented the telegraph to enhance military communication as a critical competitive advantage. The new communication technology suddenly made ambitious leaders less constrained by distance and scope in their foreign policy. Political and military leaders also obtained greater control because instantaneous communication eliminated the former need to consider contingencies in the light of changes that might occur before the message was delivered.

The invention of the telephone in the Second Industrial Revolution similarly strengthened social networks by enabling greater communication, yet the economies of scale incentivized the formation of national monopolies. The absence of competition and dominance of a single supplier thus attracted, and to some extent necessitated, greater cooperation and regulation by the state. The state subsequently also strengthened as tapping of telephones then became a common practice in both authoritarian and democratic states such as the United States.

During the Cold War, the US and Soviet governments used media to shape public opinion. While the Soviets had an openly authoritarian system with direct control over the media, the United States had to rely on more covert means to infiltrate and influence media coverage. Manipulation of media met little resistance when it was motivated by and directed against a foreign adversary. However, the Watergate scandal in 1972–1974 fuelled concerns that the President would use the CIA to target domestic political opposition. The subsequent congressional investigations produced reports, most importantly the Church Committee's final report, confirming that the CIA had infiltrated both domestic and foreign media. Two important lessons were subsequently learned in the 1970s: first, that governments do attempt to influence the media to advance their agendas, and second, that vigorous investigative journalism provides an important counterbalance. This balance has been corrupted with new developments in media advances such as the 24/7 news cycle that merges news with entertainment. Now, intelligent and informed newscasters are replaced with talking heads and pundits with political agendas. Research has found that young people in the United States are more likely to get their news from comedians hosting late-night talk shows, with the result that entertainment is widely interpreted as analysis. In order to keep ratings up, the use of sensationalism has increased. This has spurred a greater demand for violence, now supplied by attention-seeking mass shooters and terrorists.

Diplomacy was also shaken by the development and use of the telephone and digital media. George H.W. Bush's frequent phone calls with allies were met with scepticism because they sidelined the government apparatus. Former US Ambassador David Newsom argued that he 'always trembled' when President Bush picked up the phone to call allies because 'the idea of solving difficult international issues through personal rapport is a very risky one' (McManus 1989).

Digital communication technology of the Third Industrial Revolution

In the liberal view, digital technologies make it possible to go beyond the failed construct of the nation state. It was predicted as early as the 1960s that electronic and digital communication would break down barriers between individuals and societies, foster a shared identity across borders and cause the world to become a 'global village' (McLuhan 1969). The concept of the 'Netizen' was popularized in the 1990s and 2000s. It referred to Internet users who felt they had their own set of rights and responsibilities that were independent of the Westphalian state.

The belief that less power in government elevates human freedoms and creates a global village is largely informed by Lockean liberal assumptions about how the world works. The globalist expectations were premised on the idea that nationalism represents a dangerous fragmentation of identities along ethno-cultural dividing lines. As technologies enabled social networks to grow across the boundaries of the territorial state and transcend traditional cultural constraints, the world would gradually integrate towards common societal, economic and political structures under a global system of governance. Singer (2002: 14) opines:

> If the group to which we must justify ourselves is the tribe, or the nation, then our morality is likely to be tribal, or nationalistic. If, however, the revolution in communication has created a global audience, then we might need to justify our behaviour to the whole world. The change creates the material basis for a new ethic that will serve the interests of all those who live on this planet in a way that, despite much rhetoric, no previous ethic has done.

In contrast, the realist or Hobbesian view of the state is pessimistic about the possibility of transcending the state. The Social Democrat, August Bebel (1876), famously argued: 'The family forms a tribe, and several tribes form a state and the nation – and finally the close interaction of nations will result in internationality'. The organization of humanity is based on building blocks or concentric circles, and constructing a higher or broader community does not entail transcending the more distinct groupings. The nation cannot replace the family, and the international community cannot replace the nation. Rather, society crumbles if the family disintegrates and the international community similarly falters without the nation.

The weakening of collective national identity and shared narratives does not result in elevating people to a global identity, but breaks society down into rival sub-identities and gives rise to destructive identity politics. The state's weakening ability to maintain a collective identity has profound consequences. The process that 'turned peasants into Frenchmen and immigrants into American citizens is reversing' as larger identity groups fragment into smaller identities (Hobsbawm 2007: 93). Consequently, the legitimacy of the state and its ability to mobilize domestic resources in the pursuit of shared interests erodes. The emergence of a globalist economy outside the state's control further intensifies the fragmentation of identities and narratives because 'independent market power made it easier for youth to discover material or cultural symbols of identity' (Hobsbawm 2007: 328). Similarly, the development of communication technologies not bound by territory can lead to alternative and often rival identities.

Fragmentation of society

The early innovations of the digital revolution reorganized human interaction, restructuring society and the influence of the state. Digital communication became the greatest disruption to communication since the printing press. A new world has emerged in which everyone on the planet can connect with everyone else to share ideas. Although, the diminished ability of governments to construct the common and unifying narratives can also reduce trust in the authorities and among fellow citizens. Observers who were initially optimistic about the tech industry are gradually readjusting their Lockean ideals in the light of Hobbesian realities.

Early optimism was largely rooted in the assumption that the transfer of power from the state to the people would usher in a new era of enlightenment and democracy. The Internet was heralded as the greatest tool for democracy and an instrument against authoritarian governments attempting to restrict free speech. Although the Internet was at first largely seen as an important gatekeeper, as the printing press had been, that perception has changed. The Executive Chairman of Google, Eric Smith, articulated in 1997 the thin line between liberty and chaos: 'The Internet is the first thing that humanity has built that humanity doesn't understand, the largest experiment in anarchy that we have ever had' (Singer and Friedman 2014: 26). Evan Williams, the co-founder of Twitter, even apologized for developing the technological platform that helped place Trump in the White House: 'I thought once everybody could speak freely and exchange information and ideas, the world is automatically going to be a better place. I was wrong about that' (Streitfeld 2017).

Removing gatekeepers from the control over the dissemination of information democratizes and liberates information, but it also removes quality controls. When the printing press initially removed important gatekeepers from the dissemination of information, misinformation or 'fake news' proliferated rapidly. For example, it was asserted that witches live amongst us and should be burned alive at the stake, which had appalling societal consequences. The Kony 2012 video about an African warlord that went viral with more than 100 million views on YouTube in 2012 provided an early lesson about removing gatekeepers.

Initially, the Kony 2012 video was greeted with optimism, as a grassroots project that drew public attention to an important issue. However, it was soon discovered that the video was based on numerous falsehoods that should have been scrutinized by the gatekeepers in the established media.

Similar concerns emerged with regard to social media. In *Twitter for Diplomats*, former Italian Foreign Minister Giulio Terzi (2013: 7) argued that 'Twitter has two big positive effects on foreign policy: It fosters a beneficial exchange of ideas between policymakers and civil society and enhances diplomats' ability to gather information and to anticipate, analyse, manage, and react to events'. Nevertheless, Terzi (2013: 7) cautioned that 'with only 140 characters ... one cannot underestimate the potential risks of this new and much wider exposure'. Donald Trump, America's first Twitter president, could avoid relying on the country's hostile political–media establishment by speaking directly with the American people – using no more than 140 characters. Although the gatekeepers protect the increasingly oligarchic control of the political–media establishment, they also play an important role in terms of vetting – determining whether the information is accurate and in the public interest. Trump's decisions about what is real and of public interest appear to be motivated by a political agenda, one that vilifies the opposition and polarizes the country. President Trump also began to sideline the entire government apparatus by announcing decisions over Twitter even before notifying his own staff or allies. For example, Trump tweeted the replacement of his Chief of Staff and his Secretary of State. Similarly, Trump announced to the public the ban of transgender people in the US military over a series of three Tweets.

However, Trump's rise was merely a symptom of an imbalance between the state and the individual. Trump's ability to use social networks to position himself as the 'man of the people' versus a member of the elite resonated with Americans' growing resentment towards the corrupting concentration of power in the political–media establishment. Trump's ability to harness the power of digital networks meant that he did not have to be filtered through the establishment hierarchy where funding, media support and party backing are essential to get elected. Hillary Clinton, the wife of a former president and chair of the powerful Clinton Foundation, was the state-approved candidate. With distrust of the political–media establishment growing among the electorate, Trump did not win the presidential election *despite* his fight with the mainstream media and political class, but *because* of it. That feud was a testimony to his independence and ability to shake up the system, as a prerequisite to deliver change.

Technology also affects the source of governments' legitimacy and authority. Politicians need not only the support of experts, but also of online influencers without direct expertise on governance. Increasing access to information through digitalization was expected to make citizens more informed. Instead, it has given birth to a misguided intellectual egalitarianism in which knowledge from a Google or Wikipedia search demands equal status as information (Nichols 2017). Furthermore, social media platforms create a push towards conformity. Henry Kissinger astutely recognized that 'the mindset for walking lonely political paths may not be self-evident to those who seek confirmation by hundreds, sometimes thousands of friends on Facebook' (Kissinger 2015).

The growing role of the digital domain for political influence inevitably attracts new forms of manipulating public discourse. Political bots become rampant on the Internet, undermining political communication (Boyd, Levy and Marwick 2014). Political and commercial actors use political bots as technological proxies, manipulating public opinion by spreading propaganda and misinformation by retweeting contents, attacking political opponents and drowning out the conversation of activists (Woolley and Howard 2016). Even Wikipedia, a community-maintained site, has been infiltrated by 'WikiEdits bots' that spread favourable narratives (Ford, Puschmann and Dubois 2016). During the 2008 US presidential election, Obama pioneered the extensive use of voter data to make his campaign more effective (Kreiss 2016). Such use of big data is expensive and marginalizes non-establishment candidates who do not receive the same funding. It could also make political candidates more approachable by a foreign power prepared to fund the use of big data. Social media is therefore increasingly seen as a challenge to democracy:

> If you wanted to build a machine that would distribute propaganda to millions of people, distract them from important issues, energize hatred and bigotry, erode social trust, undermine respectable journalism, foster doubts about science, and engage in massive surveillance all at once, you would make something a lot like Facebook.
>
> (Vaidhyanathan 2018: 19)

Social media also reduces social cohesion by stimulating radical individualism and narcissism. Modern technology 'elevates narcissists to prominence' in politics and cultural life and 'elicits and reinforces narcissistic traits in everyone' (Lasch 1979: 235). Former Facebook President Sean Parker argued that the platform was built to consume as much human attention as possible and expressed concerns about the consequences, saying, 'God knows what this does to our kid's brains'. Indeed, the ability to obtain instant gratification and the dopamine 'high' it causes is making it more difficult for people to invest the time needed to develop deeper interpersonal relationships. People become more connected in virtual space, yet suffer more than ever from loneliness and depression.

Social media is a paradox. On the one hand, it motivates political engagement; on the other hand, it diminishes intellectual and political pluralism by eclipsing public platforms for comparing and debating ideas. Social cohesion demands recognition and respect for competing perspectives and objectives. Social media weakens the national debate and social cohesion as communities fragment into self-segregating bubbles with confirmation bias. Algorithms are designed to maximize clicks by offering similar perspectives on particular topics, as opposed to media's traditional function of introducing people to various perspectives on a multitude of issues. Newsfeeds on social media provide custom-made information and steer the user towards a relentless confirmation bias in which one's own views are constantly reaffirmed rather than challenged. Unsurprisingly, people like posts and articles with which they agree. This naturally leads to the formation of 'echo chambers' in social media as platforms feed users an endless diet of only what they like. Reinforcing existing beliefs and shielding users from opposing perspectives weakens critical thinking. Replacing public debate with echo chambers produces a less informed citizenry that is vulnerable to demagogues seeking to manipulate the truth. As US writer and commentator Walter Lippmann once famously observed, 'When all think alike, no one is thinking'.

Paradoxically, increased connectivity between people can also increase divisiveness. A similar paradox was evident in mid-nineteenth-century Britain, when railways connected the country, yet accentuated economic disparities, deepened social estrangement as people abandoned local customs, and decreased social capital in communities as people began living in isolated spheres (Guldi 2012). Furthermore, grievances towards the government grew because railways gave rise to the 'infrastructure state' – the rise of powerful bureaucrats in a centralized government that suddenly obtained an intrusive influence over citizens.

These developments are explained by the fact that human beings are inclined towards smaller social groups of similar people. Social capital is higher in more homogenous societies, and this correlates with higher levels of happiness, civic engagement, voting, empathy and trust in neighbours (Putnam 2000). Furthermore,

Inhabitants of diverse communities tend to withdraw from collective life, to distrust their neighbors, regardless of the color of their skin, to withdraw even from close friends, to expect the worst from their community and its leaders, to volunteer less, give less to charity and work on community projects less often, to register to vote less, to agitate for social reform more but have less faith that they can actually make a difference, and to huddle unhappily in front of the television.

(Putnam 2007: 150)

Political instability and revolution

The authoritarian governance that held together the Soviet Union came at a heavy prize for social networks. A totalitarian government, by definition, seeks to control every aspect of life. Gorbachev's reforms were necessary for scaling back government control over citizens and creating a more open and free society. At the same time, they unleashed internal chaos by allowing competing ethnocultural groups to form and exposing society to external influences that aimed to disrupt domestic cohesion.

Digital platforms are often used to counter the power of governments and became powerful instruments during the Arab Spring and the Occupy Wall Street movement (Wolfsfeld, Segev and Sheafer 2013; Papacharissi 2015). The events of the Arab Spring uprisings that began in 2011 demonstrated how populations could use decentralized digital communication to counterbalance the state and how Western governments could exploit it to subvert foreign governments in an attempt to expand influence in the Middle East and North Africa. Moldova experienced the world's first 'Twitter Revolution' that then spread across the post-Soviet space and the Middle East (Christensen 2011).

Although Western governments celebrated digital media as an instrument of 'people power' in other regions of the world, it labelled the technology a threat when used to challenge their own authority. The wording changed from 'revolution' to 'riots' when social media was used to organize anti-government protests in Tottenham in 2011. Government responses in the Middle East and the UK shared striking similarities, with the authorities in both places seeking to restrain and control the use of social media (Fuchs 2012: 384). Instead of celebrating 'people power', Western governments began chastising populists who employed disinformation tactics and sought to interfere in foreign governments. Populists can be defined as political figures that question issues that have been suppressed by the dogmas of the establishment. For example: Does globalization work for all when salaries have remained stagnant for more than two decades? Does NATO expansionism and endless military adventurism make us safer? Should we impose our own values abroad and encourage minority cultures at home? Although populists might not always have feasible solutions to the problems they bring up, the masses often welcome their willingness to go beyond the usual bounds of public discourse.

Governments seizing control of the Internet

The US government's initial cyber capabilities were aimed at targeting foreign powers. In the early 1990s, digital technologies were used to advance 'economic intelligence', with the US intelligence community serving national business interests (Scalingi 1992: 153). The PRISM surveillance program revealed that the NSA was conducting extensive cyber-espionage into foreign corporation such as the Brazilian energy company Petrobras, Swiss banks and Chinese telecom companies (Segal 2014). The Stuxnet cyberattack on Iran's uranium enrichment centrifuges demonstrated the capability of the United States to use digital technologies to attack the critical infrastructure and, potentially, the financial institutions of adversaries. President Obama called for a list of potential targets for cyber warfare against all adversaries. The objective of the Offensive Cyber Effects Operations program was to 'advance US national objectives around the world with little or no warning to the adversary or target and with potential effects ranging from subtle to severely damaging' (Greenwald and MacAskill 2013).

The Snowden revelations of 2013 unleashed a new power struggle between the individual and the state. Edward Snowden revealed that Big Tech was collecting a vast amount of personal data and sharing it with US intelligence services. The leaks demonstrated that the US government was also targeting its own population on an unprecedented scale. Snowden also demonstrated that governments have only a limited ability to keep secrets. Snowden's motivations were essentially those of a 'Netizen' and believed it was his responsibility to ensure that the Internet remained a forum where people around the world could exercise their right to share ideas freely without government surveillance and control. His belief in the Internet as the ultimate democratic tool of the individual had been shattered.

Julian Assange similarly proved how non-governmental organizations can curb the power of governments with digital technologies. WikiLeaks released troves of US classified cables and even revealed that the DNC rigged the primary of the Democratic Party in the 2016 US presidential election. However, even though the leak demonstrated that social networks can hold corrupt governments accountable, the political establishment was able to turn the tables by presenting WikiLeaks as an organization working for the Russian government. Snowden, Assange and even Trump were all accused of being foreign agents and puppets of the Kremlin. Irrespective of any foreign interference that might have actually occurred, the incident revealed the complex relationship between the government, social networks and foreign powers.

Towards a more authoritarian state

The United States is becoming an authoritarian, corporate state. Democratic principles prohibit the state from engaging in censorship and propaganda, but governments can engage in such activity by cooperating with private corporations that do not labour under such constraints.

The lack of any central authority that could instil order in the digital domain has emboldened governments to assert themselves. Fake news from social media platforms, much like claims of witchcraft centuries before, has become a watershed moment and warrants genuine concern (Ferguson 2019). Governments need to intervene to mitigate the chaos in social networks and restrict possible attempts by foreign powers to deliberately spread misinformation.

Governments are tasking social media giants with identifying and censoring misinformation, hate speech or offensive forms of expression, thereby endowing these corporations with immense political power. Facts are seldom self-explanatory: their meaning and significance require analysis and interpretation. Arbitrary governance thrives on ambiguous concepts such as 'hate speech' or 'offensive speech' because even distinguishing between facts and the interpretation of facts is problematic. Whoever is empowered to define the truth holds immense power, especially in international relations. Almost two centuries ago, Alexis de Tocqueville (2003: 162) cautioned:

> Whoever should be able to create and maintain a tribunal of this kind would waste his time in prosecuting the liberty of the press; for he would be the absolute master of the whole community and would be as free to rid himself of the authors as of their writings.

Governments are nonetheless moving forward with initiatives resembling Orwell's Ministry of Truth. Much like its US counterpart, the EU has begun using censorship to counter disinformation and fake news. The ability to censor is predictably vulnerable to the arbiter's vested interests. Leading EU officials indicated that combating fake news was intended to combat 'populist rhetoric' and ensure that EU-sceptics 'don't win at the ballot boxes'. It was deemed necessary to fight fake news to protect democracy and EU institutions, but no clear distinction was made between these two objectives (Williams 2018).

The state does not always behave as a unitary actor because political groups and parties envision different futures and pathways. The risk in empowering the state to act against citizens and foreign rivals is that the ability to influence political communication and organization can also be used against the political opposition at home. For example, the UK's Integrity Initiative was developed as a propaganda tool. The Integrity Initiative became a global program to mobilize academics, journalists and non-governmental organizations to target the narratives of adversaries, primarily Russia. The program is intended to deceive by depicting 'independent' observers uniting to repudiate Russia's narrative on controversial issues. However, the program was later revealed to have been turned against the domestic political opposition, the Labour party.

Powerful tech companies largely operate without full transparency, with minor adjustments to algorithms altering countless search results. There was less focus on the arbitrary power of tech giants when their tools were used against foreign rivals, but as society polarizes, these corporations become entangled in domestic politics. Because US tech giants lean to the political left, it causes an uproar among conservatives when they use their powerful digital platforms for political purposes. Researchers from Northwestern University who analysed Google's algorithms identified 'a left-leaning ideological skew' and found that conservative websites were suppressed (Flood 2019). Conservatives have been targeted and removed from these platforms. It is noteworthy that tech giants even cooperate in such activity. For example, Facebook, Apple, YouTube and Spotify coordinated their ban of conservative radio host Alex Jones. Epstein (2018) outlines a variety of ways that large tech companies, especially Google, can influence millions of votes without anyone noticing by merely changing the algorithms for search results. A leaked email revealed that a senior Google employee used the company's resources to support the Clinton campaign in the 2016 presidential elections by mobilizing pro-Clinton voters in important states (Carbone 2018).

The trend towards de-platforming people with undesirable views appears to go beyond social media. Digital currencies such as Bitcoin make it possible to transfer money directly without official oversight, greatly empowering the individual at the expense of state control. Much like in the communication sphere, however, corporations and the state can use the same technology to monitor and control. Patreon, Stripe, PayPal and other payment systems have denied individuals expressing extremist views from using their payment platforms. MasterCard has similarly been under pressure by left-wing advocacy groups to establish a human rights committee to deny services to right-wing individuals and groups. With Facebook launching its own currency, the Libra, the possibilities will grow for conducting surveillance and arbitrarily using these geoeconomic instruments to punish political adversaries. Edward Snowden argued that 'Bitcoin is freedom' because it represents 'freedom without permission'. It carries no risk of being de-platformed as could happen with corporations such as Facebook for not following their sometimes ambiguous, arbitrary and politically motivated terms and conditions (Spilotro 2019). As all aspects of human activity become digitalized, corporations and the state gain the ability to deny access to communication, payment, transportation and other functions.

Towards a Westphalian Internet

Attempts are being made to nationalize the Internet. Open markets for communications thrive when power is concentrated with a hegemon, but when new powers emerge and become more autonomous, it gives rise to a new balance of power and motivates the former hegemon to constrain market forces (Ruggie 1982: 381). A key motivation for territorializing the Internet is to defend against the narratives of foreign powers.

Government intervention to protect social media platforms from foreign interference gradually encourages tech corporations to become tools of governments. In an op-ed entitled 'Protecting democracy is an arms race: here's how Facebook can help', Mark Zuckerberg (2018) argued that Facebook is determined to confront 'bad actors' globally that seek to spread disinformation and interfere in elections. Zuckerberg demonstrated that Facebook could serve the national cause by identifying targets based on their adversarial position to the US rather than their online conduct. Zuckerberg identified these 'bad actors' as Russia, Iran and other states that Washington considers its main adversaries. However, *The Guardian* revealed as far back as 2011 that the US military played an innovative role in creating a troll army of fake online personas to manipulate social media with the purpose of 'degrading the enemy narrative' (Fielding and

Cobain 2011). The article did not, however, raise the issue of governing the behaviour of the United States and its allies, even though this arms race would require the 'combined forces of the U.S. private and public sectors' (Zuckerberg 2018). Furthermore, Facebook's ability to police the Internet for 'bad actors' seems questionable when, only a few months before Zuckerberg's op-ed, it had been revealed in the Cambridge Analytica scandal that Facebook supplied data from up to 87 million of its users to a British political consulting firm without their consent.

Facebook also made itself a foreign policy tool of the US government by agreeing to cooperate with two sub-organizations of the National Endowment for Democracy (NDI), the International Republican Institute and the National Democratic Institute. Reagan established the NDI in 1983 to take over many of the operations previously carried out by the CIA. The NDI has become a central instrument of US interference in foreign elections and regime change (Sussman and Krader 2008). Russia banned NDI for interfering in its democracy and for backing 'colour revolutions' in neighbouring states to install pro-Western/anti-Russian regimes. Facebook committed to assisting NDI by enhancing 'election integrity efforts' in the United States and around the world. Facebook is also cooperating with the NATO-funded Atlantic Council to identify and remove content on social media.

Adversaries of the United States thus have strong incentives to decouple from American social media platforms due to their manipulation of narratives. Competition had already intensified in other communication domains. Russia has been especially vocal about its intention to challenge US dominance in the information sphere as an important area of great power politics. Russian Foreign Minister Sergey Lavrov (2007) recognized that Russia's perspective is not represented in international media because 'Russia is apparently not as skilful as the West when it comes to matters of communication'. Putin (2012) stipulated:

> Russia's image abroad is formed not by us and as a result it is often distorted and does not reflect the real situation in our country ... Those who fire guns and launch air strikes here or there are the good guys, while those who warn of the need for restraint and dialogue are for some reason at fault. But our fault lies in our failure to adequately explain our position.

The Russian government launched an English-language news organization, RT that went on to become a global leader and the most-viewed news agency on YouTube. However, YouTube is also toeing the US government line to counter rivalry in the information space. After the US government listed Russian media such as RT as 'foreign agents', YouTube soon altered its algorithms to reduce RT's online traffic.

Russia has also begun asserting territorial control over the digital space by placing the Internet architecture under its governance. Virtual Private Networks are banned, encryption is restricted, online anonymity is limited, and the state is asserting control over data flows (McKune and Ahmed 2018). Mimicking developments in the West, a Russian news aggregator law in 2017 compels search engines and other digital platforms to assess the truthfulness of publicly important publications before their dissemination (Hartog 2017). A new law now before the Russian Duma, *the Digital Economy National Programme*, would require that data from Russian organizations and users remain within the country. All Internet traffic would be rerouted through exchange points managed by the Russian telecom regulator, Roskomnadzor. Nationalizing the Russian Internet with the developing of 'RUnet' will provide the authorities with a 'red button' to push in order to isolate the Russian Internet from the rest of the world if the situation demanded. Foreign providers are often required to store their data on Russian soil, while domestic platforms are linked in a partnership with the state. The founder of VKontakte, the 'Russian Facebook', gave up control over the company in 2014 when two Kremlin-linked oligarchs acquired a majority stake. In 2018, the Russian government began restricting access to Telegram, a cloud-based instant messaging application that offers encrypted person-to-person communication. The Russian authorities expressed concerns about the ability of terrorists to communicate outside the control of the government, and Telegram has, indeed, become their 'app of choice'. Nevertheless, civil society groups have voiced concerns that government limitations on encrypted messages are intended to also increase the authorities' ability to monitor the wider public.

The Chinese government is similarly working towards 'Internet sovereignty' in the format of an independent 'ChinaNet'. Establishing national control over online technologies and activities in China makes it easier to govern cyberspace and ensure non-interference in domestic affairs. Nationalizing or territorializing the internet becomes a growing priority as the digital space is increasingly capable of manipulating the physical world through innovations such as the internet of things and self-driving cars (Economy 2018: 80–2). The fragmentation of the Internet will put increasing pressure on US companies to adapt to localization policies in order to stay competitive with ChinaNet. The concept of data sovereignty is, for better or for worse, challenging the idea of an unfettered Internet that was previously considered the sole and superior alternative.

The Fourth Industrial Revolution and communication

The Fourth Industrial Revolution amplifies the aforementioned problems from the digital revolution because everything that is recorded becomes a form of communication. Schwab (2016: 7) cautions:

> As the physical, digital, and biological worlds continue to converge, new technologies and platforms will increasingly enable citizens to engage with governments, voice their opinions, coordinate their efforts, and even circumvent the supervision of public authorities. Simultaneously, governments will gain new technological powers to increase their control over populations.

The complexity of the technologies emerging from the Fourth Industrial Revolution weakens democratic governance. Democracy requires a knowledgeable populace and growing complexity results in a power shift from the electorate to the expert class. It had been common from the time of ancient Greece until early US history to limit voting rights to male landowners. The logic was that male landowners, unlike labourers and women, would have the time and cognitive abilities to acquire the requisite knowledge and assume the necessary responsibility to engage in politics. The emancipation that resulted from making political participation a universal right is being scaled back because governance over high-tech issues is creating a technocratic elite. The scope of democracy is limited when financial policies fall within the jurisdiction of central banks, international experts inform the legal system, and policies for education, human rights and immigration are set by experts and fixed in international treaties (Babones 2018c). This trend will intensify as today's algorithm-driven society becomes less comprehensible to the average citizen. This development can be defined as the tyranny of the expert class (Babones 2018c), or as Plato's ideal aristocratic government of the philosopher king.[1]

Governments will increasingly use AI to restructure the relationship between the state and citizens because capabilities tend to shape intentions. Even countries with strong democratic traditions will have great incentives to slide down this slippery slope due to their growing monitoring, tracking and surveillance capabilities. New technologies are rapidly breaking down previous political norms and dogmas in ways that would have seemed impossible only one or two decades ago. The MIT Computer Science and Artificial Intelligence Lab (CSAIL)

[1] Plato argued that the philosopher had to become king to have a ruler with love of wisdom. The aristocratic governance of experts was expected to manage the complexities of society, while in contrast a democracy would become hedonistic and gradually seek to liberate itself from the authorities and structures required to maintain order and societal cohesion.

are cooperating with the Qatar Computing Research Institute (QCRI) to develop an AI initiative that would 'stamp out fake-news outlets before the stories spread too widely'. It remains unclear whether such AI systems would also target fake news in the mainstream media such as claims of Iraq having nuclear weapons, the Doumagas attack in Syria and allegations that Trump colluded with Russia. Similarly, references to the 2014 coup in Ukraine are deemed to be fake news by the EU that instead labels those events as a 'democratic revolution'. If so, this would result in censoring leading political scientists such as Mearsheimer (2014) for spreading disinformation. Granting AI a central role in censoring information for a Ministry of Truth is laden with risks because AI technology does not explain how it learns and thinks, and any AI system is ultimately based on human biases and intentions.

The accumulation and use of data for commercial gain will gradually find more political applications. The facial recognition algorithms Facebook uses to automatically recognize friends in photos is also used for automated passport control at airports and surveillance. Without any public debate, the US Department of Homeland Security decided to use facial recognition on 97 per cent of all departing passengers by 2023 (Birnbaum 2019). Information that would have been unattainable for the Stasi is now offered voluntarily by users of social media. What's more, those companies then offer backdoor access to US intelligence agencies. As the Cambridge Analytica affair revealed, Google, Amazon and Facebook collect users' search histories to recommend books, articles or friends, and then sell that information to private companies for use in targeted advertising or political influence campaigns. Services already exist for employers and landlords that analyse the social media of applicants, including private messages, to assess personal character and develop a credit score (Zuboff 2019).

The Internet of Things – that monitors everything from users' health and driving habits to personal conversations – lays the foundation for a terrifying surveillance state that would know more about individuals than their closest friends. Seemingly altruistic motives will be cited to justify AI systems that actually undermine personal liberties. In Chicago, the police are using AI for 'predictive policing' that identifies potential victims and perpetrators to inform police officers about the most appropriate locations for patrols (Isaac and Dixon 2017). The relationship between authorities and citizens could change radically. A moral argument could be made for police practising 'pre-crime' – that is, engaging possible future victims and perpetrators. Or else it could take still another leap towards authoritarianism by using AI to assess guilt. Teachers in West Virginia were required to participate in a wellness program, monitored by a health app, with the school reinforcing 'healthy' behaviour with monetary rewards and punishing 'unhealthy' behaviour (Zuboff 2019). US presidential candidate Andrew Yang (2018) similarly argued in favour of 'Digital Social Credits'. By this arrangement, the government would pay citizens for positive behaviours such as participation in charities to mitigate the economic insecurity and mass unemployment resulting from the growing use of robotics and automation.

The contemporary challenge of online political bots – tens of millions of AI-run avatars – will worsen with deepfake technology. AI technology can extract visual and audio data from video footage to create real-looking but fake videos. This technology could prove important for political propaganda against foreign adversaries and domestic political opposition because any public figure can be 'caught' saying anything the creators want. With reality becoming increasingly ambiguous, a future awaits in which fake videos – over the authenticity of which even experts might disagree – are deliberately 'leaked', sparking a constant series of accusations and denials. Mainstream media published false accusations that the Kremlin had a 'pee tape' of Trump with prostitutes in a Moscow hotel. Despite the lack of evidence, the story dominated the news and was used to denigrate the president and portray him as a Russian agent. Similarly, LinkedIn co-founder Reid Hoffman funded an operation by Democratic operatives that created thousands of fake Russian accounts backing Alabama Republican Roy Moore. After he was successfully portrayed as a Russian agent, Moore lost the 2017 race Senate race by a small margin (Shane and Blinder 2018). In the world of deepfake, such manufactured scandals would be supplemented with manufactured videos. This will be 'disinformation on steroids' as the fake news of today becomes the deepfake news of tomorrow (Chesney and Citron 2018). Sustaining democracy and political stability will be a formidable challenge as the public grows increasingly uninformed and detached from reality. Because anyone will be able to convincingly make it seem as if anything has happened, the state will likely assert itself with technical, legislative and regulatory responses to impose order.

China leading the way

Either due to the Communist Party creed or to its technological capabilities, the Chinese government is setting itself up as a sort of 'Big Brother' and spearheading the innovative implementation of new technologies in ways that bear a striking resemblance to the Orwellian future of *1984*. China has greater ability and desire than the United States and Russia to assert government control over the information space. Beijing also exports these technologies to other states such as Zimbabwe. Vietnam and Thailand have taken the lead in emulating China's Internet laws for increased government supervision, and Malaysia and Indonesia are also following suit. Even India, the world's largest democracy, gravitates towards increased government control over the Internet (Goel 2019).

China uses AI to assimilate and process the vast data from its surveillance cameras on public streets, enhancing the government's ability to track every citizen. Because all economic, financial and social activities are linked to digital platforms, the capabilities of government surveillance further increase. For example, China has largely ended the use of cash and credit cards in favour of paying with digital QR codes. The Chinese government then collects the data from the main payment systems, AliPay and WeChat. The various sources of surveillance are then integrated. Subsequently, minor misconduct such as jaywalking is caught on facial recognition and a fine is sent instantly to the offender's WeChat account informing them that the money has already been taken from the account without their authorization.

China's Social Credit System (SCS) is slated to track all Chinese citizens by 2020. The SCS enables the government to play the patronizing role of a parent or a big brother that cultivates a well-behaved citizenry. According to the Chinese government, the social engineering of the SCS seeks to 'shape a thick atmosphere in the entire society that keeping trust is glorious and breaking trust is disgraceful' (SCS 2014). To date, the system focuses primarily on economic activities rather than political behaviour. The SCS integrates data platforms into a centralized government infrastructure and uses that data to assess citizens' social standing (Lv and Luo 2018). Social credit points are deducted for 'bad' behaviours such as posting fake news, criticizing the government, poor driving, purchasing too many video games, watching pornography, frivolous purchases, loitering, refusing military service, smoking in non-smoking zones, jaywalking, failing to pay debts or taxes, consuming excessive alcohol or junk food, visiting unauthorized websites, having close social contacts with people who have low social credit scores and similar undesirable behaviour. The same digital infrastructure then enables the authorities to distribute punishments and rewards. A low credit score can result in travel restrictions by bus, train or plane, dismissal from universities and government jobs, denial of the privilege to purchase luxury products, denial of a home loan and other negative consequences. Furthermore, social pressure mounts because an individual can be punished for the low social credit scores of his or her parents or close friends.

However, the social credit score can be increased by earning a city-level award, committing a heroic act, performing well in business, volunteering or donating to charity, helping your family through a difficult time and other acts defined as good behaviour by the government. Interestingly, the system has received some positive feedback: people have noticed some improved behaviours, such as cars now yielding to pedestrians – a very uncommon phenomenon in the past (Mistreanu 2018). As for the people forced to participate in this social experiment, how much personal liberty will they be willing to sacrifice in return for order, and will they have any say in the matter at all?

Conclusion

Throughout history, communication technologies have caused a major disruption to the triangular relationship between the state, the individual and foreign powers. Governments need to establish enough control over communication to maintain social cohesion and to rival foreign powers. The Fourth Industrial Revolution presents new challenges because market forces drive technological platforms for communication and economic power depends on amassing data through innovations linked to the Internet of Thing and other technologies. In the hands of corporations or the state, these powers undercut the privacy of individuals, and under foreign control, they can undermine state sovereignty.

It appears that these problems are being in a similar manner to the Peace of Westphalia in 1648. That Treaty clearly delineated territory and established a single source of authority within states' borders. In the Fourth Industrial Revolution, systemic incentives are similarly encouraging large powers to territorialize the digital space by nationalizing the Internet. Establishing technological sovereignty in the form of a Westphalian Internet enforces the principle of non-interference in domestic affairs. In this way, a social contract must be established between the state and domestic social networks in terms of the distribution of power. Over the next few years, it should be expected that in democratic states from the United States to Russia, the public will demand greater transparency and public ownership over digital platforms. By contrast, China appears to be developing a social contract stipulating that privacy and liberty must be surrendered in return for social order and economic growth. As states adapt to the technologies of the Fourth Industrial Revolution, it remains unclear whether democracy is tenable and whether the new choice will be between authoritarianism and anarchy.

6

Geoeconomics without capitalism: Decoupling capital from labour

Introduction

Does technology eviscerate capitalism by rewriting the fundamental and longstanding economic rules? Capitalism can reform and renew itself with the emergence of new technologies. The structures of capitalism have changed with the introduction of steam power, railways, steel, electricity, mass production, cars, petrochemicals and digital communication technologies. Do the fundamentals of market capitalism function in perpetuity or are they conditioned upon the transient technologies of the eighteenth, nineteenth and twentieth centuries? The First Industrial Revolution gave birth to capitalism and the Fourth Industrial Revolution might sound its death knell.

Enhanced productivity in the First Industrial Revolution spawned competing economic theories about the relationship between capital and labour. Feudalism and mercantilism had reigned supreme until Adam Smith introduced the market economy, according to which the demands of the market rather than the state should dictate economic relations. The rise of economic liberalism as the most prominent theory is explained by its ability to maximize efficiency. Furthermore, economic liberalism fuels political liberalism because self-regulating markets strip power from corruptible governments and decentralize decision-making, shifting it to the individual. Do these economic assumptions still hold true, however, when human beings become increasingly redundant in production processes?

The Fourth Industrial Revolution presents an existential challenge to capitalism. This inevitably affects geoeconomic cooperation and competition because it reduces the role of the market. Capitalism is fundamental to the organization of both domestic society and international relations because states must balance market efficiency and competitiveness with equity and social cohesion. The concentration of wealth and the weakening of the middle class polarizes society between capital owners and labourers. Although both the political left and right have recognized the flaws of capitalism, the ideologies of the nineteenth and twentieth centuries have failed to provide viable alternatives. The demise of communism does not necessarily guarantee the enduring victory of capitalism. In fact, capitalism might soon follow communism off the cliff. Competing solutions in response to the failings of capitalism will influence how great powers define their national interests and the extent to which they can mobilize their domestic productive resources and populations in support of these interests.

Automation of the cognitive disrupts capitalism by intensifying the decoupling of capital and labour. Traditionally, labour unions have enabled workers to use collective bargaining to achieve a balance of power vis-à-vis capital owners. Automated labour, however, puts the owners of assets in an increasingly strong position and diminishes the bargaining power of human labour. The foundation of capitalism consequently falls apart as wealth becomes more concentrated and the relationship between capital and labour decouples.

The 'creative destruction' caused by new technologies eliminates entire professions and industries. However, most of the newly automated jobs were repetitive and low-skilled and they were replaced by high-skilled and high-wage jobs. As digital technologies penetrate deeply into areas that had been exclusively physical and analogue, the scope and speed of automation will cause major disruptions to industries as diverse as manufacturing, transportation, logistics, agriculture, education and healthcare. Automating the cognitive in the Fourth Industrial Revolution could make creative destruction and 'technological unemployment' a permanent condition.

The paradox of unprecedented productivity causing widespread poverty and unemployment raises reasonable questions about the ability of capitalism to organize society. The concentration of wealth and shortage of jobs will revive old ideologies and engender new ones unless capitalism is capable of adapting and evolving. As digital capitalism penetrates manufacturing, transportation and eventually all other sectors of the economy, significant reform of the economic system will be required. Such reforms should be directed towards achieving inclusive growth.

This chapter first addresses the relationship between technology and capitalism because renowned economic theorists have suggested that the viability of capitalism could depend on transitional technologies. Second, the rise of tech giants appears to decouple capital from labour to the extent that market forces are unable to restore the equilibrium required for political stability. Third, in response to permanent technological unemployment, formerly short-term government interventions to mitigate the effects of creative destruction might need to become more permanent. Last, it explores whether the need for redistribution demands the abandonment of capitalism. It is concluded that the ideological polarization over technological unemployment and redistribution is largely a reflection of our current political climate. Leading free market capitalist thinkers have recognized that technological development might not benefit labour and have advocated redistribution as a moral imperative and as a means of maintaining political stability. Although capitalism's ability to adapt has enabled it to secure a quick victory, this success has lowered incentives for the very reforms needed to guarantee its long-term survival.

A temporary or permanent disruption to capitalism?

Two opposing narratives have consistently defined the ideological debate over capitalism. The first suggests that capitalism liberated people from hardship by unleashing the productive capacity that eventually freed many of them from poverty. In addition, property rights and the rule of law advanced economic and political freedoms. The second narrative postulates that capitalism created and legitimized new levers of power by which the rich could exploit and oppress the poor. These two narratives are not mutually exclusive because capitalism does, in fact, maximize productivity. At the same time, the concentration of wealth in the hands of capital owners has led to inequality and exploitation. This has necessitated trade-offs between opportunity and equality, productive efficiency and full employment, prosperity and environmental preservation, dynamic economic structures and rigidity, social stability and technological innovation.

Technology that elevates capital above labour will tear away at the foundations of capitalism. The concept of 'capital-biased technological change' suggests that the increasing ability to automate labour to enhance productivity will gradually shift the power and income from labour to the owners of capital (David and Klundert 1965). Capital-intensive technological undermines the ability of markets to be self-governing and intensifies the scope of labour displacement. Adam Smith's 'invisible hand', directed by market forces, has become the visible hand of big business (Chandler 1993).

Even the key thinkers behind free market capitalism recognized the limitations that technology poses to capitalism. David Ricardo (1821: 474) corrected his former assumptions about labourers sharing the benefits of enhanced productivity from new machinery: 'the opinion entertained by the labouring class, that the employment of machinery is frequently detrimental to their interests, is not founded on prejudice and error, but is conformable to the correct principles of political economy'. More efficient machinery reduces the demand for labour and the level of compensation. This means that labourers could be disadvantaged by technological innovation because they do not own the capital/machinery:

> My mistake arose from the supposition, that whenever the net income of a society increased, its gross income would also increase; I now, however, see reason to be satisfied that the one fund, from which landlords and capitalists derive their revenue, may increase, while the other, that upon which the labouring class mainly depend, may diminish, and therefore it follows, if I am right, that the same cause which may increase the net revenue of the country, may at the same time render the population redundant, and deteriorate the condition of the labourer.
>
> (Ricardo 1821: 469)

However, Ricardo did not advocate resisting technological innovation because that would merely shift productive capacities abroad, causing even greater economic pain to domestic labourers.

John Maynard Keynes (2016: 325) defined *technological unemployment* as 'unemployment due to our discovery of means of economizing the use of labour outrunning the pace at which we can find new uses for labour'. The imbalanced relationship between capital and labour also fuelled the leading criticism of capitalism. Karl Marx opined that the capitalist system would destroy itself due to its inability to cope with technological advances. Marxism originated with observations of capitalism based on the First and Second Industrial Revolutions. These convinced Marx that mechanized manufacturing would enhance the power of capital owners over workers. In his view, the concentration of wealth would eventually reach such a level that disenfranchised workers would rise up and seize the means of production from capital owners.

Decoupling capital and labour

From the Second World War to the 1970s, a seemingly harmonious relationship existed between technological innovation and reward in the United States

(Temin 2018). As new technologies rendered previous manual tasks redundant, workers were tasked with more complex tasks that entailed higher-skilled and higher-wage work that was often safer, less physically challenging and more rewarding. Both productivity and wages increased, leading to a golden age for capitalism at a time when communism challenged its legitimacy. Ever since the 1980s, however, the heightened efficiency of new technologies contributed to the decoupling of productivity from labour, resulting in a greater concentration of wealth in the hands of the owners of capital (Brynjolfsson and McAfee 2013).

Beginning in the 1990s, the digital revolution rapidly restructured the economy and intensified productivity gains. Digital copies of products amplify the economies of scale as marginal costs drop to almost zero. Reproducing perfect copies with a simple copy-paste action inevitably affects the functioning of the market (Mason 2015: 163). Corporations, especially in the tech industry, become larger and more profitable, while requiring fewer employees. In 2017, Facebook had approximately 25,000 people on staff, while Ford Motor Company, with much lower revenue, employed approximately 202,000 (Statista 2018).

Technological development increased the return on investment for wealthy capital owners, while the working class stagnated or declined (Piketty 2015). Although corporate profits have surged since the financial crisis of 2008, wages as a percentage of GDP have fallen sharply (Brynjolfsson and McAfee 2013). Economic orthodoxies and the traditional rules of capitalism are falling apart. The trend towards greater automation after the global financial crisis created the phenomenon of a jobless recovery while markets demonstrated strong growth without an increase in wages. An unusual economic situation has arisen in which companies are reporting record growth even as median salaries decline and unemployment grows.

In the past, the skewed balance of power between capital and labour was corrected by organizing collective bargaining power. Labour unions mobilized vis-à-vis capital, achieving better working conditions through negotiations with the owners of capital. However, employees' ability to resist and balance the power of capital owners has become a thing of the past. The organization of labour today can have the opposite effect because automation offers an alternative to human labour. Demands for higher wages only create more incentives for corporations to increase automation, which is why high-wage countries will automate first. As a case in point, demands for a $15 minimum wage for fast-food workers in the United States only prompted corporations such as McDonald's to rapidly automate by introducing self-order kiosks. As efficiency increases and automation costs fall, the restaurant industry will also automate kitchens and delivery. The diminishing power of labour explains why the Philips Curve on the correlation between employment and wage levels no longer appears to apply.

Furthermore, the traditional full-time position is rapidly disappearing as programming jobs are either outsourced to a global pool of freelancers or replaced with temporary and contract jobs. The 'gig economy' is ushering in an era of neo-feudalism in which today's labourers become the new serfs. Automation could turn self-employment without benefits or job security into the new normal (Frey and Osborne 2015).

The capitalist system is based on the commodification of human labour, creating a simple equation in which labour equals money. Disruptive technologies that replace human labour or place downward pressure on wages create economic and social woes for workers (Brain 2013). Silicon Valley epitomizes the growing gulf between the new elites and the rest of the population: San Francisco and San Jose have the highest average salaries in the United States, but also the highest rate of homelessness. Economic liberalism empowered the individual and laid the foundation for political freedoms. However, the diminishing significance of human labourers reduces incentives for the state to consider the interests of private citizens. The result: special interests will set public policy. Ultimately, the growing concentration of wealth tends to decouple capitalism from democracy.

The great success of capitalism has been its ability to produce abundance and material well-being. The new challenge for capitalism is not to produce enough, but to provide enough jobs (Summers 2014). Automation enhances productivity and thereby makes products and services more affordable, but by marginalizing the need for human labour, it also causes wages to fall.

> Jobs are the primary mechanism through which income – and hence purchasing power – is distributed to the people who consume everything the economy produces. If at some point, machines are likely to permanently take over a great deal of the work now performed by human beings, then that will be a threat to the very foundation of our economic system.
>
> (Ford 2009: 5)

Capitalism is premised on workers selling their labour for wages, which they then use to purchase products in the marketplace. Without workers, the fundamental question is: Who will buy the unprecedented abundance of goods produced by machines? Automation increases productivity, thereby reducing prices, which offsets the stagnating salaries of workers. For many years, these two trends have balanced each other out. Now, however, salaries are stagnating or even dropping, and yet increasingly cheap products give people more for their money. The equation is nonetheless fragile because wealth is increasingly becoming concentrated in the hands of capital owners and ever-cheaper goods will not stop the disruptive influence of labourers' weakening position.

Creative destruction and permanent technological unemployment

Austrian Economist, Joseph Schumpeter (1942), coined the term 'creative destruction' in reference to how new technologies have a disruptive effect on society by eradicating former skillsets, professions and entire industries. Unlike Keynes, Schumpeter did not believe in the possibility of structural unemployment. He argued that new jobs would continuously replace old ones. When technologies advance slowly, workers gradually become re-educated and upgrade their skills. Ideally, the erosion of professions has a generational shift that allows workers to continue their jobs with dignity until retirement. By contrast, the rapid and disruptive technological developments of industrial revolutions create rapid and widespread creative destruction to the detriment of socio-economic and political stability.

The creative destruction caused by the First Industrial Revolution in eighteenth-century England gave birth to the Luddites, a radical countermovement of textile workers who, from 1811 to 1816, protested new technologies by destroying machineries such as cotton and woollen mills. Workers feared that the efficiency of mechanization technologies would make their skills and professions redundant. Rather than causing permanent mass unemployment, however, the new technologies freed up labour to be used in more productive areas, thereby elevating the material well-being of the population. The term 'Luddite' has since become a derogatory term to ridicule irrational fear of new technologies and modernity.

One might ask, however, whether the Luddites were expressing an irrational fear of technology or were actually 200 years ahead of their time. Many neo-Luddites of today are themselves leading scientists or technological innovators. Stephen Hawking and Elon Musk warned that AI and robotics could destroy humankind. Bill Gates called for making robots pay tax to slow down the process of automation and robotics, and as a means for mitigating the rapid and broad displacement of human workers. The Luddites were not categorically opposed to technology as they used machine tools. Their failed attempt to slow down the introduction of new technologies was motivated by the fact that many thousands of people had lost their jobs to the changes. The main lesson we take from the Luddite is that 'you can't stop technological progress'.

Even rudimentary digital services in transportation and housing, primarily Uber and Airbnb, have caused major disruptions to the taxi and hotel industries. Governments around the world have intervened to protect the taxi industry by restricting and curtailing the disruptions caused by Uber, Lyft and similar ride-hailing companies (Schwartz 2018). They are also seeking to restrict Airbnb and other holiday rental websites that are driving up rental costs and subsequently pushing locals out of their own cities. It appears, however, that the implementation of new transportation technologies can only be slowed down at best. The urban landscape is expected to shift rapidly as the ride apps first eliminate the taxi industry before going on to challenge the entire bus system (Schwartz 2018). This creates a dilemma: on the one hand, Luddites try to slow down the process of technological development, but on the other hand, states that are willing to accept the creative destruction and huge social burdens it entails gain a competitive advantage.

Creative destruction in the Fourth Industrial Revolution

Digitalization and automation have, for years, replaced human labour. Professions such as bank tellers, secretaries, travel agents, gas attendants and other low-skilled and repetitive jobs have largely become remnants of a bygone era. This disruptive process intensifies with the Fourth Industrial Revolution as more human skills are rendered uncompetitive by increasingly advanced automation, robotics and computers that carry gradually decreasing price tags. It is typically low-skilled and low-wage jobs that are automated. Most recently, cashiers, bookkeepers, clerks, assembly line workers, food prepares, retailers, passport controllers, call centre representatives and other professions have seen their jobs disappear to automation.

Advances in AI, cloud computing and IoT are augmenting the efficiency and widening the application of robotics. Now capable of performing more complex tasks with greater precision and efficiency and at a lower cost, robots are replacing factory workers, legal advisers, surgeons, journalists, drivers, bricklayers, fruit pickers, waiters, chefs and other cognitively demanding professions. Automation of cognitive tasks also eliminates mid-level and high-level jobs in finance, law and similar occupations at an accelerating rate. For the moment, online shopping is devastating only shopping malls and traditional brick-and-mortar stores across the United States, but what will occur when virtually every sector of the economy can reduce reliance on human workers?

The automation of business operations and supply chains are set to rapidly eliminate tens of millions of jobs. Various estimates indicate that between 30 and 50 per cent of the United States workforce is employed in professions considered to be at 'high risk' of being automated – a number that will increase as robotics develop new capabilities and its cost declines (Frey and Osborne 2013). However, automation often replaces several tasks, not entire professions. It is estimated that more than 60 per cent of occupations will have at least made 30 per cent of their activities automated (Chui, Manyika and Miremadi 2015: 21).

A report on automation found that most jobs would be lost in manufacturing, transportation and storage (PWC 2018). Technological unemployment will be more intense among low-income workers (Frey and Osborne 2013). Although automation is reshoring manufacturing back to developed states, robots will take most of those jobs and capital owners will capture the profits. Manufacturing jobs are going the way of agricultural work: it is estimated that approximately 59 per cent of all manufacturing activities can be automated (Chui, Manyika and Miremadi 2016). Although the automation of manufacturing pushed a redundant workforce to seek refuge in the lower-skilled and lower-wage retail and service industry, these jobs are also vulnerable to the growing capabilities of a robotic workforce. The millions of low-wage hirees in the fast food industry are set to be outperformed by machines. Besides cutting labour costs, robotics prepares the food more efficiently and hygienically (Chui, Manyika and Miremadi 2016). McDonald's introduced its first all-robot restaurant without human cashiers or cooks in Phoenix, Arizona. Amazon's e-commerce platform supported with drone deliveries will contribute to closing down even more shopping malls. Approximately one-third of US shopping malls are expected to go out of business in the next few years. The consequent drop in real estate prices and social depression will replicate the socio-economic crisis caused by the closures of factories across the rust belt.

Transportation and logistics will undergo unprecedented creative destruction. More complex cognitive tasks that require the coordination of multiple human senses are next in line to be automated. As an example, self-driving cars could eliminate 5 million jobs in the United States alone (Greenhouse 2016). It is estimated that approximately one out of seven jobs in the United States is linked to transportation to some degree (Grush and Niles 2018). Amazon has already demonstrated that robotic workers and drones can completely replace their human counterparts in warehouses and distribution centres. Amazon's fleet of

Kiva robots manages warehouses without human workers and process orders four times faster than humans can. Automating office work also happens at the expense of job security. For example, approximately 7 million Americans currently work in data entry alone, a repetitive and easily automated profession that will no longer require human labourers in the near future. In Japan, robotics has also made headway into construction with the development of a drywall robot. Companies that do not automate will be forced out of business. Thus, either way, those jobs will be lost.

The poorest members of society usually bear the greatest burden of creative destruction. The Obama Administration estimated that there is an 83 per cent chance that an American earning less than twenty dollars an hour will lose his/her job (Weller 2016). The fact that middle-class jobs are particularly vulnerable to automation has raised concerns of a coming 'job polarisation' in which workers gravitate towards either low-skilled/low-paying jobs or the highly skilled/high-paying jobs in demand by the tech industry.

Automation of the cognitive is also creating a bleak future for several highly skilled professions (Ford 2015). Wall Street is a prime example of how highly skilled and high-wage employees are made redundant because most trading is now done by computers. Because the finance industry is so highly digitalized and requires a huge amount of data collection, human workers are extremely vulnerable to replacement by machine learning. Software can rapidly process huge data sets to draw connections and learn by developing its own algorithms. As AI software continues to improve its own algorithms, the growing complexity of trade is becoming less comprehensible to human traders. Financial analysts, traders, order takers, asset managers, portfolio managers and other financial industry jobs are quickly being automated. Even the legal department that authorizes the validity of trades and swaps is automated. The finance industry is growing stronger but is predicted to lose up to 50 per cent of its employees within a decade. This bears similarities to the way wealth is becoming more concentrated in the leading tech corporations – that grow larger even as they shed employees (Baer 2016). With computing power increasing exponentially while the cost of that computing drops, the number of jobs vulnerable to automation only increases.

New jobs in the Fourth Industrial Revolution

Technological change has historically increased employment opportunities and wealth as new jobs replace the old. The Agricultural Revolution and the

First Industrial Revolution freed up excess labour and capital that were directed towards manufacturing in urban centres. Similarly, when bank teller positions were automated with the invention of the ATM, banks could afford to open more branches and hire more staff. Historical precedent indicates that mundane and repetitive professions become automated, and labourers move up the career ladder by acquiring more skills and utilizing new technologies. Is this old truth about creative destruction able to stand the test of time?

By the Third Industrial Revolution, the automation and offshoring of US manufacturing resulted in the excess workforce transitioning into low-skilled and low-wage jobs in the retail and service industries. Online banking has reduced the need for branch offices, while peer-to-peer lending platforms and banking without banks might eliminate the need for banks entirely. With increasingly more sophisticated skills required, it is unreasonable to expect that former McDonald's cashiers will become developers of AI and robotics. Lawrence Summers (2014) points out that 'there are more sectors losing jobs than creating jobs. And the general-purpose aspect of software technology means that even the industries and jobs that it creates are not forever'. Furthermore, new technologies alter the quality of work. For example, technologies that can track and monitor increase efficiency, also reducing the authority that workers have traditionally held in commercial activities (Holloway, Bear and Wilkinson 2014). Similarly, 3D printing reduces the flow of labour in the workplace (Birtchnell and Hoyle 2014).

The safest jobs are creative professions devoid of repetitive tasks and less vulnerable to machine learning, or jobs where human contact is important. New jobs are subsequently expected to emerge in healthcare, scientific and technical services and education (PWC 2018). An ageing population requires more services from health care workers, more skilled workers are needed to develop and service new technologies, and education is vital to preparing people for a changing world. In the past, people completed formal education by their mid-twenties and were prepared for a lifelong career. Now, however, the rapid technological changes will make most professions similar to the IT field in which education and the upgrading of skills never end.

Exceptions exist, however. AI programs write entire articles that cover sports, politics and business. Narrative science software collects a huge amount of data from a wide variety of sources, processes the information by choosing the most insightful and interesting information and then produces well-articulated articles indistinguishable from a human author. AI has also entered the artistic world by creating symphonies, paintings and other art.

While human-to-human contact is important for emotional support in healthcare, Japanese nursing homes and hospitals are already using robots to carry patients to their beds. Eliza, the robotic psychotherapist, demonstrated that people respond positively to personal and emotional interactions with machines. Pepper, a robot friend, can read its owner's emotional state and cheer him or her up by responding appropriately with a dance, game or funny gestures (Muoio 2016). In Japan, the healthcare industry increasingly uses robotic toys for cuddling and exercise. Machines can also replace human contact when people are unaware they are interacting with robots. Experiments demonstrate that it is becoming increasingly difficult for people to distinguish human from machine call centre operators. There are also instances in which people actually prefer to interact with machines than with people. Robot brothels are opening up around the world because clients are often more comfortable engaging with and experimenting with non-human prostitutes.

Political instability and ideological alternatives

The decoupling of capital from labour and the prospect of permanent technological unemployment will create demands for economic and political reforms. Capitalism has been a resilient economic system due to its ability to evolve. Yet, the success of capitalism has created ideological orthodoxies and is used as a justification for resisting change. The triumph of capitalism in the Cold War was expected to deliver a permanent ideological victory to the West, and this reduced the political appetite for reopening the ideological debate. The ability to resist change is, nonetheless, limited. The growing pressures on capitalism will require it to reform to prevent alternative ideologies from emerging in the vacuum. Although the Fourth Industrial Revolution was born out of capitalism, it will also increasingly incentivize alternatives to capitalism.

With previously thriving manufacturing towns succumbing to socio-economic calamity, the decline of the US manufacturing industry serves as a case study of what awaits other industries. When the jobs and money left, the drugs came in and anti-social behaviour flourished. National cohesion and political stability suffered as political elites and thriving cosmopolitan regions looked down on people who had failed to adapt to the new economy. The inability of political leaders to drive change and reform led to that change being foisted upon them by an electorate that rejected the political establishment itself and voted for populists and economic nationalists. Political and media elites who reject such election results, demonize populists and attempt to overturn elections and referendums, only target the symptoms rather than the disease. In fact, capitalism's own failures might lead to its collapse.

Governments have traditionally exercised greater responsibility for mitigating the effects of creative destruction. States often intervene in the market to protect existing jobs and ensure that workers retrain for highly skilled and high-wage labour. Managing the effects of creative destruction becomes an increasingly important and ongoing task because there will not be enough new jobs to replace those that disappear. The United States has pulled back from extreme economic inequality twice before – after the Gilded Age (1870s–1900) and the Roaring '20s – and yet the market power of large corporations is more intrusive today.

The failure of capitalism leads naturally to political instability. As the labour market demands for certain skills and professions dry up, the loss of incomes, the need to relocate and the loss of career-based social status lead to social disruptions. For young people not yet established in the job market, the lack of economic opportunities and social mobility elicits feelings of frustration and a lack of purpose. It also leads to higher crime rates and causes demographic disruption because young people wait longer to start families. Political radicalism proliferates because people with fewer vested interests in the status quo are more willing to shake up the system without offering any clear assurances about viable alternatives.

Inequalities will always exist, but the population in a meritocracy generally considers them acceptable. The American dream lay in the belief that social mobility would result from hard work. Material success became a virtue and wealth was seen as the outcome of hard work and intelligence. By contrast, poverty became an indicator of laziness and, possibly, stupidity. American capitalism was an especially well-functioning system because the inequalities were interpreted to mean that the wealthy should be emulated rather than reviled. This became the new system of values.

With new technologies undermining social mobility and concentrating the wealth in the hands of a few, the growing sentiment is that the deck has been stacked (Yang 2018: 97). The meritocratic incentive for upward mobility falters as wealth is delegitimized. In a society polarized by large wealth gaps, the affluent and privileged are deemed to have earned their wealth through exploitation and the poor are absolved of personal responsibility for self-improvement because their suffering is blamed on the higher-performing individuals. Once reasonable calls for the redistribution of wealth become radicalized due to this, victim complex and belligerence call for retribution against the wealthy. Although creative destruction caused by disruptive technologies is the principal cause of unemployment, political leaders have great incentives to place a disproportionate share of the blame for these problems on immigration and imports.

As a case in point, during a visit to the manufacturer Carrier in 2016, President-elect Trump promised assistance to prevent the company from offshoring its production. The effort was seemingly a gesture to the voters who had put him in the White House to reverse the decimation of US manufacturing. However, Carrier used that financial support to automate its factory and remain competitive. The company remained in the United States thanks to the taxpayers, but workers were laid off anyway. Politicians have strong incentives to blame the loss of jobs on offshoring and immigration: it is easier to invoke nationalist sentiments as a 'quick fix' to a pressing problem. Addressing permanent technological unemployment without having a clear solution or anyone to blame is not a winning platform for career politicians.

The rise of the super-rich corrupts democracy and society with the result that Marxist ideals are again attracting attention as a solution to the growing economic and social malaise. Marx and Engels believed that the deepening inequality and exploitation of the masses would provoke the people to seize the means of production and stage a revolution. However, the revolutionary approach was destructive and merely replaced the rule of an efficient capitalist class with the rule of inefficient and corrupt bureaucrats. Rather than overthrowing capitalism through revolution, it would have been preferable if the capitalist system had gradually shed its weaknesses and retained its strengths. Prior to the Bolshevik Revolution in 1917, the bourgeoisie class had been growing rapidly and workers had enjoyed a relatively stable income, suggesting that redistribution would have been sufficient to even out any excessive inequalities.

Redistribution

The polarization of society can be slowed down or reversed with government intervention that either redistributes wealth or re-educates the population towards highly skilled and high-wage work. Any debate on the growing inequality should be rooted in two simple facts: first, technologies that enhance productivity tend to exacerbate inequality because wealth concentrates in the hands of capital owners; second, extreme economic inequality causes social and political instability. A debate on how and to what extent wealth should be redistributed is therefore in the common interest because nobody benefits from the destabilization of society. Unless we reach common ground, radical and polarizing alternatives will fill the vacuum. Reforming capitalism can range from taking certain institutions, such as education, out of the market, restoring competition to markets ruled by powerful monopolies, shifting the tax burden from labour to capital, or creating tax incentives for companies to share profits with workers (Pearlstein 2018).

It is imperative that we find a suitable format for the redistribution wealth that has become concentrated by the growing role of capital-intensive technologies. Authorizing bureaucrats to redistribute wealth can produce the opposite result because they are more likely to be influenced by powerful interest groups than by poor people. Energy corporations and tech giants lobby politicians to transfer wealth upwards rather than to the poor. The 2008 financial crisis was detrimental to the United States: it deepened inequalities that were viewed as the result of theft rather than merit. The crisis placed a number of major banks in jeopardy. In a true capitalist system, these banks would have been allowed to fail. Instead, politicians with the authority to redistribute wealth bailed out the banks with taxpayer money in what became the world's largest transfer of wealth from the middle class to the super-rich. All political conversations on the subject should recognize that such inequality produces political instability and that some form of redistribution is required to avoid it.

Capitalism facilitates human beings' propensity for competition and organizing in dominance hierarchies, thus encouraging innovation, efficiency and development. The call for redistribution should not be confused with holding illusions about radical equity. People have different productive capacities as shown by the Pareto principle that holds that 80 per cent of the effect comes from 20 per cent of the causes. Human beings perform unequally and incentives for work and efficiency should not be removed. The state should counter the concentration of wealth and mitigate the unfavourable social effects of capitalism. It is a caricature of the political right and left to suggest that the market is either the tool to fix everything or an instrument of oppression.

Egalitarianism is innate: humans instinctively oppose and reverse dominance hierarchies. The evolutionary origins can be traced back to primates banding together to take down the alpha male if he became too aggressive and authoritarian (Boehm 2009). Therefore, a government, as well as an individual leader, derives its authority not only by virtue of its strength and dominance, but also by its ability to demonstrate generosity and empathy (Boehm 2009). Even Adam Smith (2006: 58) recognized that private property could create social tensions and displacement, and that economic gain could corrupt our moral sentiments due to 'the disposition to admire, and almost worship, the rich and powerful'. Adam Smith argued that the 'hidden hand' of the market reduced the need for central planning, although he did not argue that the complete self-regulation of markets would always deliver social goods (Norman 2018). The notion that the CEO of a corporation should make several hundred times more than the average wage of the company was considered radical until the Reaganism and Thatcherism of the 1980s.

Redistribution has two central components: extracting resources from the population and redistributing them. Where is the money coming from and how can it be redistributed? The challenge is to ensure that the redistribution of wealth goes from the rich to the poor without undermining the benefits of capitalism. For example, 'free' university tuition can easily become a major wealth transfer from the poor to the middle class and the rich. University degrees have a high return on investment by creating higher salaries. Offering free university tuition means that people who did not attend university and will make much less money will have to subsidize the university degrees for those who will make more. Levying those taxes solely against the rich would create strong incentives to move capital and resources abroad out of simple self-interest. However, the lack of affordable education would impede social mobility and make the population less prepared for the drastic economic and societal changes caused by the Fourth Industrial Revolution. Empowering the population to adapt to a new economy requires the democratization of knowledge and affordable education (Peters 2013). This requires reversing the dangerous trend, especially in the United States, towards increasingly expensive education that does not prepare students for the professions of the future. If, as a result, the covenant between higher education and jobs begins to break, it would inhibit the ability of higher education to provide social mobility. Either way, changes will occur so rapidly in the Fourth Industrial Revolution that workers will be unable to fully adapt, regardless of how much education and training are available (Chace 2016).

Taxing companies that embrace automation and imposing tariffs to discourage companies from offshoring production is a means for collecting money for redistribution. These companies already enjoy the benefits of increased productivity without having to pay wages and benefits to their robots (Ford 2009). Bill Gates proposed placing a tax on robots and South Korea became the first country to do so, thereby shifting the tax burden and slowing down automation to mitigate the effects of creative destruction. However, taxing robots creates legislative challenges in terms of defining and quantifying automation and robotics. Alternatively, a temporary and transitional solution could be to end the taxation of labour, which is increasingly under pressure from automation. However, taxing robots or ending the tax on human labour slows down the incentives for companies to automate and become more productive. Second, who should be subsidized and how? Providing the unemployed with monthly payments as assistance rarely helps and instead creates a pernicious dependency. Creating incentives for some people to free ride while others must work leads to political opposition against an unfair system.

Competition could be restored to the market by using new technologies to decentralize market forces. Capitalism could also evolve from the bottom up because the prospect of decentralization enables people to reassert their autonomy and 'seize the means of production'. For example, a sharing economy makes it possible for people to rent out their cars or apartments at the expense of hotels and car rental agencies (Gibson-Graham 2008). Innovations such as the 3D printer could also stimulate mass differentiation by a growing number of individuals. Stiegler (2018) refers to the expansion of an 'economy of contribution' that allows people to be productive through innovative differentiation as opposed to passive employment. Because less fixed capital is needed to establish a business in the digital age, the potential for decentralizing production increases. Much in the same way that email has largely replaced 'snail mail', digital platforms are making it possible to do banking without banks.

Should economic activities be moved out of the market or into the market? One solution is to gradually expand the non-market activities of the economy. For example, Estonia provides free Internet to its citizens as a basic human right and will also make public transportation free, as Luxemburg has already done. Priority could be given to institutions such as universities and to fields such as journalism that have seen their intended functions corrupted by market forces. A prime example of destructive economic determinism was the Obama Administration's proposal to subsidize universities based on the salaries of their graduates. Journalism is similarly abandoning responsible reporting in favour of pushing the agenda of special interests or relying on sensationalist click-baiting stories. Money in politics, most noticeably the Super-PACs in the United States, has further weakened the ability of voters to influence policy. The goal is to incentivize the use of public transportation and democratize education, two of the main expenses for the poorest members of society, yet without empowering bureaucrats to redistribute wealth.

Instead of pulling economic activities out of the market, more societal activities could enter the market place to create jobs. Currently, unpaid jobs such as childcare, cooking, cleaning and gardening could also be offered on the market (Mankiya et al. 2017). The state could also facilitate expansion of the marketplace by, for example, rewarding volunteering and other activities that benefit society. Andrew Yang (2018), a US presidential candidate in 2020, suggests that the state could provide 'Digital Social Credits' as a reward for people who serve the community. Expanding the role of the market would, however, condition people's standard of living on credit points earned through state-sanctioned behaviours. This could be a slippery slope towards empowering the state with social engineering such as that in China, where the social credit system allows the state to interfere in the most private aspects of people's lives.

Universal basic income

Universal basic income (UBI) is a system whereby every person receives a regular payment to cover basic expenses. UBI resolves some of the immediate pragmatic problems associated with unemployment, but it could also undermine the work ethic and fuel tensions in class relations. The economic security the UBI system provides could either reduce the incentive for people to pursue innovative and productive industry or embolden them to take greater risks to develop new industries. While great costs could be associated with UBI, a study by the Roosevelt Institute estimates that UBI in the United States could have a positive effect on the economy by adding $2.5 trillion to GDP over eight years.

Innovative business leaders such as Elon Musk and Richard Branson have advocated UBI as a necessity for addressing the challenges of technological unemployment (Clifford 2018). Countries as diverse as Finland, the Netherlands, Spain, the United States and Kenya have experimented with UBI. This approach has also been implemented. Alaska has practised a sort of UBI since the 1980s, making a set payment to each citizen for the right to extract the state's energy resources. The extent to which UBI is deemed successful depends on which dependent variable is measured. Although there has only been limited research on UBI, the results indicate it has little if any effect on employment, but does increase measures of happiness (Yang 2018). The large-scale implementation of UBI would face significant cultural opposition, especially in the United States where the virtue of personal responsibility is treasured and Calvinism is still strong.

The simplistic ideological binary of either free market capitalism or socialism distracts from a rational debate about redistribution, and it obscures that the ideas behind UBI have been advocated from the political left to the right. UBI will inevitably influence the relationship between the state and the citizen. It might develop into a digital social credit system that rewards the most socially desirable behaviours, or else be used to reduce the intrusive influence of the state in private life. In the absence of economic freedom, the state could assert a totalitarian pedagogic role to promote good citizenship.

Friedrich Hayek (1979: 54–5), the legendary supporter of the free market, argued that when traditional societal structures fail to provide a safety net, the responsibility of the state should be to protect the most vulnerable in society:

> A society that has reached a certain level of wealth can afford to provide for all. The assurances of a certain minimum income for everyone, or a sort of floor below which nobody need fall even when he is unable to provide for himself, appears not only to be wholly legitimate protection against a risk common to all, but a necessary part of the Great Society.

Milton Friedman, the outspoken proponent and symbol of free market capitalism, was also an advocate of universal basic income. Friedman referred to basic income as 'negative income tax' or 'guaranteed income', which he argued was firmly grounded in principles of small government and market principles (Friedman 2009). Negative income tax can replace the unnecessary, inefficient and growing bureaucracy of anti-poverty programs that function poorly for redistribution. Negative income tax also empowers people as opposed to traditional anti-poverty programs that tell the poor how the money can be spent, instilling feelings of social humiliation and turning the poor into passive recipients submissive to the state (Friedman 2009). Furthermore, negative income tax would increase social mobility by reversing the 'welfare trap'. Taking up employment is not ideal for low-wage workers if welfare payments are the same or higher than salaries. In contrast, guaranteed income would not be sacrificed by becoming employed. Without the need to work for the most basic living income and thereby risk food and a roof over their heads, a significant segment of society would likely use the flexibility to take a risk on entrepreneurship, develop their own skills, increase their education, accept an internship, work for charities, provide additional care for children or parents, or pursue idealistic goals.

Conclusion

The pretence that we have free markets is becoming increasingly hollow because tech giants are establishing monopolistic positions, capital is decoupling from labour, creative destruction is causing socio-economic devastation to entire regions, and central banks around the world print money at an unprecedented rate to avoid painful market corrections. Capitalism appears to be failing, and the situation will soon get much more complicated if millions of people become unemployed and fall into permanent technological unemployment. Governments can be tasked to develop more social programs, but much broader reforms are needed. Furthermore, instead of propping up an increasingly vulnerable and disenfranchised working class, governments empowered with redistribution might transfer much of the wealth from the middle class to large corporations.

The disruption to free market capitalism presents both opportunities and risks. Although we can address shortcomings in the system, states have no clearly explored alternatives to offer. States will need to intervene in the economy as increasingly powerful digital corporations seize the means of production and new technologies such as genetic manipulation are commercialized. The ramifications of greater state involvement into the domestic economy are fraught with risks. The first industrial revolutions provided incentives for economic liberalism that also nurtured political liberalism. The Fourth Industrial Revolution could create an economy driven by technicians and bureaucrats, undermining individual freedoms. Friedman's concept of negative income tax addresses these problems by redistributing wealth without discarding the free market and without creating a larger and more intrusive government.

Capitalism has survived since the First Industrial Revolution due to its ability to reform and adapt. However, today's political polarization presents an existential threat to capitalism because it undermines the reforms necessary for adapting to current and future technologies. On the far left, advocates of socialism and communism threaten to abandon capitalism altogether, throwing out the baby with the bathwater. On the far right, staunch ideological support in favour of capitalism overlooks the fact that some of the greatest capitalist thinkers acknowledged the need for reform. David Ricardo and John Maynard Keynes recognized that increased productivity from technological developments might not benefit labourers; Adam Smith argued that wealth creation can corrupt individuals and institutions and fuels social tensions, and Friedrich Hayek and Milton Friedman advocated redistribution as a moral imperative for preserving political stability. Capitalism's success has radicalized its contemporary proponents to the point that they neglect the mechanisms designed to keep it running smoothly. Thus, the 'victory of capitalism' might ultimately rob it of its ability to reform and consign it to failure.

7

The great societal transformation:
Geoeconomics without Gemeinschaft?

Introduction

Polanyi (1944) argued in *The Great Transformation* that the Industrial Revolution and the subsequent introduction of a market economy caused social upheaval as economic activity was 'disembedded' from non-economic institutions of society. Technological advances disrupt the domestic organization of society, forcing states to mobilize their resources to maintain social cohesion. Ever since the First Industrial Revolution, technologies have helped create increasingly rational, calculative and complex societies. Nevertheless, our evolutionary biology is such that people tend to gravitate towards smaller, tribal communities based on kinship.

The rationality of mankind tends to be highly overrated, which leads to flawed expectations about the ability to adapt to new technologies. For tens of thousands of years, humans and their predecessors survived by virtue of highly developed instincts, without what we now refer to as 'rationality' and 'awareness'. The duality of man, defined by a schism between the rational and the instinctive, has been a central focus of religion and philosophy for thousands of years. This was defined by Plato as the struggle between the soul and the intellect. A dominant instinct has been to organize in homogenous groups. This urge to form into groups has been harnessed by nationalism and still serves as the foundation for meaning, security and even a sense of immortality by reproducing a distinctive group. The Industrial Revolution revived philosophy about the condition of human nature as people struggled to live and find meaning in industrial society. The dilemma of modernization is that human beings gravitate towards larger and more complex societies based on rationality, while concurrently being dependent on the smaller community based on interpersonal connections that appeal to the innate and instinctive in human nature.

The Fourth Industrial Revolution promises unprecedented opportunities, yet pursuing these opportunities requires the destruction of our existing societal arrangements. Technological innovations change the social, economic, political and cultural landscape so rapidly that it becomes difficult to get one's bearing in the resulting chaos. The balance between preserving the past and adapting to the future diminishes. Would the Industrial Revolution deliver a utopian future of leisure, freedom from poverty and devotion to intellectual and artistic development – or a dystopian future in which people are stripped of purpose and meaning and social stratification and debt increase? Do human beings thrive under less work and more rights, or is purpose found in struggles and responsibilities? It would seem that by automating the cognitive and outsourcing repetitive work to machines in order to improve productivity and replace hard work with leisure, we would make the world a better place. However, what are the social disruptions in a time when the structures of society and the meaning of life are often equated to work? What happens to our economically deterministic societies that measure all value in dollars when human labour cedes its competitiveness to machines? Will we rediscover some part of our pre-First Industrial Revolution humanity or will we be plagued by mass unemployment? Will human labour become a commodity that drops in value much as horsepower once did? The only certainty is that contemporary society will perish and be replaced by another.

This chapter first explores creative destruction as a societal phenomenon. Science and technology render former societal structures and sources of morality obsolete. Failure to reinvent societal structures that maintain a connection with people's instinctive impulses will lead to nihilism and decay. Second, it is argued that the excessive focus on the economic utility of technology distracts from its societal implications. Technology is not inherently good or bad and its use must be reconciled with human nature. Third, it is argued that the Fourth Industrial Revolution might have the tools to bridge Gemeinschaft with Gesellschaft and to establish benevolent frontiers as a remedy for industrial disruption to society. The Fourth Industrial Revolution will create powerful impulses to venture into space as a frontier to replenish the sense of meaning to offset social disruptions and traditional sources of purpose. Last, it is argued that geoeconomic rivalry between states is greatly influenced by societal stability. Revamping the morality, values and organization of society is required for a state to operate as a unitary actor. Otherwise, priorities in international affairs will polarize between the pragmatic pursuit of rational and calculative geoeconomic interests and the disenfranchised population that defines its interests in cultural and spiritual terms. It is concluded that great powers must also use technologies to rejuvenate Gemeinschaft and the people's instinctive traits in order to compete geoeconomically as a unitary and rational actor.

The societal aspect of creative destruction

Pablo Picasso opined that 'every act of creation is first of all an act of destruction'. The Beatles' famous song *Revolution* contains the pacifist statement: 'But when you talk about destruction, don't you know that you can count me out?' – which is a bit ironic given that all revolutions involve destruction. Today's creative destruction is no different. In political and industrial revolutions, destruction is an intrinsic part of creation because the existing system must be taken apart to give way to the new. The manner in which it is destroyed influences the nature of the new system that replaces it. This is why it is necessary to examine the disruption of society in detail.

Technological development presents a linear evolution of human knowledge that has outpaced our biological evolution. Although new technologies have rendered former societal structures obsolete, the rational mind is not capable of shedding innate and irrational traits. Mankind developed primordial instincts over tens of thousands of years to survive in nature and cannot replace them completely with rational processes that developed only relatively recently. Instincts are biologically entrenched in the nervous system and brain to reward 'correct' behaviours with a sense of security and meaning, and to punish deviations with feelings of discomfort, insecurity and nihilism.

Should technologies liberate us from the traditions of the past or connect us more closely with innate impulses? Productive forces increasingly come into conflict with the organization of society. Thomas Paine had been adamant about rejecting the power of tradition, Gilbert Keith Chesterton characterized traditions as democracy for the dead, and John Stuart Mill (1869: 65) referred to 'the despotism of custom' as a limitation on human advancement. In the spirit of revolutionary movements that deconstruct the past, Marx (1971: 245) similarly argued: 'The tradition of all dead generations weighs like an alp on the brains of the living'. By contrast, Edmund Burke championed the virtues of continuity and tradition as a counterweight to destructive revolutionary movements that would destroy society.

The struggle to reinvent a civilization increasingly dominated by machines was at the centre of nineteenth-century European philosophy. Intellectuals recognized that industrialization had revealed and exacerbated the duality of man. The schism in human nature resulted from having been confined to nature and a society based on instinct for thousands of years, and then being abruptly forced to live according to rationality and calculative considerations that ran counter to those instincts. Philosophy, therefore, focused on the competing impulses towards the traditional versus the modern, the organic versus the mechanical, the instinctive versus the rational, the distinctive versus the universal, the past versus the future and the soul versus the intellect. To some extent, these ideas built on those of Plato, who posited that Man must balance two orders – the internal and instinctive order of the soul and the external and calculative order of the commonwealth.

Creative destruction and its remedies focus primarily on economics. However, work is also a source of dignity, morality and meaning. Creative destruction makes it necessary for political leaders to address social issues beyond the economic implications of job loss, and this requires a philosophical understanding of purpose. Technological innovations and industrialization impose a reorganization of society that goes against human nature. Schumpeter's creative destruction as an economic concept was largely founded on the philosophy of Friedrich Nietzsche (Santarelli and Pesciarelli 1990). It is not clear whether Schumpeter borrowed the concept directly from Nietzsche or indirectly through the economic ideas of Werner Sombart (1913: 207), who based his writing directly on the ideas of Nietzsche. Either way, the economic principle is closely tied to a philosophical understanding of human nature, society and the source of meaning.

Nietzsche (1968: 23) argued that the creator is also the breaker of values and laws, because the destruction of the old must precede the creation of the new. The creator must, therefore, be conscious of the old and prepared to destroy it so that the new can replace it (Nietzsche 1968: 64). Conversely, reluctance to let go of the past and destroy it leads to stagnation and decay because the old eventually dissipates its energy and withers away. But, destruction itself does not automatically lead to creation. Destroying the past without creating a future is the goal of nihilists and anarchists who strive to dismantle structures altogether. What replaces the old? A common misunderstanding about modernization is that it entails eviscerating and transcending the past. Instead, modernization requires that the new build on the old, in much the same that generational continuity and change are facilitated by the ageing father passing on his legacy and traditions to the son.

Nietzsche's embrace of creative destruction in Europe did not entail replacing European culture with something completely different and superior. Rather, it was the stagnant and decadent aspects of European culture that had to die to allow the culture to renew its foundations by creating something new that conformed with contemporary realities. Jung (2014) similarly argued in 'The Spiritual Problem of Modern Man' that the new must develop in profound familiarity with the past. He cautioned that modernization often displays 'ineradicable aversion to traditional opinions and inherited truths'. Jung (2014) feared that technology would estrange Man from his individual consciousness, usefulness and instincts.

Nietzsche (1968: 23) himself appears to have borrowed the concept of creative destruction from ancient religious and philosophical thought. Nietzsche (1968: 64) argued that 'You must wish to consume yourself in your own flame: how could you wish to become new unless you had first become ashes!' This statement resembles the Phoenix of Greek mythology, a long-lived bird that, at the end of its life, builds a nest and sets it on fire to cleanse itself of weaknesses and decadence, and then is reborn out of the ashes stronger and more vibrant. The Phoenix also became a symbol of early Christianity through the analogy of Christ's death and resurrection as a prerequisite for the renewal of humanity. The idea that creation and destruction are contradictory, yet mutually dependent, is also found in eastern philosophies. Vishnu, the preserver, ensures stability, but can only coexist with Shiva, the destroyer, who incites change. Similarly, the Chinese philosophy of yin and yang describes the interdependence of the contradictory forces in human nature. In other words, stability demands change as the old becomes stagnant and decays.

Technology and the death of Gemeinschaft

Ferdinand Tönnies (1957 [1887]) developed a succinct social theory to explain the social tensions caused by industrialization. Tönnies distinguished between community (Gemeinschaft) and society (Gesellschaft) as sociological categories. Individuals instinctively gravitate towards small, traditional communities or Gemeinschaft that are unified by social capital and trust based on common traditions, affinities and kinship. Concurrently, the individual also gravitates towards larger and more complex societies or Gesellschaft that are rational and calculative. These two contradictory impulses must be balanced to maintain societal stability. Otherwise, as society advances it imperils the community, sparking a counteraction. Historically, creative destruction in pursuit of a more complex and advanced society has undermined community and created a counter-gravitational pull towards nostalgia, tradition and spiritual pursuits. The ability of decision-makers to act rationally and calculatedly – to maximize power and security in accordance with the logic of the neorealist balance of power – largely depends on internal cohesion to perform as a unitary actor. This, in turn, is contingent upon a sound understanding of the irrational and primordial nature of Man as recognized in classical realism.

Both the praise and criticism of capitalism have largely remained unchanged since humans first erected enclosures around plots of land. This laid the foundation for modernizing agriculture and freeing up the labour needed to industrialize. Enclosures led to the introduction of land rights and the abolishment of common rights, causing societal displacements and the formation of new hierarchical power structures. The wealthy appropriated public land while the landless working class lost its autonomy and had to rely on selling its labour in the marketplace to survive (Thirsk 1967). The development of a market economy in England led to the state delegating the governance of Game Laws to the aristocracy, who used them to force the common people into the labour market (Perelman 2012: 55). The role of the state expanded to ensure that society did not become subjugated completely to market forces due to the economic and social disruptions. The strong state from the feudal era had provided some restrictions to unfettered market forces and 'England withstood without grave damage the calamity of the enclosures' because the state had managed to 'slow down the process of economic improvement until it became socially bearable' (Polanyi 1944: 38).

Mechanization entirely reorganized society: labour itself took on new meaning, communities and traditions were torn apart, and new ideologies transformed the relationship between the individual, corporation and state. Prior to the First Industrial Revolution, economies were anchored firmly within traditional communities where commercial interactions were based on social obligations and interpersonal connections. Because the means of production were inefficient, people had to work long hours in demanding physical labour. Yet, farmers enjoyed autonomy inasmuch as they owned the capital – their land. Community, more than career or material values, defined identity, while the lack of organized work structures also made it a custom to mix work with play (Cross 1990). The distinction between work and fun/play was more obscured prior to the First Industrial Revolution. Since then, work and fun have become two separate pursuits in an effort to prepare young people for adulthood. The First Industrial Revolution turned autonomous farmers into factory employees. The reorganization of labour also divided families because transitioning from farms to factories meant that family members were separated physically for most of the working day (Cross 1990). Furthermore, technologies such as the railway and telegraph, organized by complex economic structures, were undermining people's ability to preserve traditions as the basis for stability and 'enduring characters' for society (Nietzsche 1967: 65).

The Industrial Revolution elevated the potential of humanity and eventually brought an unprecedented creation of wealth. Yet, the Industrial Revolution also inspired an old and dangerous idea – that the problems of humanity could be solved with unlimited material wealth. The First Industrial Revolution is commonly viewed from the economic perspective, while less focus has been devoted to its social ramifications. The literature of Charles Dickens and others reflected concerns about the destabilizing effects of technologies such as the railway and the effect of machinery on working-class labourers. Intellectuals and authors in Victorian Britain widely described technology as 'de-humanising'. The Luddites had not acted solely out of fears for the loss of skillsets and income, but also in response to the perceived challenge to moral values. The forceful push to transform an agricultural society into a labour market resulted in 'the wholesale destruction of the traditional fabric of society' (Polanyi 1944: 81). The following passage vividly describes how this affected communities:

> The fabric of society was being disrupted; desolate villages and the ruins of human dwellings testified to the fierceness with which the revolution raged, endangering the defences of the country, wasting its towns, decimating its population, turning its overburdened soil into dust, harassing its people and turning them from decent husbandmen into a mob of beggars and thieves.
>
> (Polanyi 1944: 37)

The reigning idea that markets were self-regulating caused radical societal changes. Technology and free-market forces produced a destructive dislocation of people from their communities:

> What 'satanic mill' ground men into masses? How much was caused by the new physical conditions? How much by the economic dependencies, operating under the new conditions? And what was the mechanism through which the old social tissue was destroyed and a new integration of man and nature so unsuccessfully attempted?
>
> (Polanyi 1944: 35)

Max Weber (1924: 413–14) later cautioned that the rational calculations of industrialized society deprive people of their humanity because it 'reduces every worker to a cog in this [bureaucratic] machine and, seeing himself in this light, he will merely ask how to transform himself from a little to a somewhat bigger cog' – a condition that eventually 'drives us to despair'.

The industrialized free-market economy represented a break with the traditional organization of human society. The market was not organized naturally: people instinctively resisted it and 'the history of nineteenth-century civilization consisted largely in attempts to protect society against the ravages of such mechanism' (Polanyi 1944: 42). The commodification of everything sacred had a devastating effect on social order and human relations. This spurred a dialectical process from which new ideologies advocating protectionism emerged. Industrial market society gave rise to two contradictory movements – one towards a self-regulating market that would maximize efficiency and a countermovement that resisted market forces disruptive to society (Polanyi 1944: 136). Stability depends on finding a balance between these two opposing impulses because a radical shift in either direction would eventually prove destructive.

It was commonly feared that the technologies of the industrial revolution had removed people from their natural environment and caused societies to become weak and decadent. The Industrial Revolution was seen as either having liberated mankind from nature or enslaved it to technology (Cooper 1995). Heidegger (2010 [1927]) depicted modern industrial society as tyrannical inasmuch as it inhibits people's ability to interact directly with pristine nature. In the effort to capture what had been lost, Heidegger's philosophy was used as justification for supporting the malignant politics of the National Socialist Party.

Enlisting technological development solely to make material progress would undermine society and civilization itself. Osvald Spengler (1921) viewed Western civilization as having exhausted itself and as in decay unless it could find a means to shed its decadent aspects and renew itself. Spengler's principal argument was that a civilization that outgrows its own culture by failing to reproduce the past will eventually wither away like a tree without roots. Giambattista Vico (2002 [1725]) argued that civilizational decay begins when the modern and rational starts to displace the imaginative and spiritual. Brooks Adams (1897) and Konstantin Leontiev (2014 [1885]) were similarly concerned about complex society eroding the social capital that keeps societies intact and in harmony. Pitirim Sorokin (1941) similarly viewed increasingly rational and material society as being in direct conflict with the spirituality and culture that sustained civilization. Sorokin cautioned that progress results from taking the middle path. Burckhardt (2010 [1878]) depicted the Renaissance and modernity as having pernicious features, with culture becoming a commodity and people subsequently losing connection with their past. The excesses of the Enlightenment and Renaissance subsequently gave birth to the Counter-Enlightenment movement and Romanticism.

Capitalism's inability to address these social disruptions opened up the door to radical alternatives. Already by the early eighteenth century, continental Europeans admired the agricultural advances in England but were concerned about the political and social consequences of urbanization and structural change (O'Brien 2017: 5). Across the Atlantic, Thomas Jefferson sought to avoid the moral decadence of Western European manufacturing societies. Concerns about the moral implications of unfettered trade continued all the way to Theodore Roosevelt, who wrote in 1895: 'Thank God I am not a free-trader. In this country pernicious indulgence in the doctrine of free trade seems inevitably to produce fatty degeneration of the moral fibre' (Eckes 1999: 30). In pre-communist Russia, there were similar political forces seeking to chart a future of social conservatism.

By the early twentieth century, the influence of technology on the contentious relationship between capital and labour had culminated in three modern ideologies: fascism, communism and liberalism. As argued by Polanyi, the push towards free-market capitalism had created an ideological counterbalance. Hitler, Mussolini and Stalin were the monsters that emerged in response to free-market capitalism: 'Fascism, like socialism, was rooted in a market society that refused to function' (Polanyi 1944: 239). Luttwak (1993) similarly predicted in the early 1990s that 'Fascism is the wave of the future', arguing that turbocharged globalization would eventually be countered by political forces committed to enhancing individual economic security and to restraining its destructive consequences to the social fabric of communities.

Meaning after labour: Humanity as a bored and neurotic housewife

Automated labour promises to liberate mankind from its history of physical struggle. Yet, to survive through the centuries, human evolution has developed instincts that reward struggle with a sense of meaning. Mankind's effort to obtain greater freedom from labour causes a dilemma because purpose is found primarily in taking on responsibilities, which derives from the taking care of the family or through labour. Modern society is under pressure because morality itself is shifting from a focus on personal responsibilities to individual rights – for example, from the responsibility of raising one's child to the right of terminating a pregnancy. Freeing humanity from both physical struggle and responsibility for others produces a dangerous combination of nihilism and narcissism that weakens contemporary society.

John Maynard Keynes also recognized that since economics and the struggle for subsistence had always been the primary struggle, the evolutionary biology of the human race had developed our impulses and instincts accordingly. Mankind should be careful to liberate itself from labour, he felt, because 'if the economic problem is solved, mankind will be deprived of its traditional purpose'. Keynes (2016: 327) cautioned that if technology and automation eliminated the need for labour, mankind might experience a nervous breakdown similar to that of a wealthy housewife without purpose:

> We already have a little experience of what I mean – a nervous breakdown of the sort which is already common enough in England and the United States amongst the wives of the well-to-do classes, unfortunate women, many of them, who have been deprived by their wealth of their traditional tasks and occupations – who cannot find it sufficiently amusing, when deprived of the spur of economic necessity, to cook and clean and mend, yet are quite unable to find anything more amusing.

It is therefore not enough to offset permanent unemployment with universal basic income because the resultant lack of meaning would also need to be addressed. Marx's 'alienation' or spiritual crisis postulated that human beings suffer without autonomy over their labour and without the ability to shape the world around them. The workplace and its struggles are an important source of meaning and it can safely be predicted that technological unemployment would have consequences beyond the attendant economic struggles. People will fall into depression, seek escape from their malaise with new technologies such as virtual reality entertainment, or seek out radical movements. Gore (2013: 367) identified a 'resurgence of fundamentalism' due to 'a spiritual crisis in modern civilization that seems to be based on emptiness at its centre and the absence of a larger spiritual purpose'. It has been found that 20 per cent of Americans who have been unemployed for more than a year are likely to suffer from depression, which is twice the rate for their working counterparts (Crabtree 2014). A check in the mail is unlikely to resolve this problem. As wealth increases, mental health declines. In 2009, the World Mental Health survey reported that more than one-fifth of Americans suffer from depression, one-third have an anxiety disorder and almost one-half exhibit symptoms of mental disorder (Kessler et al. 2009).

As a neurologist, psychiatrist and Holocaust survivor who was able to find meaning in adversity and suffering, Viktor Frankl (1992: 143) concluded:

> What man actually needs is not a tensionless state but rather the striving and struggling for some goal worthy of him. What he needs is not the discharge of tension at any cost, but the call of a potential meaning waiting to be fulfilled by him ... Without meaning, people fill the void with hedonistic pleasures, power, materialism, hatred, boredom, or neurotic obsessions and compulsions.

Dostoyevsky (2009 [1864]: 21) also posited that if Man liberates himself from struggle and establishes utopia, he would soon destroy it to rediscover his own humanity in the chaos:

> Reason is an excellent thing, there's no disputing that, but reason is nothing but reason and satisfies only the rational side of man's nature ... Even if man really were nothing but a piano key, even if this were proved to him by natural science and mathematics, even then he would not become reasonable, but would purposely do something perverse out of simple ingratitude, simply to win his point ... then, after all, perhaps only by his curse will he attain his object, that is, really convince himself that he is a man and not a piano key! If you say that all this, too, can be calculated and tabulated ... then man would purposely go mad in order to be rid of reason and win his point.

Success and victory tend to be followed by decadence because materialism and consumption become substitutes for meaning and happiness (Toynbee 1946).

Reconciling the utility of technology with human nature

Technology enables us to communicate with the entire world through the click of a button and to collect and retrieve vast amounts of information. In addition, artificial intelligence holds the promise of generating new knowledge that human beings would not always fully comprehend. Yet, by what purposes are these powerful technologies informed? Is the role of technology becoming so omnipresent that it defines its own purpose and the world itself? Whereas the Enlightenment used technology to spread philosophical ideas about humanity, reason and the world, that process appears to have reversed, with dominating technology now in search of a purpose and a guiding philosophy (Kissinger 2018).

Technology is neither inherently good nor bad: its nature depends on its purpose (Spengler 1932). Although economic growth is the principal driving force for developing new technologies, Spengler's concerns about the excessive focus on the economic utility of new technologies warrant further examination. Spengler (1932: 7) cautioned that the 'devastating shallowness' of English materialism resulted in the failure to appreciate the depth of the changes brought about by technology because the achievements of humanity and the utility of technology were defined solely by 'labour saving and amusement-making. Of the soul, not one word'. Similarly, Carl Schmitt's criticism of liberalism focused on its excessive rational and calculative treatment of economics and technology, prioritized above the traditional, cultural and sacred that instil value (McCormick 1999). More recently, Mahatma Gandhi similarly identified 'science without humanity' as one of the seven deadly sins.

The Fourth Industrial Revolution could be a disaster for societies and humanity if new technologies are aimed solely at reducing labour costs and increasing market efficiency. Economically deterministic societies allow economic interests to define their technology, culture, politics and intellectual endeavours. The Greek tragedies, Byron's plays, Shakespeare's sonnets and the novels of Dostoevsky and Goethe are losing their relevance in society due to their inability to generate profits. We have gradually shifted from being states with economies to being economies with states, where all areas of society are assessed by their economic utility. This degrades faith, the family and tradition, all of which are seen as having less utility and attractiveness. For example, demographic decline is primarily viewed as an economic problem can be remedied through mass immigration. Although economic determinism initially welcomed mass immigration, modern society's diminished need for unskilled labour could lead to a backlash against immigrants in much the same way that the homeless are dehumanized. What happens when the productive value of human beings decreases in societies where all value is measured in economic efficiency? Leontief (1983: 405) posited that the

> [I]ntroduction of new computerized, automated, and robotized equipment can be expected to reduce the role of labour and is similar to the process by which the introduction of tractors and other machinery first reduced and then completely eliminated horses and other draft animals in agriculture.

Without addressing how technology can reinvent purpose and restore Gemeinschaft, technology will merely be used to mask the symptoms of decay. Technology divests people of their interpersonal connections and denies fulfilment of their instinctive needs, while concurrently functioning as a sedative to distract them from the consequences of societal decay. George Kennan

(2014: 119) posited that 'people [were] drugged and debilitated by automobiles and advertisements and radios and moving pictures'. Kaczynski (1995: 5) argued that even as technology and modern society make the individual sick, they also numb the symptoms with drugs and mindless television. Similarly, digitally created personas replace authentic and reliable social interactions, causing greater isolation and a loss of social capital. As ever greater numbers of people decide not to marry and raise children – as is the case in Japan – the market for robots to replace human companionship grows. However, robotics is then applied to treat the symptom rather than the source of the disease that causes communities and families to disintegrate. Sex robots automate and dehumanize contact. People become de-socialized by superficial companionship that does not place demands or responsibilities on people. Research reveals that children become more attached to robotic toys with which they can interact and that mimic human or animal behaviour. This raises concerns, however, about mechanizing human emotions (Tanaka, Cicourel and Movellan 2007).

The salvation of society and civilization depends on providing philosophical anthropology that reconciles technology with human nature. The United States stands out as a case study for relative socio-economic stability during the First Industrial Revolution. President Jefferson was convinced that Western European manufacturing societies eroded morality. In addition to meeting the economic necessity of developing a domestic manufacturing base to escape British dominance, the United States introduced social codes that harmonized that process with social stability.

The American ideals of freedom – defined as self-reliance and personal responsibility supported by strong property rights – ensured that work was not reduced to merely an activity of putting food on the table, but remained a source of dignity, morality and meaning. With the appearance of mass production and large corporations in the Second Industrial Revolution, disharmony began to emerge between the economy and the social fabric. Although property rights were the source of freedom and autonomy for small-scale producers and farmers, they also provided the legal foundation for large corporations to dictate living conditions to their employees and to transform self-reliant workers into salaried labourers (Lasch 1979). The loss of American manufacturing jobs in the late twentieth century had profound consequences beyond lowering incomes for the working class. The manufacturing industry was deeply tied to American culture, and the loss these professions weakened the sense of professional pride.

After the Second World War, the Western capitalist economic system granted governments significant authorities to intervene to protect traditional communities from growing market efficiencies and the resultant creative destruction. Ruggie (1982) defined the post–Cold War capitalist system as 'embedded liberalism', which was a reference to Polanyi's argument that markets had become disembedded from society during the nineteenth century. In mixing free trade with welfare programs and social responsibilities, national governments were no longer simply administrators ensuring that nothing interrupted the free market. Although Adam Smith was hailed as the 'poster child' for free-market economics, he also recognized the need for government intervention in the market to deliver on the social obligations of the state (Agnew and Corbridge 2002: 225).

Nonetheless, ever since the Second World War, Western governments have staked their political legitimacy almost exclusively on their ability to deliver never-ending economic growth. The economic stagnation of the 1970s signified the demise of embedded liberalism, with the need to maximize market efficiency reducing the ability of governments to exercise social responsibility. The Reaganism and Thatcherism of the 1980s was a response to the stagnation, but rather than serving as a temporary fix for restarting the economy, it was hailed as an ideological solution to all problems. In the United States, traditional capitalism was undermined by radical deregulation, the acceptance of higher unemployment, the scaling back of unions and the dismissal of the state's societal responsibility (Davidson and Davidson 1988: 138). Under the new ideology, concepts such as full employment over market efficiency came to be seen as a betrayal of capitalism. Although the state previously held the status of a guarantor of the public's interest, it has now become a symbol of corruption, inefficient bureaucracy and technological inertia (Luttwak 1993). The digitalization and globalization of the economy in the 1990s raised social costs, with a flexible labour market requiring fewer regulations and worker protections and changes in the economy exerting downward pressure on salaries (Rodrik 1997). Subjugating society to market forces produced economic determinism as the nation state. The significance of religion, culture, the family and tradition declined due to their lack of economic utility.

Social responsibility began to wither in politics as the political left abandoned economic redistribution and the political right abandoned social conservatism. The Clinton administration began distancing itself from the traditional platform of redistribution and economic justice associated with the left (Rorty 1998). When the free market became the highest value, conservatives began neglecting the social responsibilities that defined traditional values, family, faith and community.

The desolation of settled communities and the ruin of established expectations will not be mourned and may well be welcomed by fundamentalist market liberals. For them, nothing much of any value is threatened by the unfettered operation of market institutions. Communities and ways of life which cannot renew themselves through the exercise of consumer choice deserve to perish. The protection from market forces of valuable cultural forms is a form of unacceptable paternalism. And so the familiar and tedious litany goes on.

(Gray 1995: 100)

These sentiments were also part of the manifesto of the Unabomber, a prominent American academic-turned terrorist:

They whine about the decay of traditional values, yet they enthusiastically support technological progress and economic growth. Apparently it never occurs to them that you can't make rapid, drastic changes in the technology and the economy of a society without causing rapid changes in all other aspects of society as well, and that such rapid changes inevitably break down traditional values.

(Kaczynski 1995: 7)

Vague references to traditional values and morality were also translated into specific concerns about governance, meaning and the ability to understand and shape the world. During the digital revolution in the 1990s, Sagan (1996: 25) questioned the ability of society to adapt to rapid technological changes:

Science is more than a body of knowledge; it is a way of thinking. I have a foreboding of an America in my children's or grandchildren's time – when the United States is a service and information economy; when nearly all the key manufacturing industries have slipped away to other countries; when awesome technological powers are in the hands of a very few, and no one representing the public interest can even grasp the issues; when the people have lost the ability to set their own agendas or knowledgeably question those in authority; when, clutching our crystals and nervously consulting our horoscopes, our critical faculties in decline, unable to distinguish between what feels good and what's true, we slide, almost without noticing, back into superstition and darkness.

The societal dilemma of geoeconomics

From the late nineteenth century to the early twentieth century, Russia embraced industrialization and, under the policies of Sergei Witte, became the fastest growing economy among the great powers. The Tariff Act of 1891 boosted Russian cotton, iron and industrial machinery, while Stolypin later advanced agriculture with market-based reforms and the Peasant Land Bank in 1906. Railway networks stretching from St. Petersburg to the Pacific created unprecedented economic connectivity in Russia, convincing Mackinder (1904: 434) that the markets of the British Empire would also fall to Russia. However, by 1917 the Bolshevik Revolution abandoned capitalism and thus reduced its ability to exercise economic statecraft. Failing to recognize and mitigate societal disruptions and poor working conditions during Russia's rapid industrialization set the stage for a radical Marxist alternative that could not perform economically and, with destructive force, sought to create Communist Man liberated from his past and instinctive impulses.

The societal dilemma of contemporary geoeconomics is that it values technologies primarily for their economic utility and develops Gesellschaft to gain market efficiency and strength even as the resultant destruction of Gemeinschaft undermines societal stability. The polarization of society and political instability threatens the ability of the state to act as a unitary actor and mobilize resources towards strategic ends.

The first wave of globalization in the 1870s and 1880s saw an explosion in cross-border international trade and movements of people. In Germany, economic and social interests diverged, with corporations and the government needing immigrants to fill the demand for labour and the population beginning to grow wary about demographic disruptions. They wanted workers but got people. The disconnect between economic and social development was also evident in California, where union leader Denis Kearney demanded a reduction of Chinese labour and immigration with the slogan, 'The Chinese must go'.

Populist movements past and present have embraced rhetoric about the growing disconnect between the interests of the elites and those of the common people. Societies are split between the cosmopolitan elites who consider the demise of the past as progress, and the 'internal proletariat' that seeks to rejuvenate traditional society. Toynbee (1946) understood that polarized civilizations would eventually fail to act with shared interests in international affairs because the 'internal proletariat' has always reached out to an 'external proletariat' – a rival Gemeinschaft-based civilization at the periphery – for a common cause against their cosmopolitan elites.

Huntington suggested that social disruptions would eventually be elevated above rational interests as defined by economists, driving geoeconomic competition. The rise of the economically powerful 'Davos Man', as described by Samuel Huntington and then Steve Bannon, is a cosmopolitan creature unattached to the past or a place, a person who is only loyal to his self-interest. Davos Man is the target of the increasingly successful populists across the West – a phenomenon deeply rooted in identity issues and culture. At the same time, ordinary citizens instinctively seek to preserve traditional values, national identity, culture and manufacturing jobs.

> [F]or many elites, these concerns are secondary to participating in the global economy, supporting international trade and migration, strengthening international institutions, promoting American values abroad, and encouraging minority identities and cultures at home. The central distinction between the public and elites is not isolationism versus internationalism, but nationalism versus cosmopolitanism.
>
> (Huntington 2004: 5)

Rorty (1998) expected that excessive economic liberalism supported by detached cosmopolitan elites would produce political radicalism:

> Members of labour unions, and unorganized and unskilled workers, will sooner or later realize that their government is not even trying to prevent wages from sinking or to prevent jobs from being exported. Around the same time, they will realize that suburban white-collar workers – themselves desperately afraid of being downsized – are not going to let themselves be taxed to provide social benefits for anyone else. At that point, something will crack. The nonsuburban electorate will decide that the system has failed and start looking around for a strongman to vote for – someone willing to assure them that, once he is elected, the smug bureaucrats, tricky lawyers, overpaid bond salesmen, and postmodernist professors will no longer be calling the shots ... Once the strongman takes office, no one can predict what will happen.

National interests and alliances are then changed from economic pragmatism to cultural protectionism. Patrick Buchanan (2013) argued that the world would be reorganized along a globalist-nationalist divide in the years to come.

> As the decisive struggle in the second half of the 20th century was vertical, East vs. West, the 21st century struggle may be horizontal, with conservatives and traditionalists in every country arrayed against the militant secularism of a multicultural and transnational elite.

Populists have typically viewed immigration, radical secularism and multiculturalism as the key threats to culture, but the robotics and AI used by tech giants will increasingly join the list of reasons for the growing split between elites and the people. Much as the Luddites destroyed the machinery that disrupted their way of life, the growing fury will be directed against technologies that elevate economic interests above those of society.

Bridging Gemeinschaft and Gesellschaft

AI 'attempts to understand intelligent entities. Thus, one reason to study it is to learn more about ourselves. But unlike philosophy and psychology, which are also concerned with intelligence, AI strives to build intelligent entities as well as understand them' (Russell and Norvig 1995: 3). As long ago as ancient Greece, Socrates attempted to define the characteristics of piety, understood in modern terms as an algorithm to distinguish piety from non-piety (Russell and Norvig 1995: 8). Plato argued that Man must balance the instinctive order of the soul and the calculative external order of the rational mind. Therefore, AI must aspire to satisfy more than the rational and material.

The Fourth Industrial Revolution offers tools for rebalancing Gemeinschaft and Gesellschaft. The automation of the First Industrial Revolution broke up rural communities, turning once-autonomous farmers into dependent wage workers at factories. Technology made it possible to develop larger and more rational and complex societies, encouraging mankind to look beyond small and limited communities. Technologies of the Fourth Industrial Revolution enable people to connect with complex society for knowledge, science and to develop rational thinking. At the same time, without the centralization of strenuous physical labour, they can withdraw to local communities. New technologies can enhance self-sufficiency and ownership overproduction, make economic activity regional again and spur a radical reshoring of manufacturing. Instead of making Man into a machine as was feared in the First Industrial Revolution, technologies of the Fourth Industrial Revolution could enable Man to recapture his humanity.

The Fourth Industrial Revolution could also develop new and benign frontiers as a remedy for societal disruption. Advances in science and technology have caused creative destruction in the moral order and meaning. Nietzsche argued that the Enlightenment increasingly led to the 'death of God', which was problematic as belief in God provided people with meaning. As the source of values and morality diminished, nihilism would destroy society. Creative destruction of society and culture, therefore, sparked demand for Übermensch – the creator of new values and morality to fill the vacuum left by the loss of belief in a divinely ordained moral order. Unlike God, Übermensch belongs to the physical world and is defined as highly capable and powerful because it embodies the duality of Man. Übermensch is a powerful warrior that can manage the chaos resulting from instinctive impulses, but also brilliant in its ability to advance the rational and scientific.

Übermensch represents a deep truth that itself laid the foundation for religion – namely, that transcendent values are found in Man's ability to balance the instinctive with the rational. In Greek mythology, Zeus had two sons: Apollo was the God of rational thinking, logic and order, while Dionysus was the God of the irrational, instincts and chaos. The mythology of ancient Mesopotamia tells a similar story about two original Gods: Abzu, the father, representing order, and Tiamat, the mother, embodying primordial chaos. Correspondingly, the Egyptian God of Osiris embodied a paternal spirit by ruling with wisdom and virtue, and his wife, Isis, was the Goddess of Darkness and Chaos. With the decline of religion and God, the Übermensch of this world would instil new values and morality by balancing the duality of Man.

The societal disruptions caused by the Industrial Revolution spurred the rise of colonialism, with the settler becoming an expression of Übermensch. Although the expansion of markets was imperative, the encounters with wild frontiers and barbarism also rejuvenated the sense of community by developing a shared purpose and spirit. Industrial capitalism was commonly associated with cultural decay due to the disruption of traditional society. People sought to counterbalance technological disruptions to society by migrating to less developed regions in an attempt to rediscover the traditional and connect with nature. Emigration offered some relief because radicals born out of the societal changes could simply leave. Concerns emerged, however, that this drained national energies and that such emigration would 'fertilise' other states. Germany, for example, worried that waves of emigrants to the United States would cause the end of German culture. However, German culture prospered in settlements in Brazil. Colonialism became the best solution, with settlers establishing themselves in 'new lands' where the culture could be preserved and not corrupted by intermingling with the natives.

The frontier of colonial settlers instilled manufacturing societies with meaning as an amalgam of Gemeinschaft and Gesellschaft. The Machiavellian stratagem to achieve both glory and virtue appeals to the duality of mankind, and colonization gave the Europeans an outlet for acting on primitive impulses against the 'uncivilized' while remaining civilized in the eyes of their fellow Europeans. The 'frontier thesis' posited that the individualistic, progressive and virtuous character of the United States was largely a consequence of its western frontier (Turner 2008 [1893]). Westward expansion distracted people from the societal disruptions of industrialized society and instilled optimism about a glorious future. The settler essence of America's Manifest Destiny largely embodied the frontier spirit. Turner (2008 [1893]) cautioned that reaching the Pacific Coast would be a pyrrhic victory because it would compel the United States to confront the societal malaise of industrialized society. This day of reckoning could be postponed by venturing into the Pacific and imitating European colonialism because of 'the civilization which does not advance declines' (Adams 1900: 25). Theodore Roosevelt similarly believed that the process of deterioration could be reversed and society revitalized by opening new frontiers in international affairs (Dyer 1992: 149). A similar frontier thesis arose in Russia where it was thought that industrialization could be balanced by developing the railroads and venturing into the vast Eastern steppe to develop a Eurasian future:

> When we turn to Asia, with our new view of her, something of the same sort may happen to us as happened to Europe when America was discovered. For, in truth, Asia for us is that same America which we still have not discovered. With our push towards Asia we will have a renewed upsurge of spirit and strength. Just as soon as we become more independent we'll at once find out what we have to do; but living with Europe for two centuries we've become unaccustomed to any kind of activity and have become windbags and idlers.
>
> (Dostoyevsky 1994)

Space cowboys as the new Übermensch

The Fourth Industrial Revolution will create powerful incentives to establish a similar frontier as a pressure valve for societal disruptions and to instil visions of a grand future. In a world where labour and even mundane tasks such as driving are outsourced to machines, enabling mankind to reassert its autonomy and shape the surrounding world can provide meaning. The duality of human nature demands that the rational thinking and technological innovations of Apollo are used to engage with the chaos and wild nature of Dionysus.

New technologies will impel humanity towards the endless frontier of space. The exploration of space offers the world's great powers an important arena in which to compete for status, an untapped region for mining resources and a field capable of attracting leading scientists whose experiments could produce new technologies. However, space also appeals to the duality of mankind by advancing civilization and order into the realm of chaos and barbarity. Toynbee (1946) argued that thriving civilizations need a 'creative minority' capable of finding solutions and meeting meaningful challenges. Otherwise, society becomes excessively preoccupied with past achievements and begins to stagnate and decay. Space exploration is a healthy outlet for discovering new challenges as a response to nihilism.

Artists and popular culture tend to present a techno-futuristic society that borrows from the frontier aesthetics of nineteenth-century American romanticism, projecting the liberal individual into outer space in the spirit of America's Manifest Destiny (Sage 2016). From fiction novels to Hollywood, there is a common narrative about the virtuous protagonist struggling with a lack of purpose. He delves into chaos and emerges victorious with a replenished spirit. Geography is the 'obvious discipline to carry a broad range of cultural, historical, political and economic inquiries into outer space' (MacDonald 2007). The space program was vital to US efforts to conquer nature and to reinforce the idea that the country had a higher, even divine purpose. Some even argue that space exploration created the modern United States (Sage 2016). Even corporations will be able to make a profit by establishing themselves as idealized technocratic organizations akin to NASA.

If humanity fails to find a suitable frontier, states become more likely to confront adversaries on this planet. In the past, the maritime powers of Western Europe could expend their excess energy and compete with each other by developing colonies rather than engaging in direct conflict. The shrinking number of regions outside colonial control resulted in more direct confrontation between colonial powers.

Greater opportunities and fiercer competition will spur the space industry to develop substantially over the next decade. The main constraints on space exploration have been the high costs and precarious conditions for human health beyond Earth's atmosphere. In addition, the technological and economic barriers to entry meant that few could participate in space exploration, and those that did were reliant on public funding. Now, the cost of technologies required to enter space is dropping rapidly while new technologies for protecting humans from health hazards continue to improve. Inexpensive satellites can be used to improve agriculture, transportation and other industries. The key to becoming an interplanetary species is to combine economic value creation with social aspirations. As productivity exceeds demand, adventurous souls can direct the excess capacity towards expanding into space.

Technology is making space exploration cheaper and safer. Solar radiation can be addressed with advanced materials made by nanotechnology. Permanent extraterrestrial settlements could experiment with geoengineering to find ways to alter the atmosphere and thus improve living conditions on planets that are less hospitable to human biology. Synergy effects exist, with innovations in private industry improving the space-based industry, and technological advances in space providing insights and applications for human activity and markets on Earth. 3D printing can also revolutionize space exploration. A key bottleneck has been the logistical problem of bringing up and storing spare parts at the international space station – a challenge that becomes even more daunting on the Moon or Mars. Experimentation with 3D printing in space makes it possible for any spare part to be printed and made available immediately. The European Space Agency intends to use 3D printing to develop permanent colonies on Mars. Even before the first person arrives, 3D-printing robots will arrive and construct every housing and auxiliary structure, using local materials from the Moon to avoid the cost of shipping them from Earth. Similarly, although every space mission requires an abundance of spare parts, a 3D printer in space can simply print the components as they are required. In addition, the use of AI and advanced robotics in space exploration might lead to even more exciting and unforeseeable developments.

With the barriers to entry falling, competition for space exploration is intensifying among private corporations and a new host of states. Private corporations such as SpaceX and Blue Origin are taking the lead. Those involved in space exploration are searching for markets to fuel expansion. There is great potential for manufacturing in space. For example, some high-tech materials are improved if constructed in microgravity. Space tourism and hotels orbiting the earth could offer more than just the opportunity to turn a profit. Mars One signifies another commercialization effort by sourcing income from television rights. As a reality show, the Mars One endeavour also has a positive societal effect. It is driven by excitement and curiosity about space exploration, unlike the vulgar Big Brother-styled reality shows that profit from moral decadence. The initiative might fail to achieve its high-reaching goals, but it is a powerful indicator of how ambition coupled with innovativeness can make space exploration self-funding. Indirect space tourism can become available to the wider population through developments in virtual reality (VR), which is set to revolutionize the entertainment industry. The ability to experience space through VR enables the inclusion of second-tier consumption.

Nonetheless, space exploration in the Fourth Industrial Revolution presents a challenge to the state with the field becoming the domain of tech giants and billionaires such as Jeff Bezos, Elon Musk and Richard Branson. The increasing concentration of wealth among tech giants is legitimized because these billionaires are commonly depicted as lone wolves or individualistic 'space cowboys' providing a common good for humanity. However, Blue Origin and SpaceX rely on NASA's technologies and government contracts to establish technological skills in space (Mazzucato 2018). In this way, the cost of space exploration are socialized because taxpayers carry the burden, but the profits are privatized, further concentrating wealth with the tech billionaires. Although governments were previously considered guarantors of the public good, they can be sidelined by the argument that they have become too inefficient and technologically stagnant. Amazon is the largest company in the world in terms of market value, and yet it is also renowned for its poor treatment of employees. The myth that private industry is technologically savvy and governments are backward could become a self-fulfilling prophecy as tech giants increasingly attract the best-skilled workers and created the most advanced technologies. Tech giants pursue a neo-mercantilist development strategy akin to Hamilton and List by procuring both power and legitimacy, which could establish them as the highest sovereigns in space. Without the burden of serving the public good either economically or socially, space exploration could become another domain for marginalizing human beings rather than bridging Gemeinschaft and Gesellschaft.

Conclusion

The great powers must recognize that societal disruptions are an impediment to a rational and calculative foreign policy because geoeconomics cannot be practised without Gemeinschaft. Efforts to condemn and transcend the instinctive impulses in human nature will produce destructive outcomes as centuries of philosophy have cautioned. Technologies will not enable humanity to overcome its tribalism. Rather, technology can harness and manage these impulses to prevent them from being expressed in a malign manner. Although the former industrial revolutions have placed an immense burden on the environment and the innate and irrational aspects of human nature, the Fourth Industrial Revolution can reverse this pattern. Technologies restricted to their economic utility as merely a labour-saving instrument in an economically deterministic society can diminish the value of human beings rather than serve their interests. As Nietzsche explicitly argued, the source of the morality and values that enhance social capital does not derive from democratic humanitarian or other liberal and idealistic notions – rather, it derives from the ability to harmonize rational thinking and order with irrationality and chaos. It is therefore predicted and advocated that governments will direct the technologies of the Fourth Industrial Revolution towards space exploration as the ultimate frontier to mitigate societal disruption and its influence on geoeconomics.

8

Killer robots and the return
of the great power wars

Introduction

Throughout history, war has been the prevailing instrument for competition between states. The First Industrial Revolution made possible wealth creation without plunder, but paradoxically, the weapons industry has been an important driving force for technological innovation. The mass production of the Second Industrial Revolution elevated killing to an industrial scale. The Third Industrial Revolution gave mankind weapons capable of destroying the planet. However, with increasingly destructive weapons and more economic connectivity, the world appeared to shift from militarized geopolitics to geoeconomics.

Will the Fourth Industrial Revolution cause a return from geoeconomics to militarized geopolitics? The main three countries developing AI with military applications are the United States, China and Russia. After having already seen the introduction of gunpowder and nuclear weapons, the world is now facing a third revolution in warfare: fully autonomous weapons systems that operate more rapidly and use an array of different weapons. The world has not assimilated or learned how to manage these weapons. The great powers were never comfortable with placing constraints on military force as an instrument of foreign policy. The military superiority that the United States has enjoyed since the end of the Cold War has gradually declined and other great powers such as Russia and China have been catching up with modern weaponry. The Fourth Industrial Revolution could disrupt the balance of power radically: the United States could again extend its leadership or, alternatively, its adversaries could leapfrog it, with the United States devoting its funds to maintaining increasingly obsolete military hardware.

The long spear, Maxim gun, aeroplane, chemical weapons and nuclear weapons changed the way wars are fought as well as the relationship between offensive and defensive advantage. Developments in AI, robotics, nanotechnology, biotechnology and other technologies associated with the Fourth Industrial Revolution will cause a disruption by providing a temporary first-mover advantage and change warfare forever. As happened with their technological predecessors, once the knowledge has been acquired and the weapons developed, the world will have to learn to live with them.

This chapter will first explore the theoretical assumptions behind the security dilemma and the offence/defence balance as the main indicators for the extent to which war becomes more or less likely. Second, it is assessed whether the 'nuclear peace' is coming to an end with nuclear retaliatory capabilities under threat and warfare extending into space while countermeasures further intensify the security dilemma. Third, the return of proxy wars is explored where great powers project their might with automated weapons. Last, cyber weapons open up an entirely new domain for conflict as the digital world integrates with the physical world. It will be concluded that disruptions to military technologies are causing the dismantling of former arms control regimes and that treaties addressing new weapons technologies are failing to materialize as leading powers seek to obtain a strategic advantage.

The offence/defence balance and arms control

The security dilemma is a key concept in international relations and security studies. It defines the key problem of security in an anarchic international system – namely, that enhancing the security of one state undermines the security of its adversaries. This, in turn, prompts those adversaries to build up military power to improve their security. Paradoxically, while both parties have defensive intentions and seek only to enhance their security, they inadvertently end up in conflict, arms races and even war. The dilemma consists of two unfavourable options – either enhance military capabilities and thereby encourage adversaries to respond in kind out of fear, or decide not to augment military capability and risk a military offensive by adversaries (Booth and Wheeler 2008).

The offence/defence theory is an important approach for resolving the security dilemma. Weapons technologies are assessed by the extent to which they make war more or less likely. The theory optimistically suggests that war can be prevented if defence has an advantage over offense. This suggests that arms control has great potential for preventing war. Military technologies can be assessed according to whether they are offensive or defensive, and the extent that the two can be distinguished. Military technologies change the 'relative ease of attack or defence' (Lieber 2000: 75). With offensive advantage there is less incentive to negotiate, making a state more likely to pursue preventative wars and opportunistic expansion (Lynn-Jones 1995; Glaser 2010). A defensive deficiency also encourages aggressive behaviour like a first strike for survival and 'defensive expansion' (Van Evera 1998).

Innovations such as fortresses, trenches and barbed wire tend to give an advantage to defence by deterring aggressors without raising fears that they will be used for offensive purposes. In contrast, mechanized cavalry and airpower give an advantage to offence. The technological development of the German military can, therefore, be cited as the reason for Berlin's adventurism in the Second World War. However, most military capabilities have dual uses, which make it difficult to distinguish clearly between offensive and defensive weapons (Jervis 1978; Van Evera 1998). For example, defensive weapons such as air defence were necessary for Egypt to launch an attack on Israel in 1973 (Shiping 2010). However, the non-offensive defence argument – that encouraged states to organize military infrastructure to maximize defensive capabilities and minimize offensive capabilities – gained influence in the 1980s. The Soviet Union began supporting the non-offensive defence concept in 1986–7, which made NATO reconsider its previous scepticism (Møller 1995). Non-offensive defence has subsequently become a key concept in arms control.

The nuclear revolution is recognized as having shifted the offence/defence balance towards defence (Jervis 1989). Nuclear weapons are commonly cited as the main reason why the great powers have not engaged in open hostilities since the Second World War (Waltz 1990). Strategic stability is a situation in which neither side would use its weapons. This has occurred in connection with nuclear weapons: they have forced peace over fears of mutually assured destruction (MAD). Former US Secretary of Defence Robert McNamara (1983) argued, 'there is no sensible military use of any of our nuclear forces. Their only reasonable use is to deter our opponent'.

Maintaining nuclear peace depends on preserving the strategic balance. The incentive for a nuclear first strike is removed if the second-strike capabilities of the adversary (nuclear missiles that survive the first strike and can be used for retaliation) are equally destructive or at least capable of causing intolerable destruction. First-strike nuclear weapons are therefore designed to destroy the retaliatory capabilities of the adversary and second-strike capabilities are designed to deter by maximizing destruction through the incineration of entire cities.

Arms control: Between strategic advantage and strategic balance

Controlling the proliferation of weapons depends on the incentive to accept and abide by a treaty, the entry barriers to the technology and the extent of transparency required in verifying compliance. The attempts by states to ban the crossbow, firearm and submarines, all failed because whoever first broke the agreement was rewarded with military superiority. Arms control is largely dependent on a balance of technological capabilities. States do not constrain themselves and will only accept limitations on the development and use of specific weapons if they can obtain reciprocal agreements from other states. In other words, international law and agreements entail a *quid pro quo*: states are willing to sacrifice certain freedoms in their foreign policy in return for reciprocity and predictability.

New military technology causes a disruption to the system because the innovative state temporarily enjoys unregulated use of a superior weapon until a rival emerges with the same capabilities. This, in turn, creates the incentive to accept treaties and laws that govern and restrain these technologies. The United States could use the atom bomb against Japan and also reject any limitations on drones as long as it held a monopoly on those technologies. As these technologies proliferate, the United States has the incentive to cement its strategic advantage and concurrently advance strategic stability with arms control and limitations on their use.

Arms control is most effective in the format of great powers restricting weaker states from developing particular weapons. For example, the Non-Proliferation Treaty (NPT), which came into effect in 1970, has been the key instrument for preventing the proliferation of nuclear weapons. The treaty obligated nuclear states to halt the development of such weapons and to disarm and non-nuclear states to refrain from developing them. The NPT enabled nuclear powers to cement their strategic advantage and concurrently establish strategic stability. The NPT prevented horizontal proliferation of nuclear weapons to other states, but nuclear states have chosen to modernize their weaponry rather than abandon it. The NPT was therefore criticized for cementing 'nuclear apartheid'. Complex hardware, developed by states, is ideal to regulate and restrict, as advanced technological capabilities become an entry barrier. For example, the technological sophistication and need for scarce resources to develop nuclear weapons make it more governable. Furthermore, great powers can maintain a balance of power by establishing legal frameworks that endow them with special access to these weapons while denying such access to smaller powers.

Similarly, the abolishment of biological and chemical weapons provided powerful states with a monopoly on this new form of weaponry. Whereas nuclear weapons have a high technological barrier, biological and chemical weapons are much and cheaper to develop. In 1988, the speaker of the Iranian Parliament, Hashemi Rafsanjani, described biological and chemical weapons as 'the poor man's atomic bomb'. Poorer and less developed states also seek powerful weaponry offering high deterrence as an equalizer against more powerful states. Such states would immediately seize on new technologies that are not banned for moral reasons, and that are also cheap, less complicated to develop and that do not require rare materials.

The new weapons emerging from the Fourth Industrial Revolution are typically dual purpose and will, therefore, proliferate more easily. Furthermore, unlike the Manhattan Project, digital technological innovations are being made by private corporations. Growing cooperation between the military and private corporations is the trend of the future as warfare becomes increasingly reliant on technology. Even the US military is becoming increasingly reliant on cooperation with private corporations to develop new weaponry. The digital nature of new technologies also makes them easier to copy.

Ending the nuclear peace?

The nuclear peace that followed the Second World War might not be permanent because states are seeking technologies to convert nuclear weapons into offensive armaments. Only one decade after the development of nuclear weapons, states began exploring the concept of a 'limited use' of nuclear weapons with the aim of destroying the second-strike capabilities of their adversaries (Drell and Von Hippel 1976). The reasonable but dangerous logic is that if there is an offensive advantage from suffering fewer losses in a first strike as compared to a second strike, then it would be the preferable option if war appeared imminent. However, it could become a self-fulfilling prophecy because first-strike capabilities could also escalate tensions to the point that a war becomes likely. First-strike capabilities are intended to facilitate a more belligerent foreign policy by enabling escalation control or escalation dominance – which refers to the ability to increase and decrease military pressure as a condition for limited use of force. Escalation dominance implies that pressure can continuously be increased until the other side is compelled to capitulate (Snyder 1961).

The ambition of US President Ronald Reagan to develop the so-called 'Star Wars' program threatened the strategic balance. The Star Wars program was an early concept of missile defence with space-based components such as 'laser battle stations in space' that would target Soviet ballistic missiles. Missile defence threatens to convert nuclear weapons into offensive weapons because the second-strike capabilities of the adversary could be intercepted (Diesen and Keane 2018). The offence/defence balance would subsequently be disrupted because the United States would have a greater incentive to strike first if tensions intensified, while the growing prospect of a United States first strike would also encourage the Soviet Union to strike first. The desire to prevent offensive advantage by ensuring that launching a first strike would not be preferable to a second strike informed the US–Soviet decision to sign the Anti-Ballistic Missile (ABM) treaty in 1972.

A successful first strike depends on a rapid strike before the adversary can respond, which is further assisted by taking out control centres that can authorize and launch the retaliatory strike. Improvement in weapons forces states to rely on shorter response times to assess whether an attack is actually underway and prompts them to decentralize decision-making by giving more officers access to the 'red button'. Consequently, the prospect of an accidental war increases. For example, in 1983 a technical flaw caused Soviet computers to mistakenly detect a nuclear attack by the United States. Soviet officer Stanislav Petrov reviewed the data and concluded that it was probably a computer error and did not, therefore, order a retaliatory nuclear strike. Thus, the time that was available to humans to assess the information provided by machines prevented a nuclear war. The recognition of the threat from offensive advantage and accidental nuclear war motivated the United States and the Soviet Union to sign the Intermediate-Range Nuclear Forces Treaty (INF) in 1987 banning all ground-launched missiles with an intermediate range (500–5,500 km).

However, a month after the collapse of the Soviet Union, US President George Bush (1992) used his State of the Union speech to call for reintroducing missile defence with a program known as the Strategic Defence Initiative. A leaked Pentagon paper, the Defence Planning Guidance (DPG) of 1992, outlined the objective of achieving military hegemony by preventing the emergence of any rivals. The document identified Russia as 'the only power in the world with the capability of destroying the United States', and therefore urged an early introduction of a global anti-missile system (Tyler 1992). The 2002 US National

Security Strategy similarly declared that 'our forces will be strong enough to dissuade potential adversaries from pursuing a military build-up in hopes of surpassing, or equalling, the power of the United States' (White House 2002). A security strategy based on military supremacy constitutes a rejection of the concept of strategic balance that underpins arms control agreements and mitigates the security dilemma by maintaining an offence/defence balance.

By the early 2000s, the numbers and operating procedures of US nuclear weapons indicated a departure from mere deterrence and a move towards first-strike capabilities (Buchan 2003). The US Nuclear Employment Strategy of 2013 called for maintaining 'significant counterforce capabilities against potential adversaries'. In other words, it advocated having the ability to destroy an adversary's nuclear weapons and delivery systems before they could be used. United States, first-strike capabilities were advancing through the combination of first-strike weapons and missile defences capable of intercepting a retaliatory strike by an adversary's weapons that had survived a US attack. Advances in conventional deep strike capabilities are seen as enhancing the US ability to carry out a more successful first strike against Russia (Cimbala 2012). Because US offensive capabilities would leave only a 'tiny surviving arsenal' of nuclear weapons and decoys in Russia or China, it was concluded that 'even a relatively modest or inefficient missile defence system might well be enough to protect against any retaliatory strikes' (Lieber and Press 2006: 52). The offensive potential of nuclear weapons is also enhanced by making them more practical for the battlefield. Kristensen, the director of the Nuclear Information Project at the Federation of American Scientists (FAS), cautioned that the United States was upgrading its nuclear weapons in Europe to make them 'guided' and therefore more 'usable'. These technological upgrades entail adding controllable tail fins to missiles, enabling them to strike closer to their targets. The threshold for using nuclear weapons is thus lowered due to the 'lower explosive yield and reduced nuclear fallout' (Borger 2013).

The nuclear peace in the Fourth Industrial Revolution

The Fourth Industrial Revolution exacerbates the trend towards developing the offensive potential of nuclear weapons. AI and smart weapons advance nuclear weapon and missile defence capabilities. Hypersonic weapons could restructure the balance of power and be used to render missile defences obsolete. Former US Secretary of Defence, Jim Mattis, stated that 'hypersonics is the number one priority, both having them for ourselves but also the defence against them' of US military research and development. Russia openly announced its development of hypersonic weapons to counter missile defences (US Senate 2018: 127). Faster weapons that reduce the time available to decide on a response compel the decentralization of decision-making. As nuclear weapons become a greater risk, the incentive for a pre-emptive strike increases. If the United States, China or Russia make technological advances that leave other states too far behind to catch up, those states would have an incentive to launch a pre-emptive strike. Similarly, if any of the great powers were to develop weapon technology that could lay waste to their adversaries with impunity, those states would likely react by choosing an offensive fight as a more favourable strategy.

Russia's military innovations are largely motivated by the need to defend its nuclear forces from the US-NATO missile defence system. Moscow fears that the NATO's missile defence is designed to intercept the second-strike capabilities of Russia after being hit by a US first strike. Submarine drones armed with nuclear weapons are generally considered impervious to missile attack. They would lie near the seabed during an enemy's first strike, then automatically resurface and launch a retaliatory strike. This weapon has been referred to as a doomsday device (Geist 2016). Russia's Poseidon nuclear torpedo was designed to render missile defence systems useless. It is a nuclear drone that would cause a 400–500 meter high tsunami wave that would destroy everything in its path up to 1,500 km inland and spread uncontainable radioactive contamination. Kristensen from FAS defined it as 'an insane weapon in the sense that it's probably as indiscriminate and lethal as you can make a nuclear weapon' (Lockie 2019). Keeping nuclear-armed submarine drones with immense destructive power on the seabed could result in an accidental war. For example, a technical error could occur, an attack on satellites could disrupt communication with the drones or an enemy might hack into the weapons' computer system. The fact that it is possible to hack military supercomputers and operative systems raises the very real spectre of someone hacking into nuclear weapons systems in the future (Futter 2018).

With military power increasingly relying on space-based components, the theatre of war is expanding into space. The target in a first strike against another nuclear power has traditionally been that country's nuclear weapons and command centres. However, the ability to target the adversary's military satellites would further undermine its ability to retaliate. In a possible new arms race, the United States would seek hegemony by enhancing its space-based missile defence components while denying its adversaries the same capabilities.

The US National Space Policy stipulates that the United States will 'preserve its rights, capabilities, and freedom of action in space', and 'deny, if necessary, adversaries the use of space capabilities hostile to U.S. national interests' (White House 2006). In 2007, China demonstrated its capabilities in space by using a ballistic missile to destroy one of its own ageing weather satellites. India then repeated that display of force in 2019 when it shot down a satellite and declared itself a 'space power'. Russia has also tested anti-satellite missiles successfully. Furthermore, Russia's new S-500 missile defence system reportedly has the ability to target low earth orbit satellites. US Secretary of Defence, Jim Mattis, cautioned that space had become a contested domain and that the US military was deeply reliant on satellites (US Senate 2018). President Trump's 'space force' is a response to calls by the US Department of Defense to develop greater military capabilities in space. The Pentagon is planning to construct a robot swarm space station the size of a large fridge. It would carry out orbital surveillance and contribute to combat missions in support of missile defence (Peck 2019). Other great powers will respond to the US militarization of space by developing their own innovative military capabilities.

The killer robot security dilemma

Disruptions to the military balance of power can be mitigated by making weapons more destructive, threatening first use and decentralizing decision-making. Although during the Cold War, NATO had a first-strike policy to offset its inferior conventional capabilities, Russia adopted a first-strike policy after the Cold War because NATO had become the superior conventional military power. In the Fourth Industrial Revolution, states have automated more of their military decision-making to respond to potential threats more rapidly, thereby compensating for inequalities in capabilities. Although many weapons systems now in deployment are semi-autonomous, there are strong incentives to keep humans in place for the actual decision to engage and destroy targets.

The killer robot security dilemma suggests that states will face increasing pressure to automate their militaries to remain competitive, raising the risk of disrupting strategic stability and even losing control over the military. China responds to the superior military capabilities of the United States by automating its weaponry and AI in its military, navy and air force. AI-controlled weapons systems improve the ability of states to surprise the adversary with a rapid attack and deliver a swift and decisive victory. However, shorter response times also undermine strategic stability. Future wars will be faster, requiring political and military leaders to respond swiftly. That makes it imperative to rely on AI to process large amounts of intelligence data and implement decisions rapidly. Semi-automated drones will likely transition into fully automated drones because the United States could only afford the luxury of assigning kill-decisions to humans when it controlled all of the world's airspace.

The immediate challenge of AI is not to gain humanlike self-awareness or to become all powerful, but to become more effective at identifying and engaging potential targets. Because AI does not pre-program weapons systems with algorithms for identifying and engaging targets, uncertainty and mistakes are likely to result. AI relies on experience to learn continuously and refine its own algorithms. Situations might arise for which an AI-driven system has no algorithm explaining why or how to respond. Therefore, military and political leaders plan to retain a great deal of control over the military, social, humanitarian and political aspects of war. Because machines are less capable of assessing the social and political context of warfare, they are more likely to intensify conflicts in the absence of human oversight.

As a new technological revolution in automation, robotics and AI dawns, experts are attempting to constrain the technology of killer robots. With more states acquiring the technology and making advances, an 'automation security dilemma' emerges. Imposing limits on new generations of killer robots benefits everyone, but the risk of complying with those restrictions and the incentives for abandoning them are all too great. Although preventing the emergence of these new weapons is not feasible, it is vital that states lay the necessary legal groundwork for them. On the whole, new weapons technologies can disrupt the offence/defence balance between states, make it possible for non-state actors to obtain powerful weapons, negate the concept of deterrence and radically disrupt the international balance of power.

Proxy wars: Robots, drones and swarms

The possibility of using automated weapons in proxy wars could bring the great powers into conflict. After the great power acquired nuclear weapons, they turned to competing indirectly in third countries. During the Cold War, the United States and Soviet militaries fought proxy wars in the Third World. After the Cold War, in the absence of a balance of power, the United States could begin restructuring the world under the pretext of humanitarian interventionism, the global war on terror, preventing the proliferation of weapons of mass destruction and the need to confront 'rogue states'.

The US regime gradually changed and wars grew more balanced. Also, Russia intervened when US-backed and trained Georgian forces invaded South Ossetia in 2008, provided support for rebels in Donbas after the United States backed the coup in Ukraine in 2014, backed the Syrian government starting in 2015 to resist US-backed militants seeking to topple the government, and is now providing unspecified military support to Venezuela in response to US efforts to overthrow that government. The growing number of front lines between great powers increases the likelihood of a miscalculation, a problem further exacerbated by the automated weaponry of the Fourth Industrial Revolution. New weapons make military interventionism a more attractive foreign policy option.

The use of robotics for warfare represents 'the biggest revolution within the armed forces since the atom bomb' (Singer 2009). The United States initially monopolized on automated weapons technologies such as drones. And, by fighting weak and inferior states, these battles have come at little cost and with minimal casualties. Unmanned drones lowered the bar for using military force and increased the acceptability of war (Coker, Roscini and Haynes 2013; Jackson 2018). While the lower costs in blood and treasury is seemingly a positive development, it will likely make wars more acceptable as the people usually oppose wars when its soldiers come home on coffins, the national budget is drained, and the exposure to civilian suffering is challenging the moral compass and human decency. By making warfare more 'humane', it becomes a more viable foreign policy tool. Public complacency and ignorance about the government's military activities is likely to reduce civilian control over the military.

Automated weapons alter the rules of war. For example, the threshold for attacking unmanned vehicles and drones is lower than attacking manned military equipment. What is the proper response for shooting down a drone? As Waltz (1988: 623) asks: 'What is worse – miscalculation or overreaction?' This dilemma was put to the test in June 2019 when Tehran shot down a US drone that allegedly violated Iranian airspace. The lack of clarity about the rules governing drones also gave the United States the flexibility to either treat it as an attack on US forces or de-escalate by devaluing the drone as a piece of equipment.

The trend over the last few decades has been a shift from quantity to quality, with states developing more professional armies. The emphasis could shift towards quantity again with low-cost military hardware such as swarms and other inexpensive weapons platforms making it possible to create automated fighting units numbering in the millions, if not billions. Swarm technology is the central decision-making brain that controls up to tens of thousands of small drones operating as a swarm. This technology will revolutionize urban warfare and, probably, terrorism.

However, the Fourth Industrial Revolution can also diffuse power by enabling weaker states to leapfrog technologies and non-state actors to obtain new capabilities previously available only to states. The balance of power can shift rapidly if the military technologies underpinning US dominance are made increasingly irrelevant by relatively easy-to-obtain and low-cost technologies such as small submarine drones. Initially, drones required fairly complex hardware and software that provided advantages to technologically advanced states, but new drones will likely become smaller and cheaper to manufacture. The balance of power could shift rapidly if a relatively small country could develop great numbers of small, cheap and powerful drones. Less developed states could also pose a threat to larger powers by giving machines preference over humans for kill decisions, for example. Robot armies are very attractive to states that have high labour costs or small populations (Scharre 2018).

The organization of warfare must be restructured when large weaponry becomes an attractive target. For example, in 2017 there were several instances of rebels in Donbas using small, cheap drones against the Ukrainian military. On each occasion, a cheap drone available for purchase in a toy store was used to deliver a grenade. One such attack alone destroyed a billion dollars' worth of weaponry. The United States' global dominance since the 1990s was based on its ability to control the world's oceans and airspace: US battle carrier groups could be sent to any corner of the world and engage an adversary with minimal costs in blood and treasury. However, that could change with the introduction of new, lethal and inexpensive weapons technologies.

Cyber weapons: A new domain for war

Whereas the presence of nuclear weapons discouraged the great powers from direct conflict and incentivized their military confrontation in third countries, digital technologies open up an entirely new battlefield in cyberspace.

The digital revolution differs from the major changes of the past. Previously, innovation in weapons technology was gradual, with each step representing an improvement over an existing weapon. Even revolutionary innovations were comparable to previous technologies: gunpowder improved upon the bow and arrow and nuclear weapons are essentially just larger and more destructive bombs. Terminology from the physical world is often used to describe concepts such as cyber terrorism, cyber espionage and cyber warfare. But some conceptual gaps arise. For example, terrorism involves the use of force against a civilian population to spread fear as a means of achieving a political objective. This has other implications in cyberspace.

Furthermore, the theory that informs cooperation and conflict does not always apply to cyberspace in terms of, for example, arms control and deterrence. Cybersecurity has therefore developed largely as a separate and specific field within international relations and security studies. In cyberspace, it is easier to attack than to defend and the ability to deter is severely diminished. Furthermore, does the retaliation have to take place in cyberspace or do cyber attacks warrant retaliation with conventional weapons? Strategic stability is unattainable in this area without international rules and governance. The United States is adamant that other states should not engage in cyber espionage or cyber attacks, but is unwilling to make the same commitments. The Stuxnet cyber attack by the United States and Israel against Iranian nuclear centrifuges could have sparked a nuclear disaster comparable to a conventional attack. Without a clear distinction between peace and war in cyberspace, is the world moving towards endless cyber wars in which no side claims responsibility?

The United States has attempted to bridge the gap between rules governing cyberspace and those applied to the physical world. The 2011 US International Strategy for Cyberspace claims 'the right to use all necessary means – diplomatic, informational, military and economic – as appropriate and consistent with international law' in response to a cyberattack (Obama 2011). After accusing Russia of being behind the hack of the Democratic National Committee during the 2016 presidential elections, Hillary Clinton pledged: 'As president I will make it clear that the United States will treat cyberattacks just like any other attack. We will be ready with serious political, economic and military responses' (White 2016). The so-called 'Russia-gate' accusation posed several risks due to the difficulty of establishing the origin of cyber espionage or cyber attacks. Furthermore, ambiguity about events in cyberspace made it possible for relations with Russia to become an instrument in a domestic power struggle. Linking cyber attacks with attacks in the physical world was also made problematic because the United States has openly admitted to carrying out cyber attacks against Russian power grids (Sanger and Perlroth 2019). Similarly, at a US-Chinse Cyber Summit, Barack Obama's plan to lecture China on cyber attacks against the United States was undermined by Snowden's revelations that the United States had waged cyber attacks against China. The challenge in the coming years will be to establish a balance of power with regard to cyber technologies as a requirement for international law, and then to formulate agreements that can be verified and enforced. Basic definitions of cyber offences and defences must be developed. Similarly, the ways in which cyber conflicts escalate and de-escalate must be outlined to establish new norms and procedures.

Denouncing Edward Snowden or Julian Assange as Russian or Chinese spies is a dishonest way to avoid addressing the challenge of non-state actors becoming empowered. The 11 September 2001 attacks in the United States sparked concerns about the prospect of non-state actors acquiring nuclear weapons. Such fears turned out to be overblown because non-state actors could only overcome the technological impediments involved with the help of state sponsors, who would be held accountable. However, this issue should not be put to rest because new technologies are proliferating and becoming increasingly available to non-state actors.

How does deterrence work in the cyber era, when an individual sitting in his mother's basement can take down an entire electrical grid? The Fourth Industrial Revolution is ending the divide between physical security and cyber security as the digital world merges with the physical world. Society, the economy and the military are increasingly reliant on digital tools, creating new vulnerabilities and weapons that have no historical precedents. Cyber weapons will play a greater role in the future as critical infrastructure becomes digitalized with smart infrastructure. Even cyber terrorism can affect the physical world as smart cities, self-driving cars, smart grids, smart roads and other elements of the Internet of Things connect the digital with the physical world. The ability to identify and deter aggressors becomes problematic as the battlefield increasingly enters the digital domain. Even gun violence, terrorism and assassinations could also become more anonymous. For example, a decentralized network of gun advocates who link gun ownership to personal liberty are using the Internet to share the designs of 3D-printed guns that can be mounted on recreational drones.

Conclusion

The Fourth Industrial Revolution will intensify military conflict in the coming years, causing a return to war between great powers. The Third Industrial Revolution introduced nuclear power, digital technologies and opened space to exploration. Although these technological advances gave the world cyber weapons, a space race and nuclear arms, the latter could be managed with arms control. Nuclear weapons were maintained as a defensive weapon, while space and cyberspace did not become contested arenas for full military confrontation. The Fourth Industrial Revolution could unravel the nuclear peace by assigning an offensive role to nuclear weapons, while countermeasures such as nuclear-armed submarine drones could intensify the security dilemma and increase the likelihood of accidental war. Space is set to become increasingly militarized and cyber attacks are becoming more destructive as the digital world connects with the physical world. At a time when a multipolar balance of power re-emerges, the growing arenas for proxy wars will be armed with automated weaponry.

The world is in dire need of arms control to manage disruptive weapons technologies. Technological disruptions are contributing to the demise of former arms treaties: the United States withdrew from the ABM Treaty in 2002 and the INF Treaty in 2019. Meanwhile, new treaties are not being developed because states are seeking first-mover strategic advantage rather than working to achieve strategic balance. Will the growing destructiveness and chaos of new weapons technologies eventually bring mankind together once it recognizes that the weapons themselves are the greatest threat, or will new technologies push the world back into wars between the great powers?

9

Global governance: Power, legitimacy and ungovernable technologies

Introduction

Industrial revolutions disrupt the international order and the global governance of productive power. Global governance depends on two key variables – legitimacy and power. Like the decline of British power in the nineteenth century, the decline of US geoeconomic primacy in the twenty-first century is transforming global governance from a hegemonic to a multipolar system. Re-establishing a resilient system for global governance requires a balance between legitimacy and power that reflects the nature of the technologies introduced by the Fourth Industrial Revolution.

In recent decades, the world began to unite based on common interests and a convergence of guiding principles. New technologies spurred the integration of the global economy, and the world moved towards a common system of governance, as evidenced by the success of the WTO. Hundreds of millions of people were lifted out of poverty at a speed without precedent in history. Democracy has increasingly been recognized as the sole legitimate form of governance, with even non-democratic states at least taking the effort to rig elections rather than contest the legitimacy of democracy. The unprecedented connectivity of humanity with the global spread of the Internet would have seemed like science fiction only a few decades ago. Observers might reasonably have concluded that the need and conditions were opportune for advancing global governance.

However, governments failed to take into account the growing economic inequality domestically, social disruptions that tear away at the very fabric of society, diminished democratic accountability by more distant forms of global governance and a rapidly shifting international distribution of power from the West to the East. The expectation that humanity would unite based on common interests, values and a shared fate has rapidly deteriorated. To address the adverse consequences of hyper-globalization, governments are becoming more protectionists: their former emphasis of universal values has been replaced with distinct national identities. As a result, global governance institutions are under pressure to reform.

Global governance is unravelling as the Fourth Industrial Revolution dawns, reducing the international system's ability to manage disruptive technologies and establish rules for cooperation and competition. Because the technologies of the Fourth Industrial Revolution extend beyond national borders and cannot be completely territorialized or nationalized, it is necessary to develop a global system of rules, norms and laws. Global governance must balance three key priorities: establishing common interests, managing the balance of power and mediating cultural differences and conflicting value systems (Hurrell 2007: 2).

The new technologies are developing faster than domestic regulators and legislators can respond. Political leaders' very limited understanding of these technologies was on display to the world in April 2018, when Mark Zuckerberg testified before the US Congress about the functioning of social media. The questions from members of Congress revealed how little they knew about the Internet and digital platforms. Governing such technologies is complicated by the need to address the needs of a variety of stakeholders: the corporate community, civil society, government and the military all have vastly different and even competing interests. The disruptive nature of these technologies also suggests that it will not be sufficient to merely reform existing processes and institutions. Rather, a new governance infrastructure is required.

Furthermore, additional complications arise when attempting to govern technologies at the global level. For example, when one state pioneers a technology, it is unlikely to accept a multilateral approach to regulation. States do not constrain themselves and only cooperate when there is a balance of power. Global governance requires a 'balance of technological power'. For example, the United States will resist the regulation of drones, cyber espionage, AI, bioengineering and other technologies until rival powers have similar capabilities.

This chapter explores the global governance of expanding industrial power and the disruptions caused by a shift from a hegemonic system to a balanced multipolar system. How to govern an international system defined by anarchy and in which the state is the highest sovereign? International institutions facilitate global governance, yet institutions are a reflection of power and only as strong as powerful states allow them to be. Institutions are therefore only effective to the extent that they reflect the international balance of power. The international system enjoys stability under two formats – hegemonic or a balance of power. Hegemonic stability emerges with the concentration of industrial power and the mitigation of international anarchy. It is deemed legitimate if the hegemon can provide common benefits. However, the concentration of productive capacity and other geoeconomic instruments of power are only temporary because the global system naturally gravitates towards equilibrium. The dominant power then loses its legitimacy and becomes increasingly belligerent. This is because primacy depends increasingly on marginalizing rising powers, who respond by banding together to counterbalance the hegemon. The second format for global governance emerges under a balance of power, with the status quo also being based on common principles. However, this system is unstable because it encourages the formation of geoeconomic blocs to shift the balance of dependence. Geoeconomic blocs can be used to establish equilibrium as the foundation for strategic stability, but they can also be motivated to develop strategic advantage and even hegemony.

This chapter will first explore the decline of the British hegemony and the rivalry of competing industrial powers that could not constrain its economic activities within the borders of the nation state. New technologies spurred the first wave of globalization beginning in the 1870s. This trend initially appeared to weaken the role of the sovereign state, but the globalist impulses were instinctively countered by a rise in nationalism. Second, efforts to establish a United States of Europe as a format for governing European industrial power has commonly been envisioned as an initiative to transcend the nation state. The successes and failures of the EU demonstrate, however, that national causes are prioritized and sustainable European governance depends on managing these national interests. Third, post–Cold War global governance sought to establish a hegemonic peace under the legitimacy of a liberal international order. Failure to adequately accommodate China and Russia in that order has resulted in decoupling and resistance to the failed liberal hegemonic system. Systems of governance are fragmenting into regional geoeconomic blocs, making global governance dependent on inter-regional formats. Although Eurasian geoeconomic institutions are collaborating to facilitate global multipolarity, Western institutions attempting to extend their hegemony generally reject any cooperation with them. It is concluded that, much like what happened in the nineteenth century, today's transition from a hegemonic to a multipolar system is unleashing turmoil and undermining the ability to govern new technologies.

The rise and decline of British geoeconomic hegemony

The First Industrial Revolution generated a pressing need for global governance. The Westphalian state, limiting social and economic relations to territorial borders, was challenged by industrial society. Trotsky (1934) succinctly identified the challenge of attempting to fit the economic activities of increasingly productive industrial societies into the cultural and political confines of the nation state.

The story about global governance begins in Europe as the birthplace of the industrial revolution. Economies emerged that required reliable access to natural resources, markets for export, safe transportation corridors and capital. Initially, the industrial power of Britain dominated Europe. Britain's first-mover advantage culminated in control over the main industries for manufactured goods, and the banks that financed the new economic infrastructure. Furthermore, as the dominant maritime power, it also controlled the transportation corridors needed to facilitate or deny reliable trade.

Efforts to establish a European trade system under British hegemonic rule were initially challenged by France in the early nineteenth century, with the Napoleonic Continental System aiming to render continental Europe economically independent by blocking British trade. The Continental System was an early geoeconomic bloc to govern the continent. It set out to improve symmetry in relations with Britain and replace that hegemony with a balance of power. However, enforcing the Continental System by preventing countries from trading with Britain led Napoleon to invade Spain and then launch his disastrous invasion of Russia in 1812. The Russian victory over France enabled Britain to extend its rule and made possible the Cobden–Chevalier trade agreement between Britain and France in 1860 that provided a model for other European states to follow. However, the Russian victory also resulted in the creation of the first collective European security organization, the Concert of Europe, which lasted from 1815 to 1914. As the condition for stable global governance, the Concert of Europe included the major powers, including the recently defeated France.

However, the fundamental problem later identified by Trotsky (1934) had not yet been solved: How could economies with increasing productive power and expanding economic connectivity fit into the limited format of the nation state? Without governance to manage the frequent disruptions to the geoeconomic status quo, conflict and the prospect of war were always the first instincts.

Britain's first-mover advantage and geoeconomic leadership soon began to wane as other powers competed by establishing their own industries, transportation corridors and customs unions. Starting in the 1830s, economic connectivity based on railways and economic union became the 'Siamese twins' of German state-building (Earle 1943: 442). Yet, the German Customs Union, Zollverein, was also used as an instrument for region-building through the inclusion of non-German states. Zollverein was partly motivated by the Napoleonic Continental System under which Germany had prospered. Furthermore, physical infrastructure enhanced economic connectivity with markets beyond the German states. For example, Germany's Berlin–Baghdad Railway and its development of a capable navy posed a threat to British, Russian and French interests. With the objective of skewing the balance of dependence by increasing both autonomy and influence, this connectivity coincided with the goal of territorial expansion to advance autarky.

The opening of the Suez Canal in 1869 under French control threatened to undermine British dominance over global transportation corridors. London responded by protesting the use of slave labour and inciting a revolt during its construction. By 1898, the United States had emerged victorious in the US–Spanish War and seized control over several Spanish colonial possessions, such as the Philippines. This established the Untied States as a leading geoeconomic power in the Pacific. After Washington coerced Panama to secede from Colombia in 1903, the United States could also use the strategic Panama Canal to connect the Pacific with the Atlantic to challenge Britain's rule over the seas. Russia posed a unique challenge to Britain because it had become the fastest growing economy by the late nineteenth century and threatened the primacy of all maritime powers by connecting the vast Eurasian landmass with transcontinental railroads (Mackinder 1904: 434). Germany, however, became the spark that unleashed the First World War, a conflict that was largely confined to Europe. Trotsky (1934: 397) would later recognize why Europe moved towards war:

> The basic tendency of our century is the growing contradiction between the nation and economic life. In Europe this contradiction has become intolerably acute ... One of the main causes of the World War was the striving of German capital to break through into a wider arena. Hitler fought as a corporal in 1914–1918 not to unite the German nation but in the name of a supra-national imperialistic program that expressed itself in the famous formula "to organize Europe" ... But Germany was no exception. She only expressed in a more intense and aggressive form the tendency of every other national capitalist economy.

Legitimacy and the limits of global governance – the nation as the largest tribe

Globalization initially appeared to give way to a weakened nation state as the foundation for global governance. Because economic and social activities defy national borders, it seemed reasonable to deduce that the nation state would diminish in relevance. The paradox of the first wave of globalization in the late nineteenth century, however, was that it reaffirmed statehood by triggering countries to reassert their authority and the people to seek refuge in national identities.

The first wave of globalization stretched from the 1870s to 1914.[1] Major advances in manufacturing and the invention of steamships and railroads contributed greatly to the process by facilitating the unprecedented trade and movement of people and ideas. Capital began to flow relatively freely and financial integration followed. Immigration to Germany was second only to the United States, with approximately 60 million Europeans making their way to America. The imperial expansion of European powers drew the rest of the world into a complex system of global governance under European administration. Sovereignty has not been an absolute concept ever since. State sovereignty has been defined as 'organised hypocrisy', as a foundational norm of the international system that is frequently violated (Krasner 1999). However, globalization is largely incompatible with national sovereignty and democracy. Globalization will, therefore, be detested and resisted as a threat to the democratic nation state (Rodrik 2011).

Industrialization disrupted traditional communities and caused mass immigration and emigration, increasing the bureaucratic role of the state. Mass immigration required the establishment of border control, hygiene control, the issuance of travel documents and other state functions. Globalization also fuelled a nationalist backlash and nationalism among ethnic diasporas as the ethnocultural distinction between 'us' and 'them' became more pronounced. Industrial society and mass migration provoked a rise in romanticized nationalism. The fear of cultural absorption by a rival power motivated governments and people to distinguish between 'natives' and 'non-natives'. Beginning in the 1870s, France shifted its focus from universalism to national culture as an indicator of civilization (Al-Azmeh 2012). The proliferation of French culture also encouraged Germany to assert its distinctive cultural autonomy.

---

[1] The concept of globalization is contested, with some arguing that the first wave of globalization began with Christopher Columbus in the fifteenth century.

The modernization resulting from the Industrial Revolution polarized society between the bourgeoisie cosmopolitans who benefited economically from globalization and the poor people that had been displaced from their traditional communities by rapid industrialization. Workers increasingly viewed the cosmopolitan elites as advancing economic interests at the expense of the people, while the elites viewed the working class as being stuck in a bygone era. The proportion of foreign-born people living in the United States grew to 14.8 per cent in the 1890s, an all-time high. Throughout the West in the1890s, nationalism developed a strong racial component as a means for hardening the ideational border of the state. The failure to address the concerns of disenfranchised people gave rise to populists who were prepared to scale back on globalization. In California, the highly influential workers union leader, Denis Kearney – who adopted the popular slogan 'The Chinese must go' – scorned not only Chinese labour, but also capitalism, the media and the political elites for advancing an industrial society that did not benefit the people. In Germany, the huge influx of labourers from Poland and Jews from Russia sparked fears of cultural disruptions and sparked a more crude form of nationalism in response.

Transcending the nation state is a revolutionary endeavour: it eliminates the former distinctive ethnocultural foundation for the political entity and replaces it with untested characteristics that must lay the material and non-material foundations for social cohesion. Can the distinctive characteristics of the nation be transcended or is it true that 'the primitive mind is, in the fullest sense of the word, imperishable'? (Freud 1963: 119). Furthermore, is it possible to socially engineer a regional, civilizational or a global identity?

Beyond the nation state and towards geoeconomic blocs

Global governance aims to establish a set of unifying principles about how to manage the rise of industrial societies. The principal problem is to constrain the growing productive power within the territorial space of the distinctive ethnocultural Westphalian state. The Industrial Revolution gave rise to a key question that has not been solved to this day: Is the purpose of global governance to overcome and transcend the nation state or to maintain sovereignty? If nation states integrate into larger constructs, should those structures replicate the economic arrangements of the component states or reorganize their capital and productive powers?

Viewing the nation state as an archaic concept, Trotsky (1934: 397) believed that ever-increasing productive capacity demanded nothing less than the dismantling of the European nation state:

> How may the economic unity of Europe be guaranteed, while preserving complete freedom of cultural development to the peoples living there? How may unified Europe be included within a coordinated world economy? The solution to this question can be reached not by deifying the nation, but on the contrary by completely liberating productive forces from the fetters imposed upon them by the national state.

Trotsky's suggestion was translated into a gigantic social experiment with Russia responding to the First World War by abandoning the nation state and capitalism. The objective was to replace the past with a more capable format for governing industrial societies – a post-national utopia in which workers would seize the means of production. Apart from the flawed economics of communism and the authoritarian method of Soviet governance, there were two major problems.

First, as the Soviet and Yugoslav experience demonstrated, national identities could not be transcended. The ethno-federal structure of the Soviet Union was based on the recognition of ethnocultural distinctiveness as the foundation of *demos*. While transcending national identities became a long-term objective, the Soviet Union actually laid the foundation for the nation state by delineating clearly recognized administrative borders as political entities that throughout history had been non-existent.

Second, the Soviet state did not transcend rivalry in the international system because it linked the ideals of communism to an entity of power. Herz (1950a) conceptualizes 'idealist internationalism' as the attempt to link the spread of norms of human freedom in the international system to overcoming the 'realism' and power competition in international relations. However, idealist internationalism eventually becomes 'subservient to a primarily "national" cause, or rather, the maintenance of the regime of one specific "big power"' (Herz 1950a). After seizing control in Russia, the Bolshevik Party declared its intention to become subordinate to the world proletariat because Lenin expected the imminent emergence of an 'All-World Federative Soviet Republic'. Linking ideals to a unit competing for power and hegemony caused a return to national causes manifested by exclusion, expansionism, aggression and imperialism. 'Titoism' exemplifies the Soviet rejection and opposition of power structures independent of the Soviet Union due to its 'federalistic ideology' with centralized power (Herz 1950a: 172).

Towards a United States of Europe

Geoeconomic blocs range from loose economic unions to political unions that absorb the functions and prerogatives of the state. Geoeconomic blocs function much like a military alliance in terms of managing internal rivalries and competition with external adversaries. Geoeconomic blocs govern in two ways – by managing the geoeconomic rivalry between member states and by expanding governance beyond the borders of the member states. These two functions are intrinsically linked because a state's willingness to cede some sovereignty to a geoeconomic bloc is largely conditioned upon the promise of collective influence. The geoeconomic bloc has a greater ability to manage the growing productive powers of interconnected industrial societies. However, geoeconomic blocs have several limitations: their internal cohesion is weaker than nation states and, often, they merely create larger entities of power.

A bloc's member states expect the 'cost' of pooling sovereignty to be compensated by the greater collective autonomy and influence they receive through skewing the balance of dependence with the rest of the world. This state-centric and calculative approach indicates the limitations of geoeconomic blocs. When integration efforts do not produce sufficient material gains, collective autonomy and influence, states repatriate their sovereignty and nationalism returns with a vengeance. Geoeconomic blocs have incentive to become more powerful by continuously expanding. This, however, can disrupt their internal balance of power. They then lose legitimacy and the internal cohesion of the *demos* erodes. Furthermore, the geoeconomic bloc merely becomes a larger entity of power that must still develop a system of governance to interact with the rest of the world. Initially, a geoeconomic bloc can develop hegemonic peace because collective bargaining power creates asymmetrical dependence with the rest of the world. However, the international system moves towards equilibrium because other regions then develop geoeconomic blocs to correct the imbalance. At that point, global governance will shift from a hegemonic model to one of multipolarity based on geoeconomic inter-regionalism.

The First World War, with its industrial-scale destruction, motivated leaders to address the challenge of governing industrialized Europe. The problems that caused the war had not been resolved. Rather, the Treaty of Versailles merely limited Germany's ability to expand industrial capacity. This conditioned peace in Europe on perpetuating Germany's weakness. That status quo became intolerable to Germany and the national humiliation fuelled a belligerent nationalism. In the years prior to the Second World War, Karl Haushofer, a leading intellectual figure in Germany in the 1930s and 1940s, argued that great power status for Germany could only be achieved by acquiring more territory or 'lebensraum' (living space) to achieve economic autarky. Among other proposals, French politician and financier Joseph Caillaux suggested oversight to limit industrial development and technological advances, which Trotsky (1934: 399) defined as an unfeasible and undesirable Luddite strategy.

The League of Nations, that replaced the Concert of Europe, was a weak institutional framework for managing relations between states. With greater ambitions, French Prime Minister Aristide Briand called for the establishment of a United States of Europe during a speech in 1929 at the League of Nations. Richard von Coudenhove-Kalergi's publication of *Pan-Europa* in 1923 did a great deal towards uniting the continent. The idea was not new: the French National Assembly had advocated the establishment of a United States of Europe in 1871. Even Napoleon had previously said that his motivation for conquering Europe was to develop 'the United States of Europe' governed by a 'European system, a European Code of Laws, a European judiciary; there would be but one people in Europe' (Riley 2013: 30). Failing to unite Europe through diplomacy, Germany eventually sought to bring the continent together by force in what became the Second World War. Informed by militarism and a nefarious theory of race, a united Europe under German fascism would have lacked legitimacy. The international division of labour would be structured according to race, with Eastern Europeans used for hard manual labour and the Germanic peoples in the Netherlands, Belgium and Scandinavia occupying a higher station in the global pecking order (Du Bois 1941).

Following Germany's defeat, the Allies' initial impulse was to implement a sort of Treaty of Versailles 2.0 that would deindustrialize the country and permanently eradicate mechanized German aggression. According to then ex-US President Herbert Hoover, the Morgenthau Plan – also known as US Directive JSC 1067 – would have required the United States to 'exterminate or move 25,000,000 people out of it [Germany]' (Chang 2003: 455). However, the emergence of Soviet communism as a rival power and ideology convinced the Americans and British to instead partner with Germany. Reviving German industrial power was required to rebuild industrial capitalism in Western Europe and collectively confront the Soviet Union. Six months after his Iron Curtain speech, Churchill argued in September 1946 that the Soviet threat demanded that the West let go of the past and embrace Germany. Furthermore, Churchill (1994: 6) called for building 'a kind of United States of Europe'.

The organization of Europe around the leadership of maritime powers resulted in systemic incentives to contain Russia. Britain and the United States, as non-continental powers, have traditionally pursued an offshore strategy aimed at ensuring that a hegemon would not emerge in Eurasia (Mearsheimer and Walt 2016). The dominance of Britain as a maritime power was theorized by Mackinder to depend on preventing a German–Russian partnership as land powers. When the United States replaced Britain as the leading maritime power, Spykman further developed the ideas of Mackinder by advocating 'forward deployments'. Spykman (1942: 182) argued that it was the historical responsibility of Washington to encircle and contain Russia:

> For two hundred years, since the time of Peter the Great, Russia has attempted to break through the encircling ring of border states and the reach the ocean. Geography and sea power have persistently thwarted her.

Global governance is therefore premised on preserving a division and balance of power in Europe and Eurasia. The US National Security Strategy of 1988 reiterated the basic idea about containing land powers in Eurasia:

> The United States' most basic national security interests would be endangered if a hostile state or group of states were to dominate the Eurasian landmass- that area of the globe often referred to as the world's heartland. We fought two world wars to prevent this from occurring. And, since 1945, we have sought to prevent the Soviet Union from capitalizing on its geostrategic advantage to dominate its neighbors in Western Europe, Asia, and the Middle East, and thereby fundamentally alter the global balance of power to our disadvantage.
>
> (White House 1988: 1)

The need to counterbalance the Soviet Union caused the United States and Britain to reverse their position and support integration among European continental powers. The precursor to the European Union was subsequently established in 1952, *the European Coal and Steel Community*, that regulated the industrial production of six Western European states under a centralized authority.

Division emerges over the purpose of European integration, which can be categorized as either federalist or functionalist integration (Mitrany 1965). 'Federalist integration' argues that *functions follow the form*. The central political objective of federalists is to centralize power by transferring state competencies, and the function of the entity will depend on this form. For example, the European Union may become a military actor because integrating military capabilities is instrumental to federalize. By contrast, 'functionalist integration' implies that *form follows function*. In this case, integration is only pursued in areas where it provides economic, political and security benefits for member states. Without ensuring that the benefits of integration outweigh the loss of sovereignty, integration would have to be pursued without the consent of the European people, or even by coercion. Mitrany (1965) cautioned that a federalist integration approach to a 'United States of Europe' would resemble the undemocratic and authoritarian structures of the Soviet Union rather than the United States. Throughout the Cold War, United States leadership in the West limited the European Community's scope of governance. However, less than two months after the collapse of the Soviet Union, the European Union was established by the Maastricht Treaty in February1992.

The successes and failures of the EU can be attributed to geoeconomics as a nation-building development strategy. Geoeconomics is the principal instrument for creating a European state, but the geoeconomic instruments of power are still beholden to the nation state. The EU initially succeeded by managing both power and legitimacy. Governance did not transcend the nation state: rather, stability rested on a balance of power between major economies such as Germany, France, Britain and Italy. A balance of power within an alliance ensures that no single power can dominate and extract political concessions from other member states. Integration projects therefore have greater benefits when the economies of member states are similar in size (Sorhun 2014: 288). The Single Market of 1987 and the visa-free travel of the Schengen Agreement increased intra-EU trade, which translated into political loyalty and solidarity. The collective bargaining power of the EU facilitates asymmetrical dependence with neighbouring states that it uses to govern beyond EU borders. This creates the political and economic conditions necessary for favourable access to the EU's Single Market (Bretherton and Vogler 1999: 47). The EU is therefore commonly referred to as a 'regulatory power' or 'regulatory empire' because its economic dominance is used to export its legal framework (Eberlein and Grande 2005; Zielonka 2008: 474; Damro 2015). The EU can simply focus on regulating its own markets to achieve influence beyond its borders because 'the size and attractiveness of its market does the rest' (Bradford 2012: 65). The more territory and economic power the EU absorbs, the more powerful its governance becomes and the more difficult it is for other states to remain outside the Union. Non-member states such as Norway and Switzerland are included in a 'pay-without-say' model according to which they must implement all EU directives without having a voice in the decision-making. Former French President Valery

Giscard d'Estaing, a key architect of the rejected EU Constitution, argued that the new purpose of the EU was power:

> Over the decades, the basis of the EU's existence has changed. We've moved from seeking peace to seeking greatness. The goal is clear: we have to become one of the three main players in the world, so that in 20 years, the US, China and the EU will control the world's three most important currencies.
>
> (Rettman 2013)

The failure of the EU derives from its inability to move beyond national causes. Although the purpose of the Coal and Steel Community had been to regulate industrial production to overcome the problem of increasingly productive industrial societies, the newly formed EU enabled Germany to pursue a neo-mercantilist development strategy at the expense of its neighbours. While Germany produced and saved, the economies of southern member states became dependent on borrowing and consumption (Baru 2012: 53). The US Treasury Report condemned Germany for strengthening its own economy at the expense of its neighbours:

> Within the euro area, countries with large and persistent surpluses need to take action to boost domestic demand growth and shrink their surpluses. Germany has maintained a large current account surplus throughout the euro area financial crisis, and in 2012, Germany's nominal current account surplus was larger than that of China. Germany's anaemic pace of domestic demand growth and dependence on exports have hampered rebalancing at a time when many other euro-area countries have been under severe pressure to curb demand and compress imports in order to promote adjustment. The net result has been a deflationary bias for the euro area, as well as for the world economy.
>
> (US Treasury 2013: 3)

EU expansion and the euro further upset the internal balance of power. First, power began to concentrate in Germany. The German economy benefitted most from trade with new member states, while the euro provided Germany with a severely devalued currency that fuelled its export-driven development strategy. Without public support for further integration to move beyond the nation state, the political elites circumvented the consent of the people. For example, the French and Dutch rejection of the Treaty for Establishing a Constitution of Europe was resolved by merely rewriting it as the Lisbon Treaty and not holding referendums. The Euro was largely designed to achieve political integration without consent. A monetary union requires a fiscal union and a fiscal union requires a political union. Without the consent for a political union, the EU began integration at the other end in the hope that the common currency would create a crisis that would set in motion a 'chain reaction' towards political union (Padoa-Schioppa 2004: 14; Spolaore 2013).

As the EU became less capable of delivering material benefits, it became increasingly reliant on coercion. Germany took the lead, setting conditions for 'helping' the Mediterranean member states that had never recovered from their loss of productive power to Germany or from the global financial crisis (Stockhammer 2014). With fewer carrots and waning excitement about the European project, further integration and governance become increasingly reliant on the sticks of fear and threats to deter states from decoupling from the EU (Stiglitz 2016). On the other side of the Atlantic, the United States is also increasingly relying on coercion to gain compliance with its diktat. This has culminated in threats and the levelling of tariffs or sanctions against the EU, Iran, India, Russia, China and others.

Internal cohesion also eroded due to EU expansion, with the free movement of peoples between vastly different economies disrupting demographics. British politicians began winning votes by promising to reduce the number of Polish immigrants, while Polish politicians were calling for its citizens to return home to reverse the disastrous population decline. Although the increased immigration to Britain made the rich more affluent, the greater supply of immigrants also put downward pressures on wages and weakened the distinctive national culture. A YouGov poll revealed in 2011 that 62 per cent of the British people agreed with the following statement: 'Britain has changed in recent times beyond recognition, it sometimes feels like a foreign country, and this makes me feel uncomfortable'. Further pressure was put on European nation states when Germany decided to open its borders to migrants in 2015 without first consulting other EU member states. Germany promotes a concept of a European identity based on liberal values, obligating it to assist migrants and asylum seekers. However, for countries such as Hungary and Poland, European identity is based on a demos defined by shared history, culture, ethnicity and traditions, causing them to resist mass migration from the Middle East. Germany subsequently supported sanctions against member states that did not adhere to its version of 'European values'. Such failure to accommodate the distinctive values of the nation state also prompted populists to gravitate towards Russia, which is positioning itself as an international conservative power advocating the virtues of Christianity, the traditional family and the preservation of traditional culture (Diesen 2018).

The rise and decline of US geoeconomic hegemony

The United States emerged as a seemingly benign hegemon with political legitimacy rooted in its history of advancing human freedoms. US power initially appeared to be benign compared to Europe due its geography – the distance from Europe and the size of the country. The large US domestic market could absorb its growing industrial output. Comparing Germany with the United States, Brooks Adams noted: '[T]he Germans cannot increase their velocity because they cannot extend their base, and augment their mass – we can and do' (Wiebe 1967: 234). However, as the United States began extending into the Pacific, US Senator Albert Beveridge advocated for further imperial expansion as the answer to growing productive powers:

> American factories are making more than the American people can use; American soil is producing more than they can consume. Fate has written our policy for us; the trade of the world must and shall be ours ... We will establish trading-posts throughout the world as distributing points for American products. We will cover the ocean with our merchant marine. Great colonies governing themselves, flying our flag and trading with us, will grow about our posts of trade. Our institutions will follow our flag on the wings of commerce.
>
> (Bowers 1932: 67)

Liberal ideals had previously informed the US policy of regional industrial expansion in the Americas and the desire to avoid entangling alliances with Europeans. With the country growing in power, Woodrow Wilson altered the US posture from a passive beacon of democracy to be emulated to an active missionary duty in which the military defeat of Germany would be the 'war to end all wars' and make the world 'safe for democracy'. Trotsky (1934: 401–2) predicted that the imperial impulses of the United States would grow, as arguing that 'sooner or later American capitalism must open up ways for itself throughout the length and breadth of our entire planet':

> The relative equilibrium of its internal and seemingly inexhaustible market assured the United States a decided technical and economic preponderance over Europe. But its intervention in the World War was really an expression of the fact that its internal equilibrium was already disrupted. The changes introduced by the war into the American structure have in turn made entry into the world arena a life and death question for American capitalism. There is ample evidence that this entry must assume extremely dramatic forms.

After Europe brought ruin upon itself during the Second World War, the United States emerged as the largest industrial and dominant geoeconomic power, thus taking over the hegemonic position that Britain had held since the First Industrial Revolution. Global governance established the rules for a world that was divided by a bipolar international distribution of power and conflicting concepts of legitimacy resulting from two opposing ideologies. The Western European industrial control of the old colonial system was dismantled because both the United States and the Soviet Union had an interest to replace their influence. Both the capitalist and communist ideologies offered concepts for advancing human freedom that gave legitimacy to their attempts to replace Western European power in the colonies.

In the capitalist West, the United States established liberal hegemony that enabled its geoeconomic advantage. The Marshal Plan opened up Europe to more competitive US industrial power. Washington asserted its control over oil in the Middle East and in 1945 the US Chief of the Near Eastern Division stated that in 'Saudi Arabia, where the oil resources constitute a stupendous source of strategic power, and one of the greatest material prizes in world history, a concession covering this oil is nominally in American control' (US State Department 1945). The main maritime transportation corridors were placed under US control. The Bretton Woods system made the United States the leader in the IMF and World Bank. Bretton Woods also made the US dollar the world's trade and reserve currency, a position strengthened by conditioning military support for Saudi Arabia and the Gulf states on those countries trading energy exclusively in US dollars. George Kennan (1948) cautioned against overextending the United States with idealistic missions, especially in Asia, as pursuing leadership in the East would only agitate and alienate:

> We have about 50% of the world's wealth but only 6.3% of its population … Our real task in the coming period is to devise a pattern of relationships which will permit us to maintain this position of disparity without positive detriment to our national security … We need not deceive ourselves that we can afford today the luxury of altruism and world-benefaction.

However, Western international governance during the Cold War fostered the illusion of liberal peace because the main rivals were communist states largely detached from international markets. The capitalist allies, confronting a common enemy, had strong incentives to mitigate geoeconomic tensions between themselves.

Post–Cold War: Global governance without China and Russia

A world order must include the great powers to be truly international. Global governance after the Cold War failed to establish a true world order because it was structured to cement the unipolar era (Mearsheimer 2019: 11). China and Russia were expected to integrate into the system and abide by the rules. However, the West, as the incumbent, was ill-prepared to reform and reach a political settlement that adequately accommodated its former rivals. Consequently, China and Russia are countering the Western-centric order by advancing a project to collectively integrate Greater Eurasia (Karaganov 2018).

The 'unipolar moment' was presented as a liberal international order that aligned hegemony with universal values. This liberal international order recast the former capitalist/communist divide as a liberal/authoritarian divide to avoid reforms and limit the participation of former adversaries. Kennan criticized Washington for disguising national interests as values: 'Russia's democracy is as far advanced, if not farther, as any of these countries we've just signed up to defend from Russia' (Friedman 1998). Defenders of the international liberal order tend to depict it as a multilateral, rules-based and benign order that made peaceful coexistence among the Western powers possible. After the Cold War, however, the rules-based liberal international order under the collective leadership of the West became a contradiction in terms because the requirement for solidarity among Western powers will always trump consistent application of international law and rules. In other words, in the Western-led rules-based system, Russia and China will always be in the wrong.

Global governance becomes too dependent on advanced strategic advantage to sustain unipolarity and collective hegemony, undermining the ability to deliver strategic stability. With legitimacy for governance based on liberal values – as opposed to a monarchy, religion or ethnocultural distinctiveness – the United States establishes itself as the arbiter of legitimacy that can dictate moral truths.

Much like the idealist internationalism behind the French Revolution and the Bolshevik Revolution, subservient national causes have become the West's liberal democratic internationalism. The West emulates the phenomenon of Soviet 'Titoism' with liberal democracy presented as both a universal value and an international hegemonic norm (Rosow 2005). The more democratic institutions are, the more leader will defend democratic values from the rule of the majority (Herz 1950b: 165). Global governance does mitigate and harmonize competing interests, but has become for the West a means for correcting the behaviour of adversaries. Strategic documents of the West insinuate a pedagogic teacher–student relationship, casting the West as a socializing agent that civilizes Russia (Diesen 2017b: 11). Moscow was given the option of either accepting the dominant role of NATO and the EU in Europe or becoming a 'counter-civilizational force' because rejecting Western hegemony was made tantamount to rejecting liberal values (Williams and Neumann 2000). Furthermore, the liberal international order is paradoxical in that it is conditioned on preserving unipolarity but fuelled the rise of China and transformed the world from a unipolar to a multipolar order (Mearsheimer 2019).

Efforts by states and geoeconomic blocs to govern globally without including other major powers tend to fragment the international system and fuel conflict. As a case in point, efforts by the EU to extend governance to its neighbouring states in terms of regulations, standards and legislation are causing tensions with both the states it seeks to govern and rival poles of power such as Russia. The EU imposes its energy market legislation on neighbouring states by threatening them with economic isolation. Indicative of the rivalry in governance systems, the EU Commissioner for Energy accused Russia of 'pure blackmail' for offering energy discounts to Belarus if it refused to adopt EU energy legislation-based energy discounts. Without any irony intended, the EU Commissioner for Energy went on to threaten Moldova and Ukraine with economic isolation if they also accepted the Russian offer: 'It is clear that whoever leaves the Energy Community indirectly leaves the partnership with the EU. It becomes the next Belarus' (Keating 2012). The punishment of Ukraine the following year for rejecting the EU Association Agreement went beyond economics, with the EU supporting riots and the eventual overthrow of the government. Donald Tusk, the Prime Minister of Poland who became the President of the European Council in 2014, called for moving beyond political support by funding the anti-government movement in Ukraine with 3 million Euros during the height of the riots (Rettman 2014).

Using national laws to legislate digital technologies that are not bound by national borders is clearly problematic. International law itself becomes weakened as the world fragments into regions that attempt to govern beyond their own borders. There is already a trend towards extraterritoriality with states attempting to extend their legal reach beyond the territory over which they have jurisdiction, thus running counter to customary international law. The United States has been able to unilaterally impose its domestic legislation on the rest of the world because it controls key geoeconomic instruments such as the SWIFT transaction system based on US dollars. For example, a French bank, BNP Paribas, had to accept a US government fine of almost $9 billion for conducting bilateral trade with Sudan, Iran and Cuba. The arrest in Canada of the Huawei Chief Financial Officer for alleged violations of US laws and the seizure by the UK of a Syria-bound Iranian oil tanker for the breaching of EU laws demonstrate a trend towards extraterritorialism and the subsequent fragmentation of global governance. US law even replaced international law in the case of the Iranian nuclear deal, with the United States pulling out of the agreement and imposing sanctions on countries still abiding by the deal. As US Treasury Secretary Steven Mnuchin informed G7 finance ministers: 'If you want to participate in the dollar system you abide by US sanctions' (Mallet 2019).

The Fourth Industrial Revolution will exacerbate the threat of states imposing extraterritoriality. The US Cloud Act (Clarifying Lawful Overseas Use of Data) of 2018 declares the right of US corporations to extract data from foreign companies stored by US cloud services providers. The Cloud Act undermines domestic privacy laws and grants the United States a competitive advantage by enabling it to harvest more data to develop superior AI software. Extending the US domestic legislative space into the territory of other countries demonstrates a geoeconomic effort to use asymmetrical technological and economic dependence to claim a privileged position in global governance. It seems unlikely that the United States would accept the EU, China or Russia granting themselves extraterritorial jurisdiction on US soil. The resulting breakdown in global governance encourages states and geoeconomic blocs to decouple from foreign digital platforms and instead develop their own solutions.

China under the US liberal hegemony

China, Russia and other emerging powers do not accept the dual structure of the liberal international order in which the United States enforces the rules but is not bound by them. China's growing economic power and the absence of expansionist military and geoeconomic blocs along its borders is the result of Beijing having gradually and patiently built up its strength. By contrast, Russia felt an urgent need to counterbalance the West because its economy had collapsed in the 1990s and it was increasingly marginalized by an expansionist NATO and EU. Thus, China kept its head down to delay confrontation while Russia had to punch above its weight and take greater risks.

Beijing initially sought to minimize its footprint in global governance to prevent attracting unwanted attention and being counterbalanced by other large powers. Deng Xiaoping's commitment to China's 'peaceful rise', starting from the 1970s, was a strategic plan. China's intent was to 'hide and bide' – hide its capabilities and bide its time. China did not challenge US geoeconomic instruments of power, such as its strategic industries, transportation corridors and the Bretton Woods institutions.

The United States initially welcomed China's passive stance in global governance because it kept such efforts the prerogative of the West. This approach, however, gradually raised doubts, and China was encouraged to integrate and channel its influence within the Western-centric international system. The main concern was that China would only use its influence in global governance later, once it had the ability to challenge and overthrow the existing international order (Ikenberry 2008). Beijing was therefore encouraged to take greater responsibility in the international system as an indicator of its intentions and future path. Maintaining China's 'peaceful rise' is a dual process because China must be prepared to integrate into the rules-based system while the powers dominating the existing system must reform and adjust to accommodate China (Buzan 2010: 5). The United States, however, did not accommodate Beijing because it was reluctant to relinquish its dominant role in such institutions as the IMF, World Bank and Asian Development Bank (Hilpert and Wacker 2015: 2).

China's export-driven development strategy is neo-mercantilist. China became the factory of the world by offering what seemed to be an endless supply of labour from an unproductive agricultural sector that it buttressed with a suppressed currency. By demanding that foreign companies operating in China establish joint ventures with domestic companies to transfer technology and know-how, China rapidly climbed up global value chains. China's huge trade surplus was then invested in financing US debt, reducing Washington's willingness to confront Beijing.

As China's productive forces continued to grow, it was less able to limit its industrial power and economic activity within its own borders. Domestic infrastructure projects had created large corporations capable of competing in international markets. China needed to secure a reliable supply of energy resources, motivating it to make forceful inroads into Africa, Central Asia and other regions of the world (Kreft 2006: 65). By the time the global financial crisis hit in 2008, China's vast accumulation of US dollars had become a vulnerability. The United States responded to its fiscal problem of excessive borrowing and spending by borrowing and spending even more.

Over the following years, Beijing dramatically altered its approach to global governance by restructuring global value chains around China. Beijing expressed its intention to assert leadership in the key technologies of the Fourth Industrial Revolution and to develop a Digital Silk Road. In 2013, Beijing launched the Belt and Road Initiative to physically integrate the world along Chinese land and maritime corridors. In 2015, China launched the Asia Infrastructure Investment Bank (AIIB) as a rival the Bretton Woods institutions and as a means of gradually internationalizing the Chinese yuan.

Russia under the US liberal hegemony

Towards the end of the Cold War, Moscow attempted to improve global governance by changing its confrontational bloc-based security architecture. Gorbachev proposed building a 'Common European Home' from Vancouver to Vladivostok that would harmonize the interests of capitalist and socialist states. The United States countered by proposing a 'Europe Whole and Free' that would unite the East and West under common liberal democratic principles – the implication being that it would extend rather than limit US leadership. When the Soviet Union collapsed, Yeltsin largely aligned Russia with the 'Europe Whole and Free' format, essentially agreeing to integrate with the West based on the common principles of capitalism and democracy. Including Russia, however, would have unravelled the structures that upheld US leadership. Rather than withdrawing from Europe, the United States chose to expand. One month after the demise of the Soviet Union, President Bush (1992) proclaimed victoriously:

> By the grace of God, America won the cold war ... There are those who say that now we can turn away from the world, that we have no special role, no special place. But we are the United States of America, the leader of the West that has become the leader of the world. And as long as I am President, I will continue to lead in support of freedom everywhere.

The failure of the West to reach a political settlement with Russia that accommodated it in Europe and the system of global governance has been a source of conflict ever since. A newly emboldened Europe demoted Russia to a non-European state. Uniting the continent by expanding NATO and the EU subsequently made 'European integration' a zero-sum process whereby the shared neighbourhood was expected to decouple from Russia and look to Washington and Brussels for leadership. Kennan predicted NATO expansionism would be 'the beginning of a new cold war ... there is going to be a bad reaction from Russia, and then [the NATO expanders] will say that we always told you that is how the Russians are – but this is just wrong' (Friedman 1998). The Cold War ended much like other wars, with NATO representing the victorious powers expanding into the conquered territory and laying the foundation for future conflicts (Waltz 2000). Mearsheimer (2014) similarly blamed the expansionist policies of the West for the deteriorating relations with Russia and the subsequent war in Ukraine.

Russia made several overtures towards establishing a Greater Europe. Both Yeltsin and Putin initially indicated a willingness to join NATO. After the September 11 attacks, Moscow attempted to position itself as the main ally of the United States in the war on terror. In 2008, President Medvedev proposed a new European security architecture. And lastly in 2010, Putin put forward the idea of an EU–Russian Union (Diesen and Wood 2012). Putin stated:

> From the beginning, we failed to overcome Europe's division. Twenty-five years ago, the Berlin Wall fell, but invisible walls were moved to the East of Europe. This has led to mutual misunderstandings and assignment of guilt. They are the cause of all crises ever since.
>
> (Bertrand 2016)

The EU similarly had to engage with a rising Russia that was too large to include as a member or govern as a non-member. The Eastern Partnership is blatant in its objective of shifting the economic dependence of the shared neighbourhood from Moscow to Brussels. By 2013, the EU was advancing its Association Agreements with the shared neighbourhood. It was, essentially, imposing a civilizational ultimatum according to which 'they must finally choose, so the narrative goes, between East and West' (Charap and Troitskiy 2013: 50). This created a dilemma because 'it transform[ed] integration, a positive-sum process by definition, into a zero-sum game for the state that is excluded from the integration initiatives offered to its neighbors' (Charap and Troitskiy 2013: 50). The Western-backed coup in Ukraine in 2014 demonstrated the challenge of the so-called 'Mitrany paradox', whereby integration projects construct fewer, larger and less compatible entities of power (Booth and Wheeler 2008: 188–9).

Russia's Greater Europe concept, based on Gorbachev's Common European Home, was a flawed concept from a geoeconomic standpoint. By committing to a Greater Europe, Russia would have become excessively dependent on an asymmetrical partnership with the more powerful EU, thus enabling the EU to maximize its autonomy and influence. As a result, Brussels had little incentive to accommodate Russia in European institutions and instead focused on increasingly skewing the balance of dependence by diversifying away from Russian energy and decoupling Russia's neighbours from Moscow's geoeconomic orbit. Ukraine became the litmus test for the feasibility of a Greater Europe when its democratically elected leadership sought to integrate with both Russia and the EU – thereby coinciding with Russia's pan-European ambitions (Diesen and Keane 2017). The Western-backed support for the toppling of President Yanukovich in 2014 and the instalment of an anti-Russian government shattered Moscow's illusions about the prospect of gradually integrating into a Greater Europe.

Moscow replaced its plans for a Greater Europe with the Greater Eurasian Initiative. Former Russian Foreign Minister Igor Ivanov (2015), who had been an advocate of the Greater Europe plan, argued that the initiative had been utopian and instead supported the more feasible Greater Eurasia Initiative. The geoeconomics of Greater Eurasia improves the 'balance of dependence' because it would enable Russia to diversify its economic connectivity to avoid becoming overly dependent on any one state or region. The concept envisions Russia positioning itself as an essential pole of power within a multipolar and economically integrated Greater Eurasia that encompasses Europe, China, South Korea, India, Iran and everything in between. The anti-Russian sanctions that followed the Crimean annexation/reunification gave Moscow additional impetus to achieve technological sovereignty and geoeconomic independence from the West by rapidly modernizing and diversifying its partnerships.

Greater Eurasia ended the prospect of a common Europe and the prospect of centralized global governance. The Greater Eurasia concept aims to decouple from the West's geoeconomic instruments of power and develop global governance based on a balance of power. Russia intends to develop strategic industries, transportation corridors and financial instruments beyond the control of the United States. These include technological sovereignty, the Arctic corridor, Eurasian regional institutions and development banks, an international payment system and the use of regional currencies. It is inevitable that China serves as Russia's main partner in forming a Greater Eurasia due to Beijing's ability and intention to challenge the geoeconomic leadership of the West.

Globalization as inter-regionalism

Globalization is not coming to an end: rather, it has restructured as inter-regionalism. States are gravitating towards geoeconomic regions as a more feasible way to balance the need to move beyond the confines of the nation state with the need to compete against other entities of power. Regionalism among both allies and adversaries undermines US hegemony. To sustain its global hegemony, the United States relied on its ability 'to prevent collusion and maintain security dependence among the vassals, to keep the tributaries pliant and protected, and to keep the barbarians from coming together' (Brzezinski1997: 40).

In the years since the Cold War, regionalism has become an increasingly important driver of economic globalization (Rumley 2005; Vilanova 2013). Geoeconomic considerations facilitate regional integration as a means for enhancing collective bargaining power because 'self-reliance was never viable on the national level' (Hettne 1993: 227). The formation of the EU was, to a great extent, motivated by the need to improve symmetry in relations with the United States. Similarly, the North American Free Trade Agreement (NAFTA) was a response to the increased competitiveness of Europe and Japan (Hurrell 1995: 341). Such arrangements continue to proliferate because the powerful geoeconomic blocs in the West generate systemic incentives for new regional integration initiatives across Eurasia. As predicted by Hettne (1993: 227): 'the East Asian countries in view of the fortresses emerging in Europe and North America must plan for a future with a much stronger regional interdependence'. Regional integration initiatives do not always conform with the liberal international order because regionalism in Asia often aims to shield states from US influence (Breslin 2010: 714).

Eurasianism is the aim to establish formats for inter-regionalism across the vast Eurasian continent. Russia and China created the Shanghai Cooperation Organisation (SCO) to harmonize their competing interests in Central Asia and to limit the influence of Western powers. The SCO has since begun taking on economic competencies and expanding its membership to include India and Pakistan, and possibly Iran in the future. BRICS (Brazil, Russia, India, China and South Africa) and its development bank have similarly been an important institution for diversifying away from Western capital and align the foreign policy positions of the member states. The Foreign Policy Concept of the Russian Federation (2013) also identifies the Russia–India–China (RIC) format that is instrumental in restructuring global governance. In May 2015, Russia and China agreed to harmonize the Eurasian Economic Union (EAEU) with the Belt and Road Initiative under the auspices of the SCO (Gatev and Diesen 2016). At the joint EAEU-SCO-BRICS Summit in July 2015, Putin described Eurasian governance as a rejection of the US ambitions for global hegemony:

For us this [the Eurasian landmass] isn't a chessboard, it's not a geopolitical playing field – this is our home, and all of us together want our home to be calm and affluent, and for it not to be a place of extremism or for attempts to protect one's interests at the expense of others … We are united in the sense that the aims that have been set can only be achieved by acting collectively, on the basis of genuine partnership, trust, equal rights, respect and acknowledgement of each other's interests.

(Sakwa 2016)

Western institutions are less inclined to cooperate with Eurasian institutions because it dilutes their hegemony. Rather than advance strategic stability by harmonizing interests between regions, the West seeks a strategic advantage by engaging with individual states in these regions to skew the balance of dependence and maximize both its autonomy and influence. Russia's proposal in 2004 to create a Single Economic Space between Russia, Ukraine, Belarus and Kazakhstan was immediately rebuked by Washington and Brussels as an imperial ambition. The EU has resisted engaging with the EAEU, and US Secretary of State Hillary Clinton argued in 2012 that Washington was determined 'to figure out effective ways to slow down or prevent' integration of the EAEU (Sheahan 2012). Two years later, the coup in Ukraine made its possible future participation a moot point. New regions are also constructed to marginalize Russia and China. Clinton referred to the Transatlantic Trade and Investment Partnership (TTIP) between the United States and Europe as an 'economic NATO', while President Obama (2016) advocated the Trans-Pacific Partnership (TPP) to counter China, saying, 'Other countries should play by the rules that America and our partners set, and not the other way around … The United States, not countries like China, should write them'.

Conclusion

How prepared is the international system for the Fourth Industrial Revolution? New technologies are multiplying exponentially, yet the international system organizing human affairs has changed little since the Treaty of Westphalia in 1648. The system of global governance for expanding capital, productive capacity and geoeconomic instruments of power will alter slightly in the Fourth Industrial Revolution. Geoeconomic rivalries could undergo radical restructuring as digital technologies replace strategic industries, transport corridors and financial instruments.

Strategic industries are disrupted as digital technologies intensify interactions between economies, spur the creation of new weapons and prompt intrusive interactions between competing value systems. International rules and norms are needed to oversee data storage, intellectual property, drones, self-driving cars, the Internet of Things, digital currencies and distributed ledgers. Bioengineering, gene editing and neurotechnology make it possible to control the evolutionary process and create superhumans. Some countries will choose to venture carefully down this path, while manage the resulting disruptions and conflicts to maintain a competitive advantage. Geoengineering initiatives, such as manipulating the climate by spreading sulphur in the stratosphere, require a set of common rules because not all states share the potential benefits of manipulating the environment and are not equally prepared for the risks. As with all industrial revolutions, there is also the prospect of unexpected innovations. Innovations in renewable energy could have a devastating effect on energy-exporting states. The physical infrastructure of connectivity is already changing. Governance of traditional transportation corridors now also includes digital sea lanes and satellites as arteries of the global economy. Lastly, digital solutions have the potential to disrupt the vast geoeconomic power of financial instruments such as banks and currencies.

Global governance in the Fourth Industrial Revolution will share many characteristics with the European system of the late nineteenth century. At that time, Britain's primacy was in decline and competition for technological leadership, industrial power and control over markets pushed the world closer to war. In this age, no post–Cold War arrangement has yet been reached that could serve as the foundation for global governance. As Kennan argued, restructuring global governance by including Russia would have required great statesmen with imagination and courage, but unfortunately 'we are in the age of midgets' (Friedman 1998). There is widespread agreement in Washington that the 'unipolar moment' has come to an end, although there is little debate over the alternatives and consequences. Instead, the world is making a transition from unipolarity to multipolarity, with major powers of the East and West trying to push the world in both directions at once. Former Russian Foreign Minister Igor Ivanov (2018) cautioned that the world is still passing through a dangerous transitional phase:

> The previous Yalta-based global political system has been all but destroyed in the two decades since the end of the Cold War. Yet nothing has been devised to replace it. The world is increasingly sliding towards chaos, which now threatens not just individual nations or regions, but the entire international community.

It is still uncertain whether new technologies will compel mankind to unite and develop a system of global governance that can manage states' competing industrial expansion, or will thrust the world into chaos and crisis. Political leaders seem to lack the strategic thinking needed to appreciate the tectonic shift in power that is taking place or to understand its repercussions. Apparently viewing these disruptions as nothing more than an abnormality, Western leaders are simply trying to muddle through the present difficulties rather than planning for a vastly different future.

Conclusion: Towards technological sovereignty

The Fourth Industrial Revolution will likely alter the nature of geoeconomic rivalry due to the heightened significance of technological sovereignty and reduced division of labour. There will be a greater concentration of power by automating the cognitive and enabling digital technologies to take over industries in the physical world. Great powers will be more reluctant to accept technological dependence, and the new technologies incentivize the economies of scope, dismantle supply chains and alter development strategies due to reshoring. Furthermore, there are greater incentives for state intervention in the market due to socio-economic disruptions and the potential of permanent creative destruction.

Industrial revolutions generate incentives for states to further deepen and widen economic connectivity, although the international division of labour is also used to establish asymmetrical dependence to extract political power. States need to intervene in the economy to enhance their relative position vis-à-vis competing powers and to mitigate the subsequent socio-economic disruptions. The Fourth Industrial Revolution is distinctively different from previous industrial revolutions by automating the cognitive, which then can manipulate the physical world. Technological ecosystems under domestic control are imperative to maintain autonomy and influence in the international system, and to mitigate socio-economic disruptions. The elevated role of technologies infers that great power standing will largely depend on establishing technological sovereignty.

The international divisions of labour that have developed over the several decades are currently fragmenting due to a dual decoupling. First, great powers will scale back on interdependence with other large powers by repatriating supply chains in the conviction that everything now qualifies as critical infrastructure and cannot, therefore, be entrusted to rival powers. Second, great powers will shed reliance on supply chains simply because the reshoring of manufacturing will make it possible. Developing states that previously relied on an export-based development strategy will need to embrace import substitution instead to pursue growth by supplying their domestic markets and by developing domestic technological ecosystems. Geoeconomics in the Fourth Industrial Revolution incentivizes territorializing technological ecosystems. China and Russia are already making formidable efforts to reduce geoeconomic reliance on US technologies, industries, transportation corridors, financial institutions and the dollar. US foreign policy similarly seeks to reduce dependence – both its own and its allies' – on the strategic industries of rivals. The United States has banned or restricted China's 5G networks and leading technologies, and Europe considers it a strategic objective to reduce its reliance on Russian gas. As new technological platforms play an increasingly important role in the economy, states will continue to repatriate their supply chains to skew the balance of dependence. Great powers are deliberately working to dismantle the ability of other states to use technological ecosystems for influence.

Great powers need to develop regional, national and international systems to manage technological development. A *system* by definition seeks to impose order on chaos. The imminent socio-economic, political and military challenges require a system capable of mitigating the chaos that could result as the foundations of our current world order become obsolete. Most technological innovations extend beyond national borders, although some are local rather than national. This creates immense pressure to find solutions that are not based on the state alone. Friedrich List's (1885) main thesis in *The National System of Political Economy* was that cosmopolitan theories of free-market capitalism do not correspond with the realities of a world divided into competing nation states. A functioning nation state is a foundational block in a cooperative international system. The state is the principal actor in the international system and will be the main actor in developing a system of technological development that responds to domestic disruptions and restructures international relations. As a new institutional order emerges, it is crucial to understand the mechanisms of the former order. Transformation and renewal entail shedding the decadent and obsolete aspects of the former system and replacing them with a new and resilient institutional order. Revolutions that sweep away the former system often have excessively high and even intolerable transformation costs due to the absence of a sound understanding of the old order. Illusions about making a clean break with the nation state or capitalism to accommodate new technologies will likely end as most revolutions do – in tragedy. Benign intentions eventually give way to ruthless realities because there is no effective system of global government and abolishing capitalism would simply replace powerful capital owners with authoritarian bureaucrats.

Return of the state

As digital platforms absorb the products and services of the physical world and accrue capital-intensive monopolistic power, free-market capitalism becomes problematic. The state must seize greater control over the means of production through regulation or ownership to prevent tech giants from corrupting domestic politics. Simply breaking up tech giants would also eliminate the positive synergy effects they produce and cause them to become less competitive in international markets. As innovation in communications technology intensifies, states must reassert themselves to maintain control over the creation of narratives and the direction of the political discourse. States are already gravitating towards territorializing the digital space and developing a 'sovereign Internet' to mitigate the growing chaos among domestic groups and to counter malign influence by foreign powers.

The increased demand for the state to assert control over technologies, manage geoeconomic competition and overcome socio-economic disruptions will revive ideological competition. Three decades after Fukuyama (1989) declared the 'end of history' – as liberal democracy and free-market capitalism emerged victorious from the Cold War – states will increasingly revisit and reconsider a range of ideological alternatives and their philosophical underpinnings. The role of liberalism diminishes as the state asserts control over the means of production to advance foreign policy interests and to harmonize socio-economic conditions domestically. The need for states to rely increasingly on regulation to control private industry is causing them to gravitate towards the political economy of fascism. Similarly, the argument in favour of state ownership and redistribution will revive the case for socialism. The communist planned economy was largely at fault for the collapse of the Soviet Union, whereas the Communist Party in China has survived by decentralizing and embracing market reforms. Communist states were less able to benefit from the digital revolution because data processing is more efficient in decentralized states (Harari 2016). However, the ability to use AI to manage the extraction of real-time data about all economic activities in society reverses the nature of digital technologies and could lead to more centralized rather than decentralized societies.

Geoeconomic rivalry is inevitably affected by the economic and social dimensions of creative destruction. When creative destruction is more long-lasting, new jobs do not replace the old and the fundamentals of capitalism break down. Furthermore, automation decouples capital from labour, causing power to concentrate in the former and making the redistribution of wealth imperative to preserving political stability. Similarly, creative destruction as a social phenomenon creates a crisis in meaning and purpose. Innovative technologies cannot be guided by liberal economic principles alone or simply as labour-saving instruments that increase efficiency but serve hedonistic impulses. They must also address the ills of society to prevent Gemeinschaft from succumbing. Governments must not be passive and allow themselves to be shaped by new technologies. Rather, a combination of philosophical, economic and social considerations should inform the implementation of technologies. Can liberal governance use technology for purposes other than enhancing efficiency, reducing reliance on human labour and increasing self-indulgence? Governance of innovative technologies can also be used to connect with nature, keep families together, restore social cohesion and communities and establish new frontiers.

A new international system

The international system and domestic societies are not prepared for the disruptions of the Fourth Industrial Revolution. Humanity faces the prospect of losing control over AI, mass unemployment, the collapse of capitalist democracy, political instability, cyberwarfare linked to the physical world, nuclear holocaust, unforeseen consequences of genetic manipulation and other dangers. However, the status quo is also becoming untenable with humanity burdened with such problems as overpopulation, growing energy consumption, sectarianism, terrorism, environmental degradation, financial instability, scarcity of resources, the concentration of wealth, growing nihilism and others. Political leaders are tasked with nothing less than shedding the shortcomings of the former order and replacing them with optimal solutions that conform to new realities. In any industrial revolution, political leaders must be mindful of the creative destruction they are overseeing and plan for a turbulent transition.

Political leaders must navigate between the utopian delusions that disregard the significant risks and the dystopian mindset that ignores possibilities. Capitalism revealed its structural flaws with the unsustainable concentration of capital that led to exploitation. However, capitalism is adaptable and incentivizes competition. The profit motive is instrumental to efficiency and competitiveness, but technologies must have wider applications and be guided by higher considerations than profit alone. Nationalism can be divisive and expressed in xenophobic and destructive ways. However, collective identities with tribal characteristics are innate to human nature and must therefore be harnessed and managed rather than suppressed. Governmental powers can be intrusive and can suppress the full expression of individual liberties, and yet some degree of centralized authority is necessary to mitigate chaos, provide collective goods and redistribute wealth to preserve stability. Liberal impulses, universalism and global connectivity are necessary for developing connections between peoples, yet conservatism, distinctiveness and the nation state serve an important role in terms of preserving necessary borders.

Technologies could be developed responsibly, although less scrupulous adversaries could gain a competitive edge. States that fail to maximize the advantage of AI or even resist it, out of fear of potential socio-economic, political or military disruption, could fall behind other countries. This, in turn, could cause such countries to become technological 'colonies' of other states, culminating in excessive economic dependence or even defeat on the battlefield. Historically, states that have fallen behind on the geoeconomic and security advances ushered in by an industrial revolution have faced an existential threat. The organization of international relations must be based on a balance between strategic advantage and strategic stability. Governments should avoid pyrrhic victories because excessive strategic advantage can produce a reaction detrimental to strategic stability. If one state develops geoeconomic capabilities that enable it to leap far beyond the rest of the world, the remaining states would most likely strive for complete technological and economic autarky rather than accept domination. If a state develops the ability to destroy the nuclear retaliatory capabilities of an adversary, the reaction will likely be a pre-emptive strike on satellites or space-based military capabilities rather than capitulation. Similarly, unequal military capabilities will incentivize weaker states to automate more decision-making to AI systems, thereby relinquishing ever more vital human controls.

Technology is power and industrial revolutions can radically skew the international distribution of power and also disrupt the nature of the relationship between the state and domestic corporations and individuals. The current disorder resulting from the surge in populism, nativism, protectionism, trade wars and techno-nationalism is but a precursor to what awaits humanity in the Fourth Industrial Revolution. Revolutions render the past obsolete and unleash chaos. This situation continues until a new system emerges to replace the old. As with all revolutions, the Fourth Industrial Revolution will destroy the past and give way to something new. In his prison cell, Antonio Gramsci (1971: 271) wrote: 'The crisis consists precisely in the fact that the old is dying and the new cannot be born; in this interregnum a great variety of morbid symptoms appear'. Now, the 'interregnum' refers to the uncertain period between the death of the old system and the birth of the new. The geoeconomic implications of the Fourth Industrial Revolution represent nothing less than the creation of a new industrial society – one that will emerge in the wake of disruptions to the old capitalist economic system, to existing value systems, ideologies and social fabrics – and ultimately, to the role of the state.

Covid-19 intensifying the shift towards technological sovereignty

Schwab and Malleret (2020) argues that COVD-19 is a catalyst for the fourth industrial revolution. The pandemic accelerates the need to adopt new technologies to reorganise society in terms of both work and leisure. The impact of Covid-19 on the shift towards technological sovereignty remains uncertain due to a variety of unknown variable, including the prospect of the virus mutating. There was some initial and temporary repatriation of supply chains, as for example the United States aims to reshore the production of medical supplies and Russia suspended export of grain and medical equipment. The larger and long-term implications of Covid-19 entail the intensified decoupling from the US-centric international economic system. Furthermore, China appears to exit the pandemic, strengthened, and the United States further weakened its relative power. The competition to control the narrative about the responsibility for Covid-19 has fuelled the divide between the United States and China, and Washington expresses a greater sense of urgency in the mobilization of alliance against China. Covid-19 also augments domestic socio-economic tensions as smaller business were pushed into bankruptcies, while larger corporations such as Amazon has prospered greatly during the pandemic by replacing traditional retailers in the stay-at-home economy. Society also polarized further as blue-collar workers suffered the most and are thus more likely to oppose quarantine, while white-collar workers that can work from home are more capable of withstanding the crisis and be sceptical of blue-collar workers resisting the quarantine. Subsequently, responsible states will mitigate the polarization with redistribution and assert a great role.

Bibliography

Adams, B., 1897. *The Law of Civilisation and Decay*, Macmillan, London.

Adams, B., 1900. *America's Economic Supremacy*, Macmillan, New York.

Adams, H., 1956. 'The New York Gold Conspiracy', in H. Adams and C.F. Adams (eds.), *Chapters of Erie*, Cornell University Press, Ithaca, pp.100–134.

Agnew, J. and Corbridge, S., 2002. *Mastering Space: Hegemony, Territory and International Political Economy*, Routledge, New York.

Al-Azmeh, A., 2012. 'Civilization as a Political Disposition', *Economy and Society*, vol.41, no.4, pp.501–12.

Anderson, B., 2006. *Imagined Communities: Reflections on the Origin and Spread of Nationalism*, Verso Books, London.

Ashworth, W.J., 2017. *The Industrial Revolution: The State, Knowledge and Global Trade*, Bloomsbury Publishing, London.

Babones, S., 2018a. 'How Netware Apps Are Reshaping the Personal Transportation Technosystem', *The Zhongguo Institute*, 18 August.

Babones, S., 2018b. 'China Could Be the World's First All Electric Vehicle Ecosystem', *Forbes*, 6 March.

Babones, S., 2018c. *The New Authoritarianism: Trump, Populism, and the Tyranny of Experts*, John Wiley & Sons, New York.

Baer, D., 2016. 'A Lot of People Who Make Over $350,000 are about to Get Replaced by Software', *Business Insider*, 17 March.

Baldwin, D.A., 1985. *Economic Statecraft*, Princeton University Press, Princeton.

Balzer, H., 2005. 'The Putin Thesis and Russian Energy Policy', *Post-Soviet Affairs*, vol.21, no.3, pp.210–25.

Baru, S., 2012. 'Geo-economics and Strategy', *Survival*, vol.54, no.3, pp.47–58.

Baruch, L., 2001. *Intangibles: Management, Measuring and Reporting*, Brookings Institution Press, Washington, DC.

Bebel, A., 1876. *Fur und wider die Commune: Disputation zwischen den Herren Bebel und Sparig in der 'Tonhalle' zu Leipzig*, Genossenschaftsbuchdruckerei, Leipzig.

Bell, D., 1973. 'The Coming of the Post-industrial Society', *The Educational Forum*, vol.40, no.4, pp.574–9.

Bell, D., 2008. *The Cultural Contradictions of Capitalism*, Basic Books, New York.

Bendett, S., 2019. 'Putin Drops Hints about Upcoming National AI Strategy', *Defense One*, 30 May.

Benner, C., 2002. *Work in the New Economy: Flexible Labor Markets in Silicon Valley*, Blackwell Publishing, Malden, MA.

Berend, I.T., 2000. 'The Failure of Economic Nationalism: Central and Eastern Europe before World War II', *Revue économique*, vol.51, no.2, pp.315–22.

Bertrand, N., 2016. 'Putin: The Deterioration of Russia's Relationship with the West Is the Result of Many "Mistakes"', *Business Insider*, 11 January.

Birtchnell, T. and Hoyle, W., 2014. *3D Printing for Development in the Global South: The 3D4D Challenge*, Palgrave, Basingstoke.

Birnbaum, E., 2019. 'DHS Wants to Use Facial Recognition on 97 Percent of Departing Air Passengers by 2023', *The Hill*, 18 April.

Block, F., 2008. 'Swimming Against the Current: The Rise of a Hidden Developmental State in the United States', *Politics & Society*, vol.36, no.2, pp.169–206.

Boehm, C., 2009. *Hierarchy in the Forest: The Evolution of Egalitarian Behaviour*, Harvard University Press, Cambridge.

Booth, K. and Wheeler, N., 2008. *The Security Dilemma: Fear, Cooperation, and Trust in World Politics*, Palgrave, London.

Borger, J., 2013. 'Obama Accused of Nuclear U-turn as Guided Weapons Plan Emerges', *The Guardian*, 21 April.

Bowers, C.G., 1932. *Beveridge and the Progressive Era*, The Literary Guild, Boston.

Boyd, D., Levy, K. and Marwick, A., 2014. 'The Networked Nature of Algorithmic Discrimination: Data and Discrimination: Collected Essays', *Open Technology Institute*.

Bradford, A., 2012. 'The Brussels Effect', *Northwestern University Law Review*, vol.107, no.1, pp.1–67.

Bradshaw, T., 2019. 'The Start-ups Building "Dark Kitchens" for Uber Eats and Deliveroo', *Financial Times*, 21 May.

Brain, M., 2013. *Robotic Nation and Robotic Freedom – Tenth Anniversary Edition*, BYG Publishing, North Carolina.

Breslin, S., 2010. 'Comparative Theory, China, and the Future of East Asian Regionalism(s)', *Review of International Studies*, vol.36, no.3, pp.709–29.

Bretherton, C. and Vogler, J., 1999. *The European Union as a Global Actor*, Routledge, New York.

Brynjolfsson, E. and McAfee, A., 2012. *Race Against the Machine: How the Digital Revolution Is Accelerating Innovation, Driving Productivity, and Irreversibly Transforming Employment and the Economy*, The MIT Center for Digital Business, Middletown.

Brynjolfsson, E. and McAfee, A., 2013. 'The Great Decoupling', *New Perspectives Quarterly*, vol.30, no.1, pp.61–3.

Brzezinski, Z., 1997. *The Grand Chessboard*, Basic Books, New York.

Buchan, G.C., 2003. *Future Roles of US Nuclear Forces: Implications for US Strategy*, vol.1231, Rand Corporation, Arlington.

Buchanan, P., 2013. 'Is Putin One of Us?' *Official Website of Patrick J Buchanan*, 17 December.

Burns, J., 2016. 'Scientists at Northwestern Restore Fertility in Mice with 3D-Printed Ovary', *Forbes*, 7 April.

Burckhardt, J., 2010 [1878]. *The Civilisation of the Renaissance in Italy*, Dover Publications, New York.

Bush, G., 1992. 'Address Before a Joint Session of the Congress on the State of the Union', *The American Presidency Project*, 28 January.

Buzan, B., 2010, 'China in International Society: Is "Peaceful Rise" Possible?' *The Chinese Journal of International Politics*, vol.3, no.1, pp.5–36.

Carbone, C., 2018. 'Leaked Google Employee's Email Reveals Effort to Boost Latino Vote, Surprise That Some Voted for Trump', *Fox News*, 12 August.

Cellan-Jones, R., 2014. 'Stephen Hawking Warns Artificial Intelligence Could End Mankind', *BBC*, 2 December.

Chace, C., 2016. *The Economic Singularity: Artificial Intelligence and the Death of Capitalism*, Three Cs Publishing, London.

Chandler, A.D., 1993. *The Visible Hand*, Harvard University Press, London.

Chang, J., Rynhart, G. and Huynh P., 2016. 'ASEAN in Transformation: How Technology Is Changing Jobs and Enterprises', *International Labour Organisation*, Working Paper No. 10, July.

Chang, H.J., 2003. *Rethinking Development Economics*, Anthem Press, New York.

Charap, S. and Troitskiy, M., 2013. 'Russia, the West and the Integration Dilemma', *Survival*, vol.55, no.6, pp.49–62.

Chesney, R. and Citron, D.K., 2018. 'Disinformation of Steroids', *Council on Foreign Relations*, 16 October.

China State Council, 2015. 'Made in China 2025', 7 July.

Christensen, C., 2011. 'Twitter Revolutions? Addressing Social Media and Dissent', *The Communication Review*, vol.14, no.3, pp.155–7.

Chui, M., Manyika, J. and Miremadi, M., 2015. 'Four Fundamentals of Workplace Automation', *McKinsey Quarterly*, vol.29, no. 3, pp.1–9.

Chui, M., Manyika, J. and Miremadi, M., 2016. 'Where Machines could Replace Humans – and Where They Can't (yet)', *McKinsey Quarterly*, vol.30, no.2, pp.1–12.

Churchill, W.S., 1994. 'The Tragedy of Europe', in B.F. Nelsen and A. Stubb (eds.), *The European Union*, Palgrave, London, pp.5–9.

Cimbala, S.J., 2012. 'Chasing Its Tail: Nuclear Deterrence in the Information Age', *Strategic Studies Quarterly*, Summer 2012, vol.6, no.2, pp.18–34.

Clifford, C., 2018. 'Billionaire Richard Branson: A.I. Is Going to Eliminate Jobs and Free Cash Handouts Will Be Necessary', *CNBC*, 20 February.

Coker, C., Roscini, M. and Haynes, D., 2013. *Drones: The Future of War?* Chatham House, London, pp.3–4.

Columbus, L., 2018. 'IoT Market Predicted to Double by 2021, Reaching $520B', *Forbes*, 16 August.

Cooper, D.E., 1995. 'Technology: Liberation or Enslavement?' *Royal Institute of Philosophy Supplements*, vol.38, pp.7–18.

Crabtree, S., 2014. 'In U.S., Depression Rates Higher for Long-Term Unemployed', *Gallup*, 9 June.

Cross, G., 1990. *A Social History of Leisure since 1600*, Venture Publishing, London.

Cwik, P.F., 2011. 'The New Neo Mercantilism: Currency Manipulation as a Form of Protectionism', *Economic Affairs*, vol.31, no. 3, pp.7–11.

Dahl, R.A., 1957. 'The Concept of Power', *Behavioral science*, vol.2, no.3, pp.201–15.

Damro, C., 2015. 'Market Power Europe: Exploring a Dynamic Conceptual Framework', *Journal of European Public Policy*, vol.22, no.9, pp.1336–54.

David, P.A. and Van de Klundert, T., 1965. 'Biased Efficiency Growth and Capital-labor Substitution in the US, 1899-1960', *The American Economic Review*, vol.55, no.3, pp.357–94.

Davidson, G. and Davidson, P., 1988. *Economics for a Civilized Society*, W. W. Norton, New York.

Davis, G., 2011. *Managed by the Markets: How Finance Reshaped America*, Oxford University Press, London.

De Backer, K. et al., 2016. 'Reshoring: Myth or Reality?' OECD Science, Technology and Industry Policy Papers, No. 27, OECD Publishing, Paris.

De Tocqueville, A., 2003. *Democracy in America*, Barnes & Noble Books, New York.

Del Giudice, M., Campanella, F. and Dezi, L., 2016. 'The Bank of Things: An Empirical Investigation on the Profitability of the Financial Services of the Future', *Business Process Management Journal*, vol.22, no.2, pp.324–40.

Department of Defence, 2019. 'Summary of the 2018 Department of Defense Artificial Intelligence Strategy: Harnessing AI to Advance Our Security and Prosperity', *US Department of Defence*, 12 December.

Diao, X., McMillan, M. and Rodrik, D., 2019. '*The Recent Growth Boom in Developing Economies: A Structural Change Perspective*', in M. Nissanke and J.A. Ocampo (eds.), *The Palgrave Handbook of Development Economics*, Palgrave Macmillan, London, pp. 281–334.

Diesen, G., 2016. *EU and NATO Relations with Russia: After the Collapse of the Soviet Union*, Routledge, London.

Diesen, G., 2017a. *Russia's Geoeconomic Strategy for a Greater Eurasia*, Routledge, London.

Diesen, G., 2017b. 'The EU, Russia and the Manichean Trap', *Cambridge Review of International Affairs*, vol.30, pp.177–94.

Diesen, G., 2018. *The Decay of Western Civilisation and Resurgence of Russia: Between Gemeinschaft and Gesellschaft*, Routledge, London.

Diesen, G., 2020. 'Towards an EU Strategy for Technological Sovereignty', *Valdai Discussion Club*, 3 March.

Diesen, G., 2021. *Russian Conservatism: Managing Change under Permanent Revolution*, Rowman & Littlefield, London.

Diesen, G. and Keane, C., 2017. 'The Two-tiered Division of Ukraine: Historical Narratives in Nation-building and Region-building', *Journal of Balkan and Near Eastern Studies*, vol.19, no.3, pp.313–29.

Diesen, G. and Keane, C., 2018. 'The Offensive Posture of NATO's Missile Defence System', *Communist and Post-Communist Studies*, vol.51, no.2, pp.91–100.

Diesen, G. and Wood, S., 2012. 'Russia's Proposal for a New Security System: Confirming Diverse Perspectives', *Australian Journal of International Affairs*, vol.66, no.4, pp.450–67.

Dittmar, J.E., 2011. 'Information Technology and Economic Change: The Impact of the Printing Press', *The Quarterly Journal of Economics*, vol.126, no.3, pp.1133–72.

Dostoyevsky, F., 1994. *A Writer's Diary: Volume 2 - 1887–1881*, Northwestern University Press, Illinois.

Dostoyevsky, F., 2009 [1864]. *Notes from Underground*, translated by Constance Garnett, Hackett Publishing Company, Cambridge.

Dougherty, J. and Jay, M., 2018. 'Russia Tries to Get Smart about Artificial Intelligence', *The Wilson Quarterly*, vol.42, no.2, Spring.

Drell, S.D. and Von Hippel, F., 1976. 'Limited Nuclear War', *Scientific American*, vol.235, no.5, pp.27–37.

Du Bois, W.E.B., 1941. 'Neuropa: Hitler's New World Order', *The Journal of Negro Education*, vol.10, no.3, pp.380–6.

Dyer, T.G., 1992. *Theodore Roosevelt and the Idea of Race*, Louisiana University Press, Louisiana.

Earle, E.M., 1943. 'Friedrich List, Forerunner of Pan-Germanism', *The American Scholar*, vol.12, no.4, pp.430–43.

Eberlein, B. and Grande, E., 2005. 'Beyond Delegation: Transnational Regulatory Regimes and the EU Regulatory State', *Journal of European Public Policy*, vol.12, no.1, pp.89–112.

Eckes, A.E., 1999. *Opening America's Market: US Foreign Trade Policy since 1776*, University of North Carolina Press, North Carolina.

Economy, E.C., 2018. *The Third Revolution: Xi Jinping and the New Chinese State*, Oxford University Press, Cambridge.

Engelke, P. and Manning, R.A., 2017. 'Keeping America's Innovative Edge', *The Atlantic Council*, 4 April.

Eisenstein, E.L., 1979. *The Printing Press as an Agent of Change*, Cambridge University Press, London.

Epstein, R., 2018. 'Not Just Conservatives: Google and Big Tech Can Shift Millions of Votes in Any Direction', *USA Today*, 13 September.

Ermolaeva, S., 2018. 'UAVs Drove to Israel [in Russian: Bespilotniki "Yandex" doehali do Izrailya]', *Avtovzglyad*, 25 December.

Felten, E. and Lyons, T., 2016. 'The Administration's Report on the Future of Artificial Intelligence', *White House*, 12 October.

Ferguson, N., 2019. *The Square and the Tower: Networks, Hierarchies and the Struggle for Global Power*, Penguin Books, London.

Fielding, N. and Cobain, I., 2011. 'Revealed: US Spy Operation That Manipulates Social Media', *The Guardian*, 17 March.

Flood, B., 2019. 'Google Favors Left-leaning Outlets CNN, New York Times in Its Top Stories Algorithm, Study Says', *Fox News*, 13 May.

Ford, M., 2009. *The Lights in the Tunnel: Automation, Accelerating Technology and the Economy of the Future*, Acculant Publishing, New York.

Ford, M., 2015. *Rise of the Robots: Technology and the Threat of a Jobless Future*, Basic Books, New York.

Ford, M., 2018. *Architects of Intelligence: The Truth about AI from the People Building It*, Packt Publishing Ltd, New York.

Ford, H., Dubois, E. and Puschmann, C., 2016. 'Keeping Ottawa Honest – One Tweet at a Time? Politicians, Journalists, Wikipedians and Their Twitter Bots', *International Journal of Communication*, vol.10, pp.4891–914.

Fox, 2018. 'Tucker Takes on Migrant Caravan Supporter; Rep. Jim Jordan Talks Big Tech Bias', *Fox News*, 18 October.

Frankl, V.E., 1992. *Man's Search for Meaning*, Simon and Schuster, New York.

Fratocchi, L. et al., 2016. 'Motivations of Manufacturing Reshoring: An Interpretative Framework', *International Journal of Physical Distribution & Logistics Management*, vol.46, no.2, pp.98–127.

Freud, S., 1963. 'Reflections upon War and Death', in P. Rieff (ed.), *Character and Culture*, Collier Books, New York, pp.107–134.

Frey, C.B. and Osborne, M.A., 2013. 'The Future of Employment: How Susceptible Are Jobs to Computerisation?' *Technological Forecasting and Social Change*, vol.114, pp.254–80.

Frey, C.B. and Osborne, M., 2015. 'Technology at Work: The Future of Innovation and Employment', *Citi GPS: Global Perspectives & Solutions*, February.

Friedman, M., 2009. *Capitalism and Freedom*, University of Chicago press, Chicago.

Friedmand, T.L., 1998. 'Foreign Affairs; Now a Word From X', *The New York Times*, 2 May.

Fuchs, C., 2012. 'Social Media, Riots, and Revolutions', *Capital & Class*, vol.36, no.3, pp.383–91.

Fukuyama, F., 1989. 'The End of History?' *The National Interest*, vol.16, pp.3–18.

Futter, A., 2018. *Hacking the Bomb: Cyber Threats and Nuclear Weapons*, Georgetown University Press, Washington, DC.

Gallagher, J. and Robinson, R., 1953. 'The Imperialism of Free Trade', *The Economic History Review*, vol.6, no.1, pp.1–15.

Gates, B., 2007. 'A Robot in Every Home. The Leader of the PC Revolution Predicts That the Next Hot Field Will Be Robotics', *Sci Am*, vol.296, pp.58–65.

Gatev, I. and Diesen, G., 2016. 'Eurasian Encounters: The Eurasian Economic Union and the Shanghai Cooperation Organisation', *European Politics and Society*, vol.17, no.1, pp.133–50.

Geist, E.M., 2016. 'Would Russia's Undersea "Doomsday Drone" Carry a Cobalt Bomb?' *Bulletin of the Atomic Scientists*, vol.72, no.4, pp.238–42.

Gerschenkron, A., 1963. *Economic Backwardness in Historical Perspective: A Book of Essays*, Harvard University Press, Cambridge.

Gibson-Graham, J.K., 2008. 'Diverse Economies: Performative Practices for Other Worlds', *Progress in Human Geography*, vol.32, no.5, pp.613–32.

Gilpin, R., 1983. *War and Change in World Politics*, Cambridge University Press, Cambridge.

Gilpin, R., 2001. *The Political Economy of International Relations*, Princeton University Press, Princeton.

Gilpin, R., 2011. *Global Political Economy: Understanding the International Economic Order*, Princeton University Press, Princeton.

Glaser, C.L., 2010. *Rational Theory of International Politics: The Logic of Competition and Cooperation*, Princeton University Press, Princeton.

Goel, V., 2019. 'India Proposes Chinese-Style Internet Censorship', *The New York Times*, 14 February.

Goldman, E.O., 2006. 'Cultural Foundations of Military Diffusion', *Review of International Studies*, vol.32, no.1, pp.69–91.

Gore, A., 2013. *Earth in the Balance: Forging a New Common Purpose*, Routledge, New York.

Gramsci, A., 1971. *Selections from the Prison Notebooks of Antonio Gramsci*, Lawrence & Wishart, London.

Gray, J., 1995. *Enlightenment's Wake: Politics and Culture at the Close of the Modern Age*, Routledge, London.

Greenhouse, S., 2016. 'Autonomous Vehicles Could Cost America 5 Million Jobs. What Should We do about It?' *LA Times*, 22 September.

Greenwald, G. and MacAskill, E., 2013. 'Obama Orders US to Draw Up Overseas Target List for Cyber-attacks', *The Guardian*, 8 June.

Grush, B. and Niles, J., 2018. *The End of Driving: Transportation Systems and Public Policy Planning for Autonomous Vehicles*, Elsevier, Amsterdam.

Guldi, J., 2012. *Roads to Power: Britain Invents the Infrastructure State*, Harvard University Press, Cambridge.

Guzzini, S., 1997. 'Robert Gilpin: the Realist Quest for the Dynamics of Power', in I.B. Neumann and O. Wæver (eds.), *The Future of International Relations*, Routledge, London, pp.129–54.

Hammes, T.X., 2018. 'Navy Aircraft Carriers Are Expensive and Vulnerable to Attack. Here's How to Replace Them', *The National Interest*, 17 October.

Harari, Y.N., 2016. *Homo Deus: A Brief History of Tomorrow*, Random House, London.

Hartog, E., 2017. 'How a New Law Is Making It Difficult for Russia's Aggregators to Tell What's New(s)', *The Moscow Times*, 7 April.

Hayek, F.A., 1979. *Law, Legislation, and Liberty: The Political Order of a Free People*, Chicago University Press, Chicago.

Heckscher, E., 1955. *Mercantilism*, George Allen and Unwin, London.

Heidegger, M., 2010 [1927]. *Being and Time*, State University of New York Press, Albany.

Heilmann, S., Rudolf, M., Huotari, M. and Buckow, J., 2014. 'China's Shadow Foreign Policy: Parallel Structures Challenge the Established International Order', *China Monitor*, vol.18, October, pp.1–9.

Herz, J.H., 1950a. 'Idealist Internationalism and the Security Dilemma', *World Politics*, vol.2, no.2, pp.157–80.

Herz, J.H., 1950b. 'Political Ideas and Political Reality', *Political Research Quarterly*, vol.3, no.2, pp.161–78.

Herz, J.H., 1981. 'Political Realism Revisited', *International Studies Quarterly*, vol.25, no.2, pp.182–97.

Hettne, B., 1993, 'Neo-mercantilism: The Pursuit of Regionness', *Cooperation and Conflict*, vol.28, no.3, pp.211–32.

Hilferding, R., 1910 [1985]. *Finance Capital: A Study of the Latest Phase of Capitalist Development*, Routledge, London.

Hilpert, H.G. and Wacker, G., 2015. 'Geoeconomics Meets Geopolitics: China's New Economic and Foreign Policy Initiatives', *Stiftung Wissenschaft und Politik*, June, pp.1–7.

Hilton, B., 1977. *Corn, Cash, Commerce: The Economic Policies of the Tory Governments, 1815–1830*, Oxford University Press, New York.

Hirschman, A., 1945, *National Power and the Structure of Foreign Trade*, University of California Press, Berkeley.

Hobsbawm, E.J., 1968. *Industry and Empire: An Economic History of Britain since 1750*, Weidenfeld and Nicolson, London.

Hobsbawm, E.J., 2007. *Globalisation, Democracy and Terrorism*, Little Brown, London.

Holloway, L., Bear, C. and Wilkinson, K., 2014. 'Robotic Milking Technologies and Renegotiating Situated Ethical Relationships on UK Dairy Farms', *Agriculture and Human Values*, vol.31, pp.185–99.

Hopkins, M. and Lazonick, W., 2014. 'Who Invests in the High-Tech Knowledge Base', *Institute for New Economic Thinking*, Working Paper no.6.

Horowitz, M.C., 2018. 'Artificial Intelligence, International Competition, and the Balance of Power', *Texas National Security Review*, vol.1, no.3, May.

Hruschka, J., 2012. *How Books Came to America: The Rise of the American Book Trade*, Pennsylvania State University Press, Pennsylvania.

Huntington, S.P., 1978. 'Trade, Technology and Leverage: Economic Diplomacy', *Foreign Policy*, no.32, pp.63–106.

Huntington, S.P., 1993. 'Why International Primacy Matters', *International Security*, vol.17, no.4, pp.68–83.

Huntington, S.P., 2004. 'Dead Souls: The Denationalization of the American Elite', *The National Interest*, 1 March.

Hurrell, A., 1995. 'Explaining the Resurgence of Regionalism in World Politics', *Review of International Studies*, vol.21, no.4, pp.331–58.

Hurrell, A., 2007. *On Global Order*, Oxford University Press, Oxford.

IFR, 2018. 'Robot Density Rises Globally', *International Federation of Robotics*, 7 February.

Ikenberry, G.J., 2008. 'The Rise of China and the Future of the West: Can the Liberal System Survive?' *Foreign Affairs*, vol.87, no.1, pp.23–37.

Irwin, D.A., 1989. 'Political Economy and Peel's Repeal of the Corn Laws', *Economics & Politics*, vol.1, no.1, pp.41–59.

Isaac, W. and Dixon, A., 2017. 'Why Big-data Analysis of Police Activity Is Inherently Biased', *The Conversation*, 10 May.

Ivanov, I., 2015. 'The Sunset of Greater Europe', Speech at the 20th Annual International Conference of the Baltic Forum 'The US, the EU and Russia – the New Reality', *Riga*, 12 September.

Ivanov, I., 2018. 'Russia, China and the New World Order', *Russian International Affairs Council*, 19 June.

Jackson, J.E., 2018. *One Nation Under Drones: Legality, Morality, and Utility of Unmanned Combat Systems*, Naval Institute Press, Annapolis.

Jervis, R., 1978. 'Cooperation under the Security Dilemma', *World Politics*, vol.30, no.2, pp.167–214.

Jervis, R., 1989. *The Meaning of the Nuclear Revolution: Statecraft and the Prospect of Armageddon*, Cornell University Press, London.

Jung, C.G., 2014. *The Spiritual Problem of Modern Man: Modern Man in Search of a Soul*, Routledge, London.

Kaczynski, T., 1995. 'Industrial Society and Its Future', *Washington Post*, 19 September.

Kaku, M., 2018, Author interview with Michio Kaku at the Astana Economic Forum, Kazakhstan, 17 May.

Kania, E.B., 2017. *Battlefield Singularity: Artificial Intelligence, Military Revolution, and China's Future Military Power*, Center for a New American Security, Washington DC, 28 November.

Karaganov, S., 2018. 'The New Cold War and the Emerging Greater Eurasia', *Journal of Eurasian Studies*, vol.9, no.2, pp.85–93.

Keating, D., 2012. 'Commissioner Urges EU to Face Down Russia on Energy', *Europeanvoice*, 11 October.

Keller, D., 1992. 'Should Europe Provide Selective Assistance for Key Industries?' *Intereconomics*, vol.27, no.3, pp.111–17.

Keller, W., 2010. 'International Trade, Foreign Direct Investment, and Technology Spillovers', in B.H. Hall and N. Rosenberg (eds.), *Handbook of the Economics of Innovation*, Elsevier, Amsterdam, pp.793–829.

Kennan, G., 1948. 'Report by the Policy Planning Staff', *US Department of State*, 24 February.

Kennan, G., 2014. *The Kennan Diaries*, W. W. Norton, New York.

Kessler R.C., Aguilar-Gaxiola, S., Alonso, J., Chatterji, S., Lee, S., Ormel, J., Üstün, T.B. and Wang, P.S., 2009. 'The Global Burden of Mental Disorders: An Update from the WHO World Mental Health (WMH) Surveys', *Epidemiology and Psychiatric Sciences*, vol.18, no.1, pp.23–33.

Keynes, J.M., 2016. *Essays in Persuasion*, Palgrave Macmillan, London.

Kindleberger, C.P., 1973. *The World in Depression, 1929–1939*, Allen Lane, London.

Kindleberger, C.P., 1986. *The World in Depression, 1929–1939*, University of California Press, California.

Kissinger, H., 2015. *World Order*, Penguin Books, New York.

Kissinger, H., 2018. 'How the Enlightenment Ends', *The Atlantic*, June.

Krasner, S.D., 1999. *Sovereignty: Organized Hypocrisy*, Princeton University Press, Princeton.

Krugman, P., 2018. 'Transaction Costs and Tethers: Why I'm a Crypto Sceptic', *The New York Times*, 31 July.

Kreft, H., 2006. 'China's Quest for Energy', *Policy Review*, vol.139, pp.61–71.

Kreiss, D., 2016. *Prototype Politics: Technology-intensive Campaigning and the Data of Democracy*, Oxford University Press, Oxford.

Lash, C., 1979. *The Culture of Narcissism: American Life in an Age of Diminishing Expectations*, W. W. Norton, New York.

Lavrov, S., 2007. 'Spiegel Interview with Russian Foreign Minister Sergey Lavrov: "Everyone Ought to Stop Demonizing Russia"', *Der Spiegel*, 7 February.

Lawton, T., 1999. *European Industrial Policy and Competitiveness: Concepts and Instruments*, Macmillan, New York.

Lazonick, W., 2009. *Sustainable Prosperity in the New Economy?: Business Organization and High-tech Employment in the United States*, WE Upjohn Institute for Employment Research Kalamazoo, Michigan.

Le Corre, P. and Sepulchre, A., 2016. *China's Offensive in Europe*, Brookings Institution Press, Washington.

Lee, K.F., 2018. *AI Superpowers: China, Silicon Valley, and the New World Order*, Houghton Mifflin, Boston.

Leontief, W., 1983. 'Technological Advance, Economic Growth, and the Distribution of Income', *Population and Development Review*, vol.9, no.3, pp.403–10.

Leontiev, K., 2014 [1885]. *East, Russia and the Slavs [Vostok, Rossiya i slavyanstvo]*, Respublika, Moscow.

Letzter, R., 2016. 'Our Healthy Future: How Technology and Public Health Efforts Will Transform and Extend People's Lives in the Next Ten Years', *Business Insider*, 11 November.

Lieber, K.A., 2000. 'Grasping the Technological Peace: The Offense-defense Balance and International Security', *International Security*, vol.25, no.1, pp.71–104.

Lieber, K.A. and Press, D.G., 2006. 'The Rise of US Nuclear Primacy', *Foreign Affairs*, vol.85, no.2, pp.42–54.

Lieberman, M.B. and Montgomery, D.B., 1988. 'First-mover Advantages', *Strategic Management Journal*, vol.9, pp.41–58.

Lipson, H. and Kurman, M., 2013. *Fabricated: The New World of 3D Printing*, John Wiley & Sons, New York.

Lipton, A., Shrier, D. and Pentland, A., 2016. 'Digital Banking Manifesto: The End of Banks?' *Massachusetts Institute of Technology*, pp.1–20. https://www.getsmarter.com/blog/wp-content/uploads/2017/07/mit_digital_bank_manifesto_report.pdf.

List, F., 1827. *Outlines of American Political Economy*, Samuel Parker, Philadelphia.

List, F., 1885. *The National System of Political Economy*, Longmans, Green & Company, London.

Lockie, A., 2019. Russian Media Threatens Europe with 200-megaton Nuclear 'Doomsday' Device, *Business Insider*, 14 January.

Lorot, P., 1999. *Introduction a la Geoeconomie*, Economica, Paris.

Lukin, A., 2018. *China and Russia: The New Rapprochement*, John Wiley & Sons, New York.

Luttwak, E.N., 1990. 'From Geopolitics to Geo-economics: Logic of Conflict, Grammar of Commerce', *The National Interest*, vol.20, pp.17–23.

Luttwak, E.N., 1993. 'Why Fascism Is the Wave of the Future', *London Review of Books*, vol.16, no.7, pp.3–6.

Luttwak, E.N., 2010. *Endangered American Dream*, Simon and Schuster, New York.

Lv, A. and Luo, T., 2018. 'Authoritarian Practices in the Digital Age| Asymmetrical Power between Internet Giants and Users in China', *International Journal of Communication*, vol.12, pp.3877–95.

Lynn-Jones, S.M., 1995. 'Offense-defense Theory and Its Critics', *Security Studies*, vol.4, no.4, pp.660–91.

MacCarthy, M., 2019. 'Would Breaking Up Digital Platforms Enhance Free Speech?' *Forbes*, 19 June.

MacDonald, F., 2007. 'Anti-Astropolitik – Outer Space and the Orbit of Geography', *Progress in Human Geography*, vol.31, no.5, pp.592–615.

Mackinder, H.J., 1904. 'The Geographical Pivot of History', *The Geographical Journal*, vol.170, no.4, pp.421–44.

Mallet, V., 2019. 'Abide by US Sanctions on Iran or Drop the Dollar, Mnuchin Says', *Financial Times*, 18 July.

Mandiant Report, 2013. 'Exposing One of China's Cyber Espionage Units'.

Mankiya, J., Lund, S., Chui, M., Bughin, J., Woetzel, J., Batra, P., Ko, R. and Sanghvi, S., 2017. 'Jobs Lost, Jobs Gained: What the Future of Work Will Mean for Jobs, Skills, and Wages', *McKinsey Global Institute*, 28 November.

Mann, M., 2005. *The Dark Side of Democracy: Explaining Ethnic Cleansing*, Cambridge University Press, Cambridge.

Marx, K., 1867 [1887]. *Capital: A Critique of Political Economy*, Progress Publishers, Moscow.

Marx, K., 1971. *On Revolution (Vol 1)*, McGraw-Hill, New York.

Marx, K., 2008. *The 18th Brumaire of Louis Bonaparte*. Wildside Press LLC, Maryland.

Mason, P., 2015. *Postcapitalism: A Guide to Our Future*, Macmillan, New York

May, C. and Sell, S., 2005. *Intellectual Property Rights: A Critical History*, Lynne Rienner Press, Boulder.

Mazzucato, M., 2018. *The Entrepreneurial State: Debunking Public vs. Private Sector Myths*, Penguin, London.

McBride, S. and Vance, A., 2019. 'Apple, Google, and Facebook Are Raiding Animal Research Labs', *Bloomberg*, 18 June.

McBride, W.M., 2000. *Technological Change and the United States Navy, 1865–1945* (vol. 27). The Johns Hopkins University Press, Baltimore.

McCarthy, D.R., 2017. *Technology and World Politics: An introduction*, Routledge, London.

McCormick, J.P., 1999. *Carl Schmitt's Critique of Liberalism: Against Politics as Technology*. Cambridge University Press, Cambridge.

McKeown, T.J., 1989. 'The Politics of Corn Law Repeal and Theories of Commercial Policy', *British Journal of Political Science*, vol.19, no.3, pp.353–80.

McKinsey 2018. 'China's Fast Climb Up the Value Chain', *McKinsey Quarterly*, May.

McKune, S. and Ahmed, S., 2018. 'Authoritarian Practices in the Digital Age – The Contestation and Shaping of Cyber Norms through China's Internet Sovereignty Agenda', *International Journal of Communication*, vol.12, pp.3835–55.

McLuhan, M., 1969. *The Gutenberg Galaxy: The Making of Typographic Man*, Toronto University Press, Toronto.

McManus, D., 1989. 'The Malta Summit: Bush's Personal Diplomacy Faces Tough Test at Summit', *LA Times*, 2 December.

McNamara, R.S., 1983. The Military Role of Nuclear Weapons: Perceptions and Misperceptions: Foreign Affairs, Fall. *Survival*, vol.25, no.6, pp.261–71.

Mearsheimer, J.J., 1990. 'Back to the Future: Instability in Europe after the Cold War', *International Security*, vol.15, no.1, pp.5–56.

Mearsheimer, J.J., 2009. 'Reckless States and Realism', *International Relations*, vol.23, no.2, pp.241–56.

Mearsheimer, J.J., 2014. 'Why the Ukraine Crisis Is the West's Fault: The Liberal Delusions That Provoked Putin', *Foreign Affairs*, vol.93, pp.1–12.

Mearsheimer, J.J., 2019. 'Bound to Fail: The Rise and Fall of the Liberal International Order', *International Security*, vol.43, no.4, pp.7–50.

Mearsheimer, J.J. and Walt, S.M., 2016. 'The Case for Offshore Balancing', *Foreign Affairs*, vol.95, no.4, pp.70–83.

Mellon, J. and Chalabi, A., 2017. *Juvenescence: Investing in the Age of Longevity*, Fruitful Publications, Suffolk.

Metz, C., 2017. 'Teaching A.I. Systems to Behave Themselves', *The New York Times*, 13 August.

MIIT, 2017. 'Three-Year Action Plan to Promote the Development of New-Generational Artificial Intelligence Industry', Ministry of Industry and Information Technology, 12 December.

Milberg, W. and Winkler, D., 2013. *Outsourcing Economics: Global Value Chains in Capitalist Development*, Cambridge University Press, London.

Mill, J.S., 1869. *On Liberty*, Longmans, Green, Reader, and Dyer.

Mistreanu, S., 2018. 'Life Inside China's Social Credit Laboratory', *Foreign Policy*, 3 April, pp.1–9.

Mitrany, D., 1965. 'The Prospect of Integration: Federal or Functional', *Journal of Common Market Studies*, vol.4, no.2, pp.119–49.

Moisio, S., 2018. 'Towards Geopolitical Analysis of Geoeconomic Processes', *Geopolitics*, vol.23, no.1, pp.22–9.

Mott, W.H., 1997. *The Economic Basis of Peace: Linkages between Economic Growth and International Conflict*, Greenwood Publishing Group, Westport.

Moyer, J.W., 2014. 'Why Elon Musk Is Scared of Artificial Intelligence – and Terminators', *The Washington Post*, 18 November.

Muller, J. and Pandey E., 2019. 'Amazon's Autonomous Vehicles Bet Could Make Deliveries Even Cheaper', *Axios*, 20 February.

Muoio, D., 2016. 'This "Emotional" Robot Is Coming to the US – and It Wants to Live in Your Home', *Business Insider*, 28 July.

Murgia, M. and Yang, Y., 2019. 'Microsoft Worked with Chinese Military University on Artificial Intelligence', *Financial Times*, 10 May.

Murphy, M., 2017. 'Building the Hardware for the Next Generation of Artificial Intelligence', *MIT News*, 30 November.

Møller, B., 1995. *The Dictionary of Alternative Defence*, Lynne Rienner Publishers, Boulder.

Nichols, T., 2017. *The Death of Expertise: The Campaign against Established Knowledge and Why It Matters*, Oxford University Press, New York.

Nietzsche, F., 1967. *The Will to Power*, Random House, New York.

Nietzsche, F., 1968. *Thus Spoke Zarathustra*, Penguin Books, London.

Norman, J., 2018. *Adam Smith: What He Thought, and why It Matters*, Penguin, UK.

O'Brien, P., 2017. Was the First Industrial Revolution a Conjuncture in the History of the World, LSE, Economic History Working Papers, No: 259/2017.

Obama, B., 2011. *International Strategy for Cyberspace: Prosperity, Security, and Openness in a Networked World*, White House, 29 May.

Obama, B., 2016. 'President Obama: "The TPP Would Let America, Not China, Lead the Way on Global Trade"', *The Washington Post*, 2 May.

Oracle, 2016. *Cloud: Opening Up the Road to Industry 4.0*, Oracle, California.

Padoa-Schioppa, T., 2004. *The Euro and Its Central Bank: Getting United after the Union*, MIT Press, Massachusetts.

Panzar, J.C. and Willig, R.D., 1981. 'Economies of Scope', *The American Economic Review*, vol.71, no.2, pp.268–72.

Papacharissi, Z., 2015. *Affective Publics: Sentiment, Technology, and Politics*. Oxford University Press, New York.

Pearlstein, S., 2018. *Can American Capitalism Survive?: Why Greed Is Not Good, Opportunity Is Not Equal, and Fairness Won't Make Us Poor*, St. Martin's Press, New York.

Peck, M., 2019. 'The Pentagon Wants a Robot Swarm Space Station', *The National Interest*, 14 July.

Perelman, M., 2003. *Steal This Idea: Intellectual Property and the Corporate Confiscation of Creativity*, Palgrave Macmillan, New York.

Perelman, M., 2006. *Railroading Economics: The Creation of the Free Market Mythology*, New York University Press, New York.

Perelman, M., 2012. 'The Power of Economics versus the Economics of Power', *Challenge*, vol.55, no.6, pp.53–66.

Peters, M.A., 2013. *Education, Science and Knowledge Capitalism: Creativity and the Promise of Openness*, Peter Lang, New York.

Piketty, T., 2015. *Capital in the Twenty-first century*, Harvard University Press, Cambridge.

Polanyi, K., 1944. *The Great Transformation*, Beacon Press, Boston.

Prechel, H., 1997. 'Corporate Form and the State: Business Policy and Change from the Multidivisional to the Multilayered Subsidiary Form', *Sociological inquiry*, vol.67, no.2, pp.151–74.

Prechel, H., 2000. *Big Business and the State: Historical Transformation and Corporate Transformation, 1880s–1990s*, State University of New York Press, Albany.

Putin, V., 2012. 'Russia in a Changing World: Stable Priorities and New Opportunities', Meeting with Russian Ambassadors and Permanent Representatives in International Organisations, President of Russia, July.

Putnam, R. D., 2000. *Bowling Alone: The Collapse and Revival of American Community*, Simon & Schuster, New York.

Putnam, R.D., 2007. 'E pluribus Unum: Diversity and Community in the Twenty-first Century the 2006 Johan Skytte Prize Lecture', *Scandinavian Political Studies*, vol.30, no.2, pp.137–74.

PWC, 2018. 'UK Economic Outlook', *PWC*, July.

Quigley, C., 1979. *The Evolution of Civilizations: An Introduction to Historical Analysis*, Macmillan Company, New York.

Raza, W., 2007. 'European Union Trade Politics: Pursuit of Neo-Mercantilism in Different Flora', in W. Blaas and J. Becker (eds.), *Strategic Arena Switching in International Trade Negotiations*, Ashgate, Hampshire, pp.67–96.

Reagan, R., 1975. Interview with 60 Minutes, *CBS*, 14 December.

Rettman, A., 2013. 'D'Estaing: Eurozone Should Shut Its Doors after Poland', *EUObserver*, 26 March.

Rettman, A., 2014. 'EU Chairman Blames Yanukovych for "destabilising" Ukraine', *EUObserver*, 27 January.

Ricardo, D., 1821. *On the Principles of Political Economy and Taxation*, John Murray, London.

Richter, F., 2019. 'China's Electric Vehicle Market Races Ahead', *Statista*, 14 January.

Rifkin, J., 2016. 'The 2016 World Economic Forum Misfires with Its Fourth Industrial Revolution Theme', *Industry Week*, 15 January.

Riley, J.P., 2013. *Napoleon and the World War of 1813: Lessons in Coalition Warfighting*, Routledge, New York.

Rodrik, D., 1997. 'Has Globalization Gone Too Far?' *California Management Review*, vol.39, no.3, pp.29–53.

Rodrik, D., 2011. *The Globalization Paradox: Democracy and the Future of the World Economy*, W. W. Norton, New York and London.

Rodrik, D., 2018. 'New Technologies, Global Value Chains, and the Developing Economies', *Pathways for Prosperity Commission Background Paper Series*; no. 1. Oxford. United Kingdom.

Rogers, E.M., 2010. *Diffusion of Innovations*, Simon and Schuster, New York.

Rorty, R., 1998. *Achieving our Country: Leftist thought in Twentieth-century America*, Harvard University Press, Cambridge.

Rose, G., 1998. 'Neoclassical Realism and Theories of Foreign Policy', *World Politics*, vol.51, no.1, pp.144–72.

Rosow, S.J., 2005. 'Beyond Democratic Idealism: Borders', Speed and Cosmopolitan Ethos, International Studies Association Annual Meeting, Hawaii, 1–5 March.

Ruggie, J.G., 1982. 'International Regimes, Transactions, and Change: Embedded Liberalism in the Postwar Economic Order', *International Organization*, vol.36, no.2, pp.379–415.

Rumley, D., 2005. 'The Geopolitics of Asia-Pacific Regionalism in the 21st Century', *The Otemon Journal of Australian Studies*, 31, pp.5–27.

Russell, S.J. and Norvig, P., 1995. *Artificial Intelligence: A Modern Approach*, Prentice Hall, Englewood.

Russian Federation, 2013. Concept of the Foreign Policy of the Russian Federation, 12 February.

Rüstow, A., 1949 [2009]. *Die Religion der Marktwirtschaft*, LIT Verlag, Münster.

Sagan, C., 1996. *Demon-Haunted World: Science as a Candle in the Dark*, Ballantine Books, New York.

Sage, D., 2016. *How Outer Space Made America: Geography, Organization and the Cosmic Sublime*, Routledge, London.

Sakwa, R., 2008. *Putin: Russia's Choice*, Routledge, London.

Sakwa, R., 2016. 'How the Eurasian Elites Envisage the Role of the EEU in Global Perspective', *European Politics and Society*, vol.17, pp.4–22.

Sanger, D.E. and Perlroth, N., 2019. 'U.S. Escalates Online Attacks on Russia's Power Grid', *The New York Times*, 15 June.

Santarelli, E. and Pesciarelli, E., 1990. 'The Emergence of a Vision: The Development of Schumpeter's Theory of Entrepreneurship', *History of Political Economy*, vol.22, no.4, pp.677–96.

Sberbank, 2018. Sberbank strategy 2020.

Scalingi, P.L., 1992. 'US Intelligence in an Age of Uncertainty: Refocusing to Meet the Challenge', *Washington Quarterly*, vol.15, no.1, pp.145–56.

Schaake, M., 2019. Microsoft, Alibaba and Others Are Setting Norms Online, but That's Not Automatically a Good Thing, Bloomberg, 17 January.

Scharre, P., 2018. *Army of None: Autonomous Weapons and the Future of War*, W. W. Norton, New York.

Sheahan, F., 2012. 'Clinton Challenges "Soviet" Plans for Europe', *The Irish Independent*, 7 December.

Schelling, T.C., 1980. *The Strategy of Conflict*, Harvard University Press, London.

Schmoller, G., 1897. *The Mercantile System and Its Historical Significance*, Macmillan, London.

Schumpeter, J., 1942. *Creative Destruction – Capitalism, Socialism and Democracy* (vol. 825), Harper and Brothers, New York City.

Schwab, K., 2016. 'The Fourth Industrial Revolution: What It Means and How to Respond', in G. Rose (ed.), *The Fourth Industrial Revolution: A Davos Reader*. Foreign Affairs, 12 December, pp.3–11.

Schwab, K., 2018. *Shaping the Fourth Industrial Revolution*, World Economic Forum, Geneva.

Schwab, K. and Malleret, T., 2020. *COVID-19: The Great Reset*, World Economic Forum, Geneva.

Schwartz, S.I., 2018. *No One at the Wheel: Driverless Cars and the Road of the Future*, Hachette, London.

SCS, 2014. 'State Council Notice Concerning Issuance of the Planning Outline for the Construction of a Social Credit System (2014–2020)', China State Council, GF No. (2014) 21, 14 June.

Segal, A.M., 2014. 'Cyberspace: The New Strategic Realm in US–China Relations', *Strategic Analysis*, vol. 38, no.4, pp.577–81.

Sell, S.K., 2003. *Private Power, Public Law: The Globalization of Intellectual Property Rights*, Cambridge University Press, Cambridge.

Semmel, B., 1970. *The Rise of Free Trade Imperialism*, Cambridge University Press, Cambridge.

Serfati, C., 2008. 'Financial Dimensions of Transnational Corporations, Global Value Chain and Technological Innovation', *Journal of Innovation Economics* 2, pp.35–61.

Shadlen, K., 2005. 'Policy Space for Development in the WTO and Beyond: The Case of Intellectual Property Rights', Global Development and Environment Institute Working Paper No. 05–06, Tufts University.

Shane, S. and Blinder, A., 2018. 'Secret Experiment in Alabama Senate Race Imitated Russian Tactics', *The New York Times*, 19 December.

Shiping, T., 2010. 'Offence-defence Theory: Towards a Definitive Understanding', *The Chinese Journal of International Politics*, vol.3, no.2, pp.213–60.

Sil, R. and Katzenstein, P.J., 2010. 'Analytic Eclecticism in the Study of World Politics: Reconfiguring Problems and Mechanisms Across Research Traditions', *Perspectives on Politics*, vol.8, no.2, pp.411–31.

Singer, P., 2002. *One World: Ethics Of Globalisation*, Yale University Press, New Haven.

Singer, P., 2009. *Wired for War: The Robotics Revolution and Conflict in the 21st century*, Penguin Books, London.

Singer, P. and Friedman, A., 2014. *Cybersecurity: What Everyone Needs to Know*, Oxford University Press, Oxford.

Skolnikoff, E.B., 1994. *The Elusive Transformation: Science, Technology, and the Evolution of International Politics*, Princeton University Press, Princeton.

Smith, A., 2006. *The Theory of Moral Sentiments*, Dover Publications, New York.

Smith, N.R., 2018. 'Can Neoclassical Realism Become a Genuine Theory of International Relations?' *The Journal of Politics*, vol.80, no.2, pp.742–9.

Smith, N.R., and Dumieński, Z., 2018. 'Rise of Cryptocurrencies Could Curb American Power', *The Conversation*, 29 March.

Snyder, G., 1961. Deterrence and Defense: Toward a Theory of National Security, Princeton University Press, Princeton.

Sombart, W., 1913. *Krieg und kapitalismus*, Duncker&Humblot, Leipzig.

Sorhun, E., 2014. *Regional Economic Integration and the Global Financial System*, IGI Global, Hershey.

Sorokin, P.A., 1941. *The Crisis of Our Age*, E.P. Dutton, New York.

Spengler, O., 1991 [1921]. *The Decline of the West*, Oxford Paperbacks, Oxford.

Spengler, O., 1932. *Man and Technics*. Alfred A. Knopf, Inc, New York.

Spilotro, T., 2019. 'Privacy: Bitcoin Is Freedom Because It's Permissionless', *NewsBTC*, 2 July.

Spolaore, E., 2013. 'What Is European Integration Really About? A Political Guide for Economists', *Journal of Economic Perspectives*, vol.27, no.3: 125–44.

Spykman, N.J., 1942. *America's Strategy in World Politics: The United States and the Balance of Power*, Transaction Publishers, New Brunswick.

Spykman, N.J., 1966. *America's Strategy in World Politics: The United States and the Balance of Power*, Harcourt, Brace, and Co., New York.

Statista, 2018. 'Number of Facebook Employees From 2007 to 2017 (full-time)', and 'Number of Ford Employees from FY 2011 to FY 2017 (in 1,000s)', *Statista.com*.

Steuart, J., 1770. *An Inquiry into the Principles of Political Economy*, J.J. Tourneisen, Dublin.

Stiegler, B., 2018. *Automatic Society: The Future of Work*, John Wiley & Sons, New Jersey.

Stiglitz, J., 2016. *The Euro: And its Threat to the Future of Europe*, Penguin Books, London.

Stiglitz, J., 2019. *People, Power, and Profits: Progressive Capitalism for an Age of Discontent*, Penguin, London.

Stockhammer, E., 2014. 'The Euro Crisis and Contradictions of Neoliberalism in Europe', *Post Keynesian Economics Study Group*, Working Paper 1401, pp.1–18.

Streitfeld, D., 2017. '"The Internet Is Broken": @ev Is Trying to Salvage It', *The New York Times*, 20 May.

Summers, L., 2014. 'Lawrence H. Summers on the Economic Challenge of the Future: Jobs', *The Wall Street Journal*, 7 July.

Sussman, G. and Krader, S., 2008. 'Template Revolutions: Marketing US Regime Change in Eastern Europe', *Westminster Papers in Communication & Culture*, vol.5, no.3, pp.91–112.

Szabo, S.F., 2015. *Germany, Russia, and the Rise of Geo-Economics*, Bloomsbury Publishing, London.

Tanaka F., Cicourel A., Movellan J.R., 2007. 'Socialization between Toddlers and Robots at an Early Childhood Education Centre'. *Proceedings of the National Academy of Sciences (PNAS)*, San Diego, vol.104, no.46, pp.17954–8.

Taylor, M.Z., 2016. *The Politics of Innovation: Why Some Countries Are Better than Others at Science and Technology*, Oxford University Press, New York.

Teece, D.J., 1980. 'Economies of Scope and the Scope of the Enterprise', *Journal of Economic Behavior & Organization*, vol.1, no.3, pp.223–47.

Temin, P., 2018. *The Vanishing Middle Class: Prejudice and Power in a Dual Economy*, MIT Press, Cambridge.

Tepper, J., 2018. *The Myth of Capitalism: Monopolies and the Death of Competition*, John Wiley & Sons, New Jersey.

Terazono, E., 2018. 'The Billion-dollar Agritech Start-ups Disrupting Farming', *Financial Times*, 10 December.

Terzi, G., 2013. 'Preface', in A. Sandre (ed.), *Twitter for Diplomats, DiploFoundation and IstitutoDiplomatico*, Diplo, Belgrade, pp.7–8.

Thirsk, J., 1967. 'Enclosing and Engrossing', *The Agrarian History of England and Wales*, 4, pp.1500–640.

Thompson, N., 2018. 'Emmanuel Macron Talks to Wired about France's AI Strategy', *Wired*, 31 March.

Toynbee, J.A., 1946. *Study of History*, Oxford University Press, Oxford.

Tönnies, F., 1957 [1887]. *Community and Society*, Dover Publications, New York.

Trotsky, L., 1934. 'Nationalism and Economic Life', *Foreign Affairs*, vol.12, pp.396–402.

Tsygankov, A., 2006. *Russia's Foreign Policy: Change and Continuity in National Identity*, Rowman & Littlefield Publishers, New York.

Tsygankov, A.P., 2009. *Russophobia*, Palgrave Macmillan, New York.

Turner, F.J., 2008 [1893]. *The Significance of the Frontier in American History*, Penguin Books, London.

Tyler, P.E., 1992. 'US Strategy Plan Calls for Insuring No Rivals Develop', *The New York Times*, 8 March.

US State Department, 1945. 'Memorandum by the Under Secretary of State (Acheson) to the Secretary of State', *US State Department*, 9 October.

US Senate, 2018. 'Hearing to Receive Testimony on the Department of Defense Budget Posture in Review of the Defense Authorization Request for Fiscal Year 2019 and the Future Years Defense Program', in *United States Senate: Committee on Armed Services*, Washington, DC, 26 April. https://www.armed-services.senate.gov/imo/media/doc/18-44_04-26-18.pdf.

US Treasury, 2013. 'Report to Congress on International Economic and Exchange Rate Policies', *US Department of the Treasury Office of International Affairs*, 30 October.

Vaidhyanathan, S., 2018. *Antisocial Media: How Facebook Disconnects us and Undermines Democracy*, Oxford University Press, New York.

Van Evera, S., 1998. 'Offense', *Defense, and the Causes of War, International Security*, vol.22, no.4, pp.5–43.

Van Tyne, C.H., 1927. *England and America*, Cambridge University Press, New York.

Varian, H., 2018. *Artificial Intelligence, Economics, and Industrial Organization* (No. w24839), National Bureau of Economic Research, Cambridge.

Vaughan, A., 2016. 'Google Uses AI to Cut Data Centre Energy Use by 15%', *The Guardian*, 20 July.

Vico, G., 2002 [1725]. *Scienzanuova, The First New Science*, translated by Leon Pompa, Cambridge University Press, Cambridge.

Vilanova, P., 2013. 'The Fragmentation of Political Science and "Methodological Pluralism": Regionalism and Geopolitics', *Geopolitica(s)*, vol.4, no.1, pp.11–33.

Walt, S. M., 1998. 'International Relations: One World, Many Theories', *Foreign Policy*, no.110, pp.29–46.

Waltz, K.N., 1970. 'The Myth of Interdependence', in C.P. Kindleberger (ed.), The International Corporation, MIT Press, Cambridge, pp. 205–23.

Waltz, K.N., 1979. *Theory of International Politics*, Addison-Wesley Publishing Company, Massachusetts.

Waltz, K.N., 1988. 'The Origins of War in Neorealist Theory', *The Journal of Interdisciplinary History*, vol.18, no.4, pp.615–28.

Waltz, K.N., 1990. 'Nuclear Myths and Political Realities', *American Political Science Review*, vol.84, no.3, pp.730–45.

Waltz, K.N., 1993. 'The Emerging Structure of International Politics', *International Security*, vol.18, no.2, pp.44–79.

Waltz, K.N., 2000. 'Structural Realism after the Cold War', *International Security*, vol.25, no.1, pp.5–41.

Ward, S., 2012. *Neoliberalism and the Global Restructuring of Knowledge and Education*, Routledge Press, London.

Weber, M., 1924. *GesammelteAufsditzezurSoziologie und Sozialpolitik*, Mohr, Tübingen.

Weber, M., 1958. *The Protestant Ethic and the Spirit of Capitalism*, Scribner, New York.

Webster, G. et al., 2017. *Full Translation: China's 'New Generation Artificial Intelligence Development Plan'*, New America, 1 August (Webster, G. et al. RogierCreemers, Paul Triolo and Elsa Kania).

Weller, C., 2016. 'Obama Just Warned Congress about Robots Taking Over Jobs That Pay Less than $20 an Hour', *Business Insider*, 10 March.

White, D., 2016. 'Read Hillary Clinton's Speech Touting "American Exceptionalism"', *Time*, 31 August.

White House, 1988. 'National Security Strategy of the United States', *White House*, April.

White House, 2002. 'The National Security Strategy of the United States of America', *White House*, September.

White House, 2006. 'US National Space Policy', *White House*, 31 August.

White House, 2019. Remarks by Vice President Pence at the 2019 Munich Security Conference, Munich, Germany, 16 February.

Whiteley, P., 2007. 'The Era of Prosperity is Upon Us', *China Daily*, 19 October.

Wiebe, R.H., 1967. *The Search for Order, 1877–1920*, Hill and Wang, New York.

Wiener, N., 1950. *The Human Use of Human Beings: Cybernetics and Society*, Houghton Mifflin, Boston.

Williams, M., 2018. 'EU vs Fake News: The Truth about Brussels' Fight Against Disinformation', *Channel 4 News*, 18 December.

Williams, M.C. and Neumann, I.B., 2000. 'From Alliance to Security Community: NATO', Russia, and the Power of Identity, *Millennium-Journal of International Studies*, vol.29, no.2, pp.357–87.

Williams, W.A., 2011. *The Contours of American History*, Verso Books, New York.

Winkler, R., 2017. 'Elon Musk Launches Neuralink to Connect Brains with Computers', *The Wall Street Journal*, 27 March.

Wolfsfeld, G., Segev, E. and Sheafer, T., 2013. 'Social Media and the Arab Spring: Politics Comes First', *The International Journal of Press/Politics*, vol.18, no.2, pp.115–37.

Woolley, S.C. and Howard, P.N., 2016. 'Social Media, Revolution, and the Rise of the Political Bot', in P. Robinson, P. Seib and R. Frohlich (eds.), *Routledge Handbook of Media, Conflict and Security*, Taylor & Francis., Routledge, New York, pp.282–92.

World Bank, 2018. 'Competing in the Digital Age: Policy Implications for the Russian Federation', *World Bank*, September.

Yang, A., 2018. *The War on Normal People: The Truth about America's Disappearing Jobs and Why Universal Basic Income Is Our Future*, Hachette, UK.

Zhan, J. et al., 2019. 'Modelling Face Memory Reveals Task-generalizable Representations', *Nature Human Behaviour*, vol.3, no.8, 17 June (Jiayu Zhan, Oliver G. B. Garrod, Nicola van Rijsbergen, and Philippe G. Schyns).

Zhavoronkov et al., 2018. 'Artificial Intelligence for Aging and Longevity Research: Recent Advances and Perspectives', *Ageing Research Reviews* (A. Zhavoronkov, P. Mamoshina, Q. Vanhaelen, M. Scheibye-Knudsen, A. Moskalev and A. Aliper).

Zielonka, J., 2008. 'Europe as a Global Actor: Empire by Example?' *International Affairs*, vol.84, no.3, pp.471–84.

Zuboff, S., 2019. *The Age of Surveillance Capitalism: The Fight for the Future at the New Frontier of Power*, Profile Books, New York.

Zuckerberg, M., 2018. 'Protecting Democracy Is an Arms Race. Here's How Facebook Can Help', *The Washington Times*, 4 September.

Index

www.ingramcontent.com/pod-product-compliance
Lightning Source LLC
Chambersburg PA
CBHW050414280326
41932CB00013BA/1855